The Economic Dimension of Eurasian Integration

Natalia A. Piskulova
Editor

The Economic Dimension of Eurasian Integration

palgrave
macmillan

Editor
Natalia A. Piskulova
Moscow State Institute of International Relations
Moscow, Russia

ISBN 978-3-030-59885-3 ISBN 978-3-030-59886-0 (eBook)
https://doi.org/10.1007/978-3-030-59886-0

This Palgrave Macmillan imprint is published by the registered company Springer Nature Switzerland AG.
The registered company address is: Gewerbestrasse 11, 6330 Cham, Switzerland

Foreword

This book offers a holistic, albeit critical, overview of current trends of economic integration taking place in the Eurasian Economic Union (EAEU). It enriches the existing area of studies by providing a systematic vision on the EAEU from the perspective of International Economic Relations. It may be useful for a broad audience of scholars, graduates, and post-graduates interested in Eurasian integration and post-Soviet studies, as well as policymakers. Contributors to this volume hold solid expertise in the related areas of research. Their individual chapters are structured in a way to thoroughly investigate major dimensions of economic integration in the EAEU, that is, trade, foreign direct investments, manufacturing, energy, transport and logistics, science and education, digital economy, labor, and ecology. Particular attention is paid to the analysis of the conceptual grounds behind Eurasian integration. The book also evaluates the existing trade agreements, and highlights potential ones, between the EAEU and both individual countries and regional trading blocks. Finally, Russia's role as a key regional player in sustaining Eurasian integration has been critically studied. Overall, the authors conclude that the EAEU is the most advanced regional entity in the post-Soviet space to have achieved certain economic results. However, economic integration in the EAEU is not without problems, given both internal and external factors. These challenges could be overcome through creating a full-fledged common regulative framework within the EAEU and exploring the modalities of interregional dialogue.

The authors are grateful to REGION Group (Moscow, Russia) for financial support in the implementation of research projects.

Moscow, Russia Natalia A. Piskulova

Acknowledgments

This book would not have been possible without the support of the Moscow State Institute of International Relations (MGIMO University) and personally its Rector Prof. Anatoly V. Torkunov.

We are also grateful to the MGIMO University Department of Research Policy for their continued support and encouragement while writing the book. Besides, we would like to thank respective academic departments at the MGIMO University as well as the REGION Group (Moscow, Russia) for financial support in the implementation of research projects.

Our sincere thanks also go to the publisher and to the editor's finishing touches on our manuscript.

Finally, I would like to express my sincere gratitude to Dr. Egor Pak for his great organizational work to make this book happen and his constant communications with the authors.

Contents

1 **Economic Framework for Eurasian Integration: Theory and Practice** 1
Yaroslav D. Lissovolik, Egor V. Pak, and Henglong Zhang

2 **EAEU Intra-Regional Trade** 27
Andrey N. Spartak

3 **Foreign Direct Investments in the EAEU** 67
Galina M. Kostyunina

4 **Industrial Cooperation in the EAEU** 93
Yuri A. Savinov and Evgenya V. Taranovskaya

5 **Perspectives of Common EAEU Oil and Gas Markets** 107
Olga L. Garanina

6 **Transport and Logistics in the EAEU** 125
Egor V. Pak

7 **Scientific, Technical, and Educational Cooperation in the EAEU** 143
Petr I. Kasatkin, Ludmila S. Salnikova, and Veronika M. Fatykhova

8 Digital Economy Developments Within the EAEU 161
Anna V. Abramova and Elina Thorne

9 Labour Mobility in the Eurasian Economic Union: New Opportunities and Challenges 175
Anna N. Tsibulina

10 Environmental Issues in the Eurasian Economic Union 189
Natalia A. Piskulova

11 EAEU-Third Countries Cooperation: Opportunities and Limitations 209
Maria A. Maksakova and Stevan Gajić

12 Russia in the EAEU 227
Alexander S. Bulatov

Index 235

Notes on Contributors

Anna V. Abramova is an associate professor at MGIMO University, School of International Economic Relations. She is also Head of the Department of Digital Economy and Artificial Intelligence ADV group, Academic Director for the Masters' Programme on Artificial intelligence. She has more than ten years of experience in research and lecturing on e-commerce, ICT market and digital trade developments, as well as official development assistance in ICT sector. She has worked as a consultant for UNCTAD and World Bank.

Alexander S. Bulatov is Professor and Senior Research Scholar at the World Economy Department at MGIMO University, former head of this department. He is the author and editor of numerous publications on the World and Russian economy, including the Economy of other post-Soviet countries.

Veronika M. Fatykhova is Master of Arts in International Relations and postgraduate student at the Department of World Politics, MGIMO University. She is pursuing a diplomatic career at the Ministry of Foreign Affairs of the Russian Federation. Her research interests focus on post-Soviet and European integration processes and the political dimensions of science and higher education and their role in furthering integration.

Stevan Gajić is a researcher at the Institute of European Studies in Belgrade, Serbia. His academic expertise includes European and American studies, Russian and post-Soviet politics, and international relations. He obtained his PhD (Political Science) from the University of Belgrade.

Olga L. Garanina is an associate professor at the Graduate School of Management, St. Petersburg University, where she teaches courses in energy markets and international political economy. She holds a PhD in economics from Grenoble Alpes University in France. Her research interests include international oil and gas market trends, business strategies of Russian energy companies and energy transition.

Petr I. Kasatkin is Doctor Habilitatus, Head of Science Policy Department at MGIMO University. He is also a professor at the Department of World Political Processes, where he teaches courses on International Relations and World Politics, professional activity in the international environment, and negotiating (workshop), and also supervises Master's and PhD theses.

Galina M. Kostyunina is Doctor in World Economy, Professor of the Department of International Economic Relations and Foreign Economic Affairs, MGIMO University. Her research interests include economic integration and international investments. She has authored many books and articles on those issues. She conducted research for UNCTAD (World Investment Report 2012), UNESCAP (Growing Together: Economic Integration for Inclusive and Sustainable Asia Pacific Century, 2013), and Virtual Institute of UNCTAD (Module 3 VI Training Package on Technology Transfer, 2009).

Yaroslav D. Lissovolik is Head of Research at Sberbank Investment Research (CIB). He holds his PhD in Economics from MGIMO University. His primary research expertise embraces modern theories of international politics, global governance, regional integration, and Eurasian integration.

Maria A. Maksakova is an associate professor at the Department of International Economic Relations and Foreign Economic Affairs and Deputy Dean of the Faculty of International Economic Relations, MGIMO University. She is also a Leading Research Fellow of the Center for Eastern European Studies at the Institute of Economics of the Russian Academy of Sciences. She holds her PhD in International Economics. Her professional and research interests include regional economic integration, international economic organizations, and Western Balkans' economic and post-crisis development. She is also a member of International Union of Economists and expert of the Alexander Gorchakov Public Diplomacy Fund.

Egor V. Pak is an associate professor at the Department of International Economic Relations and Foreign Economic Affairs, MGIMO University. He holds his PhD in Economics from MGIMO University. Eurasian integration has been in the neat focus of his expertise since 2011. His main research interests include regional integration, post-Soviet studies, Eurasian integration, transport and logistics in the EAEU.

Natalia A. Piskulova is a professor at the Department of International Economic Relations and Foreign Economic Affairs, MGIMO University. She holds a Doctorate degree from MGIMO University. She has written articles and books in national and international journals and had project leadership responsibilities in international research and development projects. Her main research interests include environmental and economic issues in global and regional trade and investments, international environmental policy, green economy, climate policy, and economic integration.

Ludmila S. Salnikova is an assistant professor, Candidate of Social Sciences, Department of Public Relations, MGIMO University. She is Scientific director of programs in the School of Business and International Competencies. She is the author of more than 200 publications. She is an expert in the field of strategic communications management and has a certificate of professional qualification in the PACO field of public relations. She is also Director General of L.S. Consulting Communication Agency, and member of the Russian Union of Journalists.

Yuri A. Savinov is a professor at the Department of International Trade Transaction Technology, Russian Foreign Trade Academy of Ministry of Economic Development. His research interests extend to a wide range of problems: international trade in high-tech goods, the development of Russian exports of these goods, the impact of international industrial cooperation on the expansion of exports for certain goods, the effectiveness of foreign trade transactions, use of digital technologies in foreign trade, state support for exports, and a number of other areas. His current research interests include foreign trade in finished goods and raw materials, international e-commerce, commercial document flow in e-business, and outsourcing in international trade.

Andrey N. Spartak is Corresponding Member of the Russian Academy of Sciences, Professor and Head of the Department in the Russian Foreign Trade Academy of Ministry of Economic Development, Professor in the

Plekhanov Russian University of Economics. He is also the Director of the All-Russian Market Research Institute, Chairman of the Committee on the Economic Integration and Foreign Economic Activity in the Chamber of Commerce and Industry of Russia, and a member of several Consultative Committees in the framework of the Eurasian Economic Commission. He has been intensively involved in research and expert support on the issues of post-Soviet economic integration, the creation and functioning of the Eurasian Economic Union, conjugation of building of the EAEU and Chinese Belt and Road Initiative, multilateral and bilateral cooperation in the CIS region, and trade policy agenda for Russia and the EAEU. His last three books on global issues received the Russian Academy of Sciences Award for the outstanding scientific research in the field of world economy.

Evgenya V. Taranovskaya is an associate professor at the Department of Finance, Monetary and Credit Relations, Russian Foreign Trade Academy, Ministry of Economic Development. She worked as Dean of Professional Refresher Department, Professor in Accounting in Moscow High School of International Business, Chief-Accountant in JSC Promstroytema, and General Director of RAM-Engineering. Her scientific interests include the issues of export financing and its state support, the development of the international investment process, the terms of payment in foreign trade contracts, and international trade and economic activities.

Elina Thorne is Investment Advisor in AdventaWealth, multi-family office, investing in startups and VC funds. She is also Investment Advisor in Collectly, a digital debt collection service that helps healthcare providers improve medical bill collections. Elina has graduated from INSEAD, a business school located in France and Singapore. Elina Thorne has more than seven years of experience in research analysis, consulting on digital transformation and growth.

Anna N. Tsibulina is an associate professor of the Department of Integration Studies at MGIMO University. She is also a senior research fellow at the Institute of Europe of the Russian Academy of Sciences (RAS). She holds a PhD in Economics from the Institute of Europe of the RAS. Her research interests include economic and monetary integration, the economy of the Central and Eastern European countries, the EU Single Market, and Eurasian integration.

Henglong Zhang is a professor at School of Economics, Shanghai University, China. He holds a PhD in Economics from Shanghai Academy of Social Sciences. His major research interest lies in the areas of international relations, globalization, global governance, and South-South cooperation.

Abbreviations

1PL	First-Party Logistics Provider
2PL	Second-Party Logistics Provider
3PL	Third-Party Logistics Provider
4PL	Fourth-Party Logistics Provider
AfCFTA	African Continental Free Trade Area
AfT	Aid for Trade
AIIB	Asian Infrastructure Investment Bank
APEC	Asia Pacific Economic Cooperation
ASEAN	Association of South East Asian Nations
AU	African Union
BIMSTEC	Bay of Bengal Initiative for Multi-Sectoral Technical and Economic Cooperation
BIT	Bilateral Investment Agreement
BRI	Belt and Road Initiative
BRICS	Brazil, Russia, India, China, South Africa
CAU	Central Asian Union
CDB	China Development Bank
CELAC	Community of Latin American and Caribbean States
CER	Australia-New Zealand Closer Economic Relations
CIS	Commonwealth of Independent States
CU	Customs Union
DBSA	Development Bank of South Africa
EAEU	Eurasian Economic Union
EBRD	European Bank for Reconstruction and Development
EDB	Eurasian Development Bank
EEC	Eurasian Economic Commission

EIA	Economic Integration Agreement
EIB	European Investment Bank
EIC	Eurasian Intergovernmental Council
EPI	Environmental Performance Index
ESCAP	United Nations Economic and Social Commission for Asia and the Pacific
EU	European Union
EurAsEC	Eurasian Economic Community
FAO	Food and Agriculture Organization
FDI	Foreign Direct Investment
FOCEM	Structural Convergence Fund
FTA	Free Trade Agreement
GATS	WTO General Agreement on Trade in Services
GATT	WTO General Agreement on Tariffs and Trade
GCC	Gulf Cooperation Council
GDP	Gross Domestic Product
GUAM	Organization for Democracy and Economic Development
GVC	Global Value Chain
ICIDS	International Center for the Investment Disputes Settlement
ICT	Information-Communication Technology
IIB	International Investment Bank
IMF	International Monetary Fund
IOM	International Organization for Migration
ITC	International Trade Centre
ITU	International Telecommunication Union
LAI	Latin American Integration
LAS	League of Arab States
LPI	Logistics Performance Index
MEA	Multilateral Environmental Agreement
MERCOSUR	Southern Common Market
MFN	Most Favored Nation
MIGA	Multilateral Investment Guarantee Agency
NAFTA	North American Free Trade Agreement
NDB	New Development Bank
NTB	Non-Tariff Barrier
OECD	Organization for Economic Cooperation and Development
OIC	Organization of Islamic Countries
PRC	People's Republic of China
PTA	Preferential Trade Agreement
RCEP	Regional Comprehensive Economic Partnership
RFA	Regional Financing Arrangement
RFTA	Russian Foreign Trade Academy

RIAC	Russian International Affairs Council
RTA	Regional Trade Agreement
SADC EPA	Southern Africa Development Community
SAARC	South Asian Association for Regional Cooperation
SACU	Southern African Customs Union
SCO	Shanghai Cooperation Organization
SDG	Sustainable Development Goals
SEEC	Supreme Eurasian Economic Council
SES	Single Economic Space
SRF	Silk Road Fund
TCM	Thousand Cubic Meters
TEU	Twenty-Foot Equivalent
TKM	Ton per Kilometer
TPP-11	Trans-Pacific Partnership
TRIA	Trilateral Intercontinental Alliance
TRIMs	WTO Agreement on Trade-Related Investment Measures
TRIPS	WTO Agreement on Trade-Related Intellectual Property Rights
UNASUR	Union of South American Nations
UNCTAD	United Nations Conference on Trade and Development
UNECE	United Nations Economic Commission for Europe
USMCA	United States-Mexico-Canada Agreement
USSR	Union of Soviet Socialist Republics
WBG	World Bank Group
WTO	World Trade Organization

List of Figures

Fig. 2.1 Dynamics of the EAEU intra-regional exports of goods in 2010–2019 ($ billion). (Source: Calculated by the author based on the EAEU countries national statistical sources. Retrieved from: http://www.belstat.gov.by; http://www.customs.gov.by/; http://www.armstat.am; http://www.stat.kz; http://e.customs.kz/wps/portal/customs/; http://www.stat.kg; http://www.customs.ru) 37

Fig. 2.2 Comparison of EAEU intra-regional exports and exports to third countries commodity structure in 2018 (per cent of the total). (Source: Calculated by the author based on the EAEU countries national statistical sources. Retrieved from: http://www.belstat.gov.by; http://www.customs.gov.by/; http://www.armstat.am; http://www.stat.kz; http://e.customs.kz/wps/portal/customs/; http://www.stat.kg; http://www.customs.ru) 41

Fig. 2.3 Share of intra-regional trade in the overall foreign trade in services of the EAEU countries in 2018 (per cent). (Source: Calculated by the author based on the balance of payments statistics of the National/Central banks of the EAEU countries. Retrieved from: http://www.cbr.ru; http://www.nbrb.by; https://nationalbank.kz; https://www.nbkr.kg, https://www.cba.am) 44

Fig. 2.4 Share of mutual trade in the structure of supply for the consumption on the EAEU internal market, by sector and industry in 2018 (per cent of the total supply*, in brackets—the share of imports). * Consists of three components: supply of national products to national markets, mutual trade, imports from third countries. (Source: Calculated by the author based on EEC data. Retrieved from: http://www.eurasiancommission.org/ru/act/integr_i_makroec/dep_stat/tradestat/Pages/default.aspx) 46
Fig. 2.5 Share of receipts (payments) in national currencies in the EAEU mutual trade in goods and services (per cent). (Source: Compiled by the author based on data from Eurasian Economic Commission. Retrieved from: http://www.eurasiancommission.org/ru/act/integr_i_makroec/dep_stat/fin_stat/express_information/Pages/express_payments.aspx) 54
Fig. 3.1 FDI inflow into the economy of Armenia ($ million). (Source: Compiled on the basis of data of the Central Bank of Armenia. Retrieved from: https://www.cba.am/RU/SitePages/Default.aspx) 83
Fig. 4.1 Correlation of the index of increase of trade turnover from the dynamics of the Spearman's coefficient in mutual trade of Russia and the Republic of Belarus. (Note: The dynamics of Spearman's correlation coefficient is marked on the abscissa axis, the movement of the trade turnover index of Russia and the Republic of Belarus on the ordinate axis. Calculated based on: https://www.trademap.org) 102
Fig. 4.2 Dependence of the dynamics of the growth rate of mutual trade in machinery and equipment on the indicator of cooperation between Russia and Kazakhstan for 2014–2018. On the ordinate axis—indicators of the Spearman's coefficient; on the abscissa axis—indicators of the growth index of mutual trade in machinery and equipment between Russia and Kazakhstan. The coefficient of determination in the equation is quite high. It shows that with an increase in the degree of coincidence of mutual export structures (i.e., with an increase in the degree of mutual intra-industrial cooperation) by 1, the export growth rate increases by 0.85. This indicates a significant impact of the development of intra-industry cooperation on the growth rate of mutual exports. Calculated based on: https://www.trademap.org 103

Fig. 8.1 ICT connectivity in EAEU member-states, 2018. (Source: Compiled by the author based on ITU ICT database. Retrieved from: https://www.itu.int/net4/ITU-D/icteye/#/countries. *The latest data for Armenia and Kyrgyzstan for percentage of individuals using Internet is available for 2017) 165
Fig. 8.2 Fixed broadband basket for EAEU member-states, 2008–2017, in $. (Source: Compiled by the author based on ICT Price Baskets (IPB). Retrieved from: https://www.itu.int/net4/ITU-D/ipb/) 166
Fig. 9.1 Personal remittances, received (per cent of GDP). (Source: Compiled by the author based on data from the World Bank. Retrieved from https://data.worldbank.org/indicator/BX.TRF.PWKR.DT.GD.ZS?end=2019&start=1993&view=chart) 183
Fig. 9.2 Migration inflow (+) and outflow (−). (Source: Compiled by the author based on data from Eurasian Economic Commission. Retrieved from http://www.eurasiancommission.org/ru/act/integr_i_makroec/dep_stat/econstat/Pages/express_demography.aspx) 184

List of Tables

Table 2.1	Indicators of Russia's economic leadership in the EAEU in 2018	31
Table 2.2	Importance of Russia as a trade partner for the EAEU countries (share in total goods foreign trade turnover, per cent)	32
Table 2.3	Importance of Russia for the EAEU countries as a source of currency and capital receipts in 2018	34
Table 2.4	Share of intra-regional trade in the total EAEU countries foreign trade in goods in 2010–2019 (per cent)	38
Table 2.5	Commodity structure of the EAEU intra-regional exports by analytical groups (per cent of the total)	40
Table 2.6	Diversification levels of the EAEU countries merchandise exports to major trade partners (number of the four-digit HS codes actually traded in 2018)	42
Table 2.7	Difference between exports of textiles, clothing, and footwear from China to Kazakhstan and Kyrgyzstan and respective imports by Kazakhstan and Kyrgyzstan from China (based on mirror statistics, $ million)	48
Table 2.8	Volume of violation by Belarus of the Russian counter-sanctions regime in 2016–2017 (thousand tons)	50
Table 2.9	Assessment of intra-EAEU trade growth due to full elimination of non-tariff barriers (based on 2015 values)	53
Table 2.10	Shares of the EAEU countries in mutual trade in goods and trade imbalances in 2018	55
Table 2.11	Assessment of the size of Russia's oil and gas transfer to Belarus in 2010–2018	56

Table 2.12 Ranking merchandise trade partners of the EAEU countries in 2018 (per cent of the total foreign trade turnover) 60
Table 3.1 Accumulated FDI inflow into EAEU ($ million) 76
Table 3.2 FDI inflow into Russia ($ million) 77
Table 3.3 FDI inflow into Kazakhstan ($ million) 80
Table 3.4 FDI inflow into Belarus ($ million) 81
Table 3.5 Geographical distribution of FDI in the Armenian economy (per cent) 83
Table 3.6 FDI inflow into the economy of Kyrgyzstan ($ million) 84
Table 3.7 Matrix of mutual accumulated FDI of the EAEU countries in 2017 ($ million) 85
Table 3.8 Key indicators for calculating the Investment Intensity Index of mutual accumulated FDI in the EAEU in 2014 and 2017 ($ million) 87
Table 5.1 EAEU energy space: an overview 111
Table 5.2 Oil industry and trade in the EAEU in 2015 (million tons) 113
Table 5.3 Natural gas industry and trade in the EAEU in 2015 (billion cubic meters) 115
Table 6.1 Freight turnover of the EAEU states in 2010–2018 (billion tkm) 128
Table 6.2 Freight turnover of the EAEU by modes of transport in 2010–2018 (per cent) 129
Table 6.3 Volume of goods transported in the EAEU states in 2010–2018 (billion tons) 130
Table 6.4 Volume of goods transported of the EAEU by modes of transport in 2010–2018 (per cent) 131
Table 6.5 Structure of the EAEU market of transport and logistics services in 2018 (per cent) 132
Table 6.6 Exports of transport and logistics services from the EAEU states in 2010–2018 ($ billion) 135
Table 6.7 Share of regional economic entities in world trade in transport and logistics services in 2010–2018 (per cent) 135
Table 6.8 Global LPI scores of the EAEU states in 2012, 2014, 2016 and 2018 136
Table 6.9 Ecological characteristics of Belarus, Kazakhstan and Russia auto fleet in 2018 (per cent) 137
Table 8.1 International indexes covering ICT and digital facilities development in EAEU (the latest available data) 164
Table 8.2 Aid for Trade disbursements 2006–2017 in selected EAEU member-states ($ million) 172
Table 9.1 Dynamics of the main labour market indicators in the EAEU member states 177

Table 10.1	Environmental Performance Index 2018	193
Table 10.2	Greenhouse gas emissions in EAEU countries	194
Table 10.3	Energy intensity in the EAEU countries	196
Table 12.1	Share of the EAEU in merchandise trade and FDI inflow of its member countries in 2018–2019 (per cent)	228
Table 12.2	Share of Russia and China in foreign trade of some EAEU member countries (per cent)	231
Table 12.3	Annual GDP growth of the EAEU leading economies (per cent)	232

CHAPTER 1

Economic Framework for Eurasian Integration: Theory and Practice

Yaroslav D. Lissovolik, Egor V. Pak, and Henglong Zhang

1.1 Introduction

As of today, the global economy and global architecture at large are facing rises in protectionism, trade wars, institutional erosion and looming global risks. In this context, region-related formats are vastly reinforcing their economic, political and social roles in structuring the world order. For instance, regional trading blocks have substantially raised their role when settling the global economic agenda. According to World Trade Organization (WTO) estimates, as of 2019 there are 301 Regional Trade

Y. D. Lissovolik
Sberbank Investment Research, Moscow, Russia
e-mail: ylisovol@mail.ru

E. V. Pak (✉)
MGIMO University, Moscow, Russia
e-mail: egor_pak@mail.ru

H. Zhang
Shanghai University, Shanghai, China
e-mail: henglongzhang@126.com

N. A. Piskulova (ed.), *The Economic Dimension of Eurasian Integration*, https://doi.org/10.1007/978-3-030-59886-0_1

Agreements (RTAs) in force (really functioning), out of which the European Union (EU) is party to 41 (WTO 2019).

Besides, there are also a number of interregional formats (e.g. Southern Common Market [MERCOSUR], Southern African Customs Union [SACU], Preferential Trade Agreement [PTA], the Economic Partnership Agreement between the EU and the Southern Africa Development Community [SADC EPA Group]). In its turn, the Eurasian Economic Union (EAEU) in 2018 signed memoranda on mutual cooperation with the Association of South Asian Nations (ASEAN) and MERCOSUR. Simultaneously, mega-regional deals also sustain the emergence of region-related global architecture (e.g. in the Pacific region there are the Trans-Pacific Partnership [TPP-11] and the Regional Comprehensive Economic Partnership [RCEP]; in Africa it is the African Continental Free Trade Area [AfCFTA] launched in 2018).

In the post-Soviet region, the EAEU is the most advanced integrative project. Prior to its establishment the region had seen various economic-oriented integrative initiatives, such as the Commonwealth of Independent States (CIS), Central Asian Union (CAU), Organization for Democracy and Economic Development (GUAM), Union of Russia and Belarus and Eurasian Economic Community (EurAsEC). However, due to economic turbulence from the aftermath of the dissolution of the USSR and the explicit nation-building rhetoric of new elites, all these integration projects either have predominantly failed or have been largely inefficient.

Marking its fifth anniversary, the EAEU is already an established regional trading block. In the EAEU format, Armenia, Belarus, Kazakhstan, Kyrgyzstan and Russia account for 2.2 per cent of global GDP (measured in current prices) and almost 90 per cent of the GDP of the CIS. EAEU states secure 2.8 per cent of world merchandise exports and 1.4 per cent of global service exports. The EAEU represents a solid market of 183.8 million people. The Union holds 14.5 per cent of global reserves in oil and 20.2 per cent of global reserves in gas. In terms of industrial potential, the EAEU accounts for 2.2 per cent of global industrial output. This Union is ranked second in global production of fertilizers, third in global grain production, fourth in global iron output and fifth in global steel output (EEC 2018a).

In the EAEU framework, its member-states have committed to exploit their trade, investment, energy, industrial, transport, labor, digital, ecological and humanitarian potential. Such multidimensional cooperation coupled with the overall economic and technological modernization required for the region at large meets the developmental agenda of all of the EAEU members.

So far, deepening Eurasian integration via various economic dimensions might contribute to the overall efficiency, development of industrial cooperation, greater connectivity and global competitiveness of the EAEU.

1.2 Distinctive Features of Eurasian Integration

When studying the theoretical and practical grounds of Eurasian integration in the existing realm of regionalism, it is worth pointing out a number of its specific features.

First, from the theoretical side, EU-centered classical integration theories have generally failed to explain the Eurasian case. Both old regionalism (largely) and new regionalism (to some extent) view the economic factor as the most decisive one in the integration process, which is understandable for the EU though less reasonable for the EAEU. As a result, research suggests that the EAEU should be conceptualized from the perspective of comparative regionalism rooted primarily in historical, cultural, identity and security traditions and only after that through economic traditions via which the integration evolved.

Theoretical discourse on regionalism has historically been centered around the European integrative pattern laying the basis for major schools of thought, that is, old regionalism and new regionalism. However, viewing the EU as *sui generis* has diminished the legacy of European integration on regional projects around the world (Fabbrini 2008; Kelemen 2006; Söderbaum and Sbragia 2010). As Warleigh-Lack and Rosamond (2010) stress, an exclusively EU-sided approach limits further understanding of region-building practices elsewhere. In turn, Moravcsik (1998) claims that classical EU-centered theories can no longer fully explain the processes happening in the EU itself. Indeed, the Eurozone crisis, Brexit, and the so-called migration invasion have undermined the salience of the EU integrative model (Shaw 2018).

Striving for theoretical grounds to conceptualize the specifics of integrative projects elsewhere (including post-Soviet region) has resulted in the emergence of comparative regionalism. As Hettne (2005) puts it, after several decades of new regionalism it is now time to move 'beyond the new regionalism' on the basis of multifold interactions between state and non-state actors, institutions and processes at a variety of levels ranging from bilateral to regional, interregional and multilateral. Under this framework, regions are to be studied comparatively in constructivist traditions, that is, from the perspective of social interactions given unique historical, social, political and economic specifics of a particular region (Acharya 2016; De Lombaerde et al. 2010; Farrel et al. 2005; Warleigh-Lack and Van Langenhove 2010; Torkunov 2018). By studying a divide between EU studies and other regional cases, regions can and should be compared in time as well as across different spaces and forms of organizations (Söderbaum 2015; Warleigh-Lack et al. 2010). Therefore, the emerging field of comparative regionalism is an eclectic concept, in the sense that it is enriched by studies from many regions, including both the EU and the EAEU.

Besides, by critically analyzing regional processes in various parts of the world, comparative regionalism empirically challenges the classical argument that economic interdependence and regionalism are interrelated (Hooghe et al. 2019). In this context, Börzel and Risse (2019) argue that economic interdependence (measured by intra-regional trade) and the strength of integration (measured by the depth of integration achieved in regional organizations) are not interrelated in major regions. Out of the major regions selected, only in Europe (i.e. the EU) do economic interdependence and strong regionalism evolve together. Africa, Latin America and the post-Soviet region are characterized by relatively low economic interdependence and stronger regionalism, whereas North America and South-East Asia show substantially high economic interdependence and lower regionalism.

As such, stronger regionalism in the case of the EAEU might be a consequence of other factors not limited to economic interdependence. Such factors include security externalities, regime stability and common values.

Second, and more fundamentally, EAEU economies have generally managed to sustain the complementarity of their manufacturing, energy, transport and further systems which they inherited from the USSR. However, the EAEU still displays modest integration-induced economic results. This fact lays the grounds for the excessive politicization of Eurasian integration. As Shishkov (2007) encapsulates, the whole concept of post-Soviet integration remains not as a matter of research *per se* but is more about ideology.

Again, under the framework of classical theories of integration, modest economic results achieved in the EAEU could be regarded as a sign of its predominant political nature. To be more specific, in terms of depth of integration (according to the Balassa classification), the EAEU has reached the level of Common Market (yet, still functioning with quite a number of exemptions), while intra-regional trade accounts for only 13.7 per cent of the overall EAEU trade (EEC 2018a).

However, such an approach toward Eurasian integration might mislead the research. Indisputably, a lack of tangible economic breakthrough in EAEU states in 2014–2019 supports the argument that Eurasian integration is primordially flawed and economically unsustainable (Kirkham 2016; Popescu 2014). In the same vein, the whole idea of the Eurasian project might also be concluded as Russia's strive to reintroduce its dominance in the region (Sergi 2018). In their turn, Roberts and Moshes (2016) stress that the EAEU is largely limited to 'reproducing sovereignty rather than transforming it', claiming geopolitics first in the integrative process.

Simultaneously, Rotaru (2018) asserts that the EAEU does not promise much in economic terms to Russia (which accounts for almost 82 per cent of the EAEU GDP) but might be of greater economic benefits for other members. In the same vein, Knobel et al. (2019) admit few economic results have been achieved (mainly at the expense of Russia, e.g. pointing at Russia's lower prices on gas for Belarus and Armenia) but stress that trade liberalization within the EAEU is challenged by non-tariff barriers (NTB). At the same time, Libman and Vinokurov (2010) view regional integration as a public good and logically justify Russia's decisive part in producing such public good.

In contrast, taking a comparative regionalism perspective on Eurasian integration, Vinokurov and Libman (2014, p. 344) assert the economic status of the EAEU, pointing at the logical desire of post-Soviet member-states to preserve their existing economic ties rather than 'venturing into uncertain alternative integration prospects that require costly reforms, for instance, EU'. Moreover, security issues that do matter to the region (i.e. terrorism, drug trafficking), requiring a solid and inclusive defense system, objectively could be sustained only by Russia (Kazantsev 2016; Hancock and Libman 2016). Indeed, Börzel and Risse (2019) strongly claim regime stability (whether democratic or authoritarian) to be one of the most daring drivers for Eurasian integration. Overall, as Dragneva and Wolczuk (2017) put it, the EAEU is intended to strengthen Russia's global influence, but given global economic turbulence and global risks the Eurasian project might evolve from a geopolitical agenda to the geoeconomic one. In doing so, Russia and its EAEU partners might pioneer a new geoeconomic strategy for the whole Greater Eurasia (Diesen 2019).

Therefore, the Eurasian integration incontestably has an economic dimension rooted in long-lasting, mutually dependent and complementary economic ties between its integrating states. However, its economic dimension is proceeding under a strong political will for integration, as displayed by the EAEU leaders. Overall, from the very beginning, economic integration could be objectively sustained only by Russia as the region's major economic power and the main provider of regional stability.

Third, all five nations share a common history, culture, unique lingua franca—Russian—and, more crucially, identity. Overall, Armenia, Belarus, Kazakhstan, Kyrgyzstan and Russia do share some common values should they agree on such depth of integration (according to the Balassa classification).

Armenia, Belarus, Kazakhstan and Kyrgyzstan have been a part of the Russian civilization for centuries, cemented by the Russian language. For instance, Russian is the 'state language' in Belarus, 'language of interethnic communication' in Kazakhstan and 'official language' in Kyrgyzstan. According to the Russkiy Mir Foundation (2017), almost 99 per cent of the Belarusian and Kazakhstani population have command of Russian, while in Kyrgyzstan and Armenia this figure is 87 and 93 per cent, respectively.

Public opinion in all the EAEU states is considerably welcoming the evolvement of Eurasian integration, despite some dwindling in 2015–2017 (EDB 2017). With the EAEU facing adverse external shocks, on the one hand this decline is a logical result of people's exaggerated expectations of rapid integration-induced benefits, but on the other hand the decrease was secured by the increase in the share of people who are indifferent to Eurasian integration (e.g. in 2017 these people constituted 33 per cent of the Belarusian population and 30 per cent of the Armenian population). Nonetheless, as of 2017, the highest public support for involvement into the integration process was captured in Kyrgyzstan (83 per cent). Out of the troika states, the Kazakhstani population displays greater approval of Eurasian integration leveled at 76 per cent, ahead of the populations of Russia (68 per cent) and Belarus (56 per cent). In its turn, only half of Armenian citizens are supporting state's membership in the EAEU.

Fourth, given its unique geoeconomic and geopolitical location, the EAEU is destined to become one of the decisive elements in new multilayered global architecture. One of the promising directions of the EAEU's involvement into the process might be widening the array of free-trade accords and forming interregional trade alliances with other regional blocs.

From the perspective of comparative regionalism, the multifactorial nature of regional integration bodies has made Acharya (2014) and Van Langenhove (2011) look at the emerging region-centered architecture of the global economy and politics. As of today, a 'world of regions' comprises the global regions of European, Asia-Pacific, Latin America and EAEU origin (Lagutina 2018). However, what might be missing in the emerging region-centered system of the global economy and global governance is greater coordination among regional arrangements—a system of syndicated regionalism (Regionalism Inc.). Syndicated regionalism might fill the voids in regional economic cooperation by exploiting the potential of regional integration arrangements as well as their key institutions, such as regional development banks and regional financing arrangements (RFAs) (Lissovolik 2018; Shaw 2018).

If there is an attempt to imbue regionalism with a more coordinated approach toward institutions and financing arrangements, it is likely to happen in Eurasia, with Eurasian integration set to be at the front (Lissovolik and Vinokurov 2019). On the one hand, Eurasia is witnessing the launch of one of the most ambitious and large-scale integration efforts—the Belt and Road Initiative (BRI). On the other, it is in Eurasia where there are several solid regional development banks, such as Asian Infrastructure Investment Bank (AIIB), Silk Road Fund (SRF), China Development Bank (CDB), New Development Bank (NDB), European Investment Bank (EIB) and Eurasian Development Bank (EDB). Thus, syndicated regionalism under the umbrella of comparative regionalism offers the EAEU additional opportunities for greater economic cooperation and connectivity, at a time when fragilities in the global economy are transcending national borders and taking on regional dimensions.

To sum up, the research stresses that comparative regionalism with its eclectic nature is one of the most tailored tools to track the integrative process of the EAEU states, taking into account historical, cultural, social, political and economic context in which they emerged.

1.3 Mapping Eurasian Integration

In chronological terms, Eurasian integration could be broken down into three approximate periods spanning from 1991 to 2019: first period (1991–2000), second period (2000–2015) and third period (2015–till present).

The starting point of Eurasian integration is the formation of the CIS. According to Libman (2007), its establishment in 1991 was just 'an instrument of civilized divorce', an attempt to minimize the aftershocks of dismantling the centralized Soviet state. Nonetheless, in 1994 the states immediately agreed to form a Free Trade Area and Common Financial

Zone, with prospects of deeper integration and the creation of the Economic Union. Simultaneously, in 1994 then President of Kazakhstan N. Nazarbayev, during his public speech at the Lomonosov Moscow State University (Russia), pioneered the idea of Eurasian integration (as it is understood in its present pragmatic context). Nazarbayev introduced Eurasian integration as a rescue tool for the CIS states to overcome the post-Soviet economic and social disintegrative agenda. However, a massive economic downturn (and induced social crisis), national elite building, as well as Euro- and Atlantic vectors undertaken by some of the CIS states, have made all economic initiatives predominantly stay on paper. Overall, post-Soviet states in 1990s were locked in the 'shadow of the future', when national elites and business circles saw no additional benefits from integration with Russia (Michalopoulos and Tarr 1997).

The second period (2000–2015) is characterized by 'a diverse speed integration' (Libman 2007), when integration evolved only among the states mostly prepared to accept it. Russia, Kazakhstan and Belarus (referred to as troika states) formed an integrative core of Eurasian integration. In 2000, together with Kyrgyzstan and Tajikistan, they established the EurAsEC, aimed at facilitating and deepening Eurasian integration by creating first the Customs Union (CU) and further on the Single Economic Space (SES) of the five. However, the 'color revolution' that swept Kyrgyzstan in 2005, and relative inertness displayed by the Tajik government, put their active participation in the integration process on a pause. As such, in 2009, during the Minsk Summit, the Presidents of Russia, Kazakhstan and Belarus signed the Agreement on the Creation of the CU, which was introduced in 2010. In 2012 it was upgraded to the SES. The SES format ensured free movement of goods (yet with some exemptions still in place), services, capital and labor, as well as some degree of economic policy being coordinated. Moreover, it is at this stage where, for the first time since 1991, these states have relinquished part of their sovereignty in favor of the supranational body of the Eurasian Economic Commission (EEC). Finally, troika states signed the Treaty on the Eurasian Economic Union (EAEU) in 2014 in Astana (Kazakhstan).

The third period was launched by the creation of the Eurasian Economic Union (EAEU) with troika states and Armenia entering it straightway at the beginning of 2015, and Kyrgyzstan later on in 2015. In the EAEU format the states initiated massive work on further institutionalization of common regulative mechanisms (including technical regulation) in selected areas of the economy. Simultaneously, in 2015 the EAEU members signed its FTA (covering goods and services) with a third economy—Vietnam. In 2018 the EAEU launched an interim FTA with Iran. In 2019 the EAEU free-trade accords were enriched with its second FTA with Singapore. Negotiations on prospective FTAs are being held with Serbia, Israel, India and Egypt.

Thus, Eurasian integration has evolved from disintegrative tendencies dominant in 1990s to its integrative breakthrough in 2010s. Overall, it took integrating states roughly five years to pass from the CU to the Economic Union, which is, however, still functioning with serious exemptions.

1.4 EAEU Institutional Framework

The institutional framework of the EAEU is very similar to that of the EU. As Risse (2016) explains, there is a 'diffusion' of European integrative approaches and practices in the Eurasian integration-building process. Diffusion does not imply 'copying and pasting' but is about the selective adoption and transformation of integrative models, of which the EU is indisputably the most sophisticated one.

Under the Treaty on EAEU, the institutional structure of the EAEU comprises the Supreme Eurasian Economic Council (SEEC), the Eurasian Intergovernmental Council (EIC), the EEC and the Court of the EAEU. The EAEU financial regulator is to be created by 2025 and placed in Almaty (Kazakhstan).

The SEEC is the highest EAEU body, which is formed by the Heads of the EAEU states rotated annually. The Council defines the strategic objectives of further development of the EAEU and gathers not less than once a year. Its decisions are binding upon all members and bodies. The decision-making process is set as consensus. In 2019, the first President of Kazakhstan, N. Nazarbayev, was appointed as the Honorary Chair of the SEEC.

The EIC is built up of the Prime Ministers of the EAEU members. It gathers not less than two times a year. Its scope of responsibilities involves the implementation of the decrees passed by the SEEC and maintenance of the execution of the Treaty on the EAEU, as well as all the agreements signed by the EAEU. Besides, the Council is authorized to scrutinize the cases discussed at the platform of the EEC, on which consensus has not been reached. The decisions of the EIC are also made by consensus and are to be executed by the member-states in accordance with their national legislature.

The EEC is a constantly operating supranational body headquartered in Moscow (Russia). The organizational layout of the EEC is two-layered. The Council of the Commission, composed of five Deputy-Ministers, tracks Eurasian integration and supervises the Board of the Commission. The Board of the Commission includes a Chairman of the Board and nine Members of the Board-Ministers (two per each EAEU member), all appointed for a four-year term to execute day-to-day operational duty. The Board focuses on distinct functional areas, such as integration and macroeconomics, economy and financial policy, industry and agriculture, trade, technical regulation, customs operation, energy and infrastructure, competition and antitrust regulation, and IT and digitalization. Decisions of the Council of the Commission are to be made by consensus, whereas the decisions of the Board of the Commission are passed either by consensus or by qualified majority (yet, the Supreme Eurasian Economic Council sets a number of sensitive areas in which the decisions of the Board are to be made by consensus). Besides, the EEC can be empowered by the SEEC to sign international agreements on behalf of the EAEU.

The Court of the EAEU is headquartered in Minsk (Belarus) and is a constantly operating judicial body of the EAEU. It was introduced in 2015. Its main function is to monitor the uniform of how member-states and EAEU bodies apply the norms of the Treaty on EAEU, as well as international agreements within the EAEU and those with third countries. The Court is made up of two judges from each EAEU member, appointed for nine years by the SEEC. The Court reviews disputes on the implementation of the Treaty on EAEU, international agreements within the EAEU, and those with third countries, initiated either by a member-state or by a business unit.

Thus, as of today, the EAEU has an institutional structure that overall allows it to deepen integration and raise its competitiveness globally.

1.5 Integration in the EAEU: Major Results

Eurasian integration has led to a number of inbound and outbound economic results, as well as has somewhat progressed in creating common regulative mechanisms for free movement of goods, services, capital and labor. However, adverse external pressure (i.e. volatility in commodity prices in 2014–2016 as well as sanctions imposed on Russia in 2014) deprives the research of objective analysis of integration-induced results, as, for instance, all major economic indicators predominantly showed a downward trend in 2014–2016.

Major inbound quantitative achievements stem from the overall rise in mutual trade and investment volumes. According to EEC statistics (2018), EAEU mutual trade showed an immense increase in 2010–2011 (having risen from $47.1 billion to $63.1 billion) and reached their peak in 2012 ($67.8 billion). Further on, mutual trade volumes were constantly falling and leveled at a bottom of $42.9 billion in 2016. It is worth mentioning that in 2015 trade within the EAEU fell less than trade with third economies (25.8 per cent against 33.6 per cent), which could be treated as a true success of Eurasian integration. In 2016–2018, on the contrary, mutual trade rebounded the track and reached $60.2 billion in 2018.

According to EDB figures (2017), EAEU mutual foreign direct investments (FDI) in stock generally followed the related dynamics of mutual trade in 2010–2018. They rose from $21.2 billion in 2010 to $27.1 billion in 2013, and then bounced back to $24.1 billion in 2014. In 2016, after a three-year decline, mutual FDI in stock showed growth and reached $26.8 billion (+15.9 per cent to the value of 2015). As of 2018, EAEU mutual FDI in stock leveled at $27.0 billion. The Russia-Kazakhstan partnership accounts for roughly a half of the overall EAEU FDI stock. When broken down to states, Russia remains the largest investors within the EAEU securing almost 80 per cent of the overall EAEU FDI stock.

Primary inbound qualitative results imply a relative non-energy shift in mutual trade as well as green shoots in industrial and technological cooperation. Cumulative shares of mineral products and metals have diminished from 53.8 per cent in 2011 to 41.7 per cent in 2018 (EEC 2018). As for machine building, its share showed a steady growth in 2016–2018 (from 17.5 per cent to 19.1 per cent) but is still less than its peak in 2014 (21.5 per cent). Another qualitative sign comes from the relative rise in intra-industry status of mutual trade in machine building. As Pak (2020) puts it, out of the troika states, mutual trade in machine building between Belarus and Russia is predominantly of the intra-trade status (Grubel-Lloyd index equals to 0.9 in 2018). Relative potential for intra-trade growth has been identified in Kazakhstan-Armenia, Kyrgyzstan-Belarus and Kyrgyzstan-Kazakhstan pairs. Thus, the greater role of the non-energy sector observed might be a sign of the development of industrial cooperation in the EAEU.

As far as free movement of the labor force is concerned, citizens of the EAEU states are free to work in any of the five states under the common diploma acceptance policy. Moreover, labor migrants from EAEU members are subject to similar income taxes like locals. A common pension system of the EAEU and related social welfare is also under discussion.

In its outbound economic development, the EAEU has relatively succeeded in setting an array of free-trade accords with states. As of 2019, the EAEU runs two FTAs with Vietnam (signed in 2015) and with Singapore (signed in 2019). An interim EAEU-Iran FTA was also launched in 2018. Discussions on FTA agreements are also underway with Serbia, India, Egypt and Israel.

From the regulative side, the EAEU states have generally advanced in the creation of common markets, the harmonization of technical regulation, the elimination of NTBs and the creation of regional digital platforms. More fundamentally, integrating states came up with the EAEU Customs Code in 2018 to facilitate these processes. The Code introduced several major innovations, including electronic customs declarations, automated operations, shorter goods-release periods, authorized economic operators and a 'one-window' system.

The EAEU has overall moved forward in setting a common regulative framework in selected areas of the economy in 2016–2019. As of today, major progress has been captured in the common medicinal drugs market; the common market of electricity; common oil, gas and petroleum markets; common alcohol and tobacco markets and the common services market. The full introduction of regulative mechanisms in these EAEU markets is to be completed by 2025 on the bases of informatization and digitalization.

In the common medicinal drugs market, the EAEU members have stated to maintain good distribution practices setting common rules for storage, transportation and distribution, to prevent the circulation of counterfeit. A transition period for manufacturers of pharmaceuticals from national to common regulation, until 2025, has been set.

The EAEU states have also taken a step toward the creation of a common electricity market. The Treaty on the formation of the EAEU common electric power market defined the basis for the formation, operation and development of the market, as well as access of electric power providers on the markets of the EAEU members. It has been agreed to launch a common electric power market in a trial version in 2024, with full operation set for 2025.

The EAEU has moved forward to one of the most sensitive common markets (causing serious tensions between Russia and Belarus, for instance)—EAEU common oil, gas and petroleum market—by adopting the Program for passing to the common oil, gas and petroleum market in the EAEU, which is to be put into operation in 2025.

Work on the creation of a common alcohol and tobacco market in the EAEU has gone ahead by working out common indicative excise rate, which is to be applied in 2022–2024.

As far as a common services market is concerned, the EAEU members have added 9 sectors (subsectors) of services to the existing 43, where common regulative mechanisms had already been introduced, such as construction services, engineering services, real estate and renting services, leasing services, consulting services, retail services, tourism services, research and development services, cargo handling and warehousing services and so on. Newly added sectors (subsectors) include services related to the production and distribution of motion pictures and video films, advertising services, tourism, geology consulting services, agricultural services and other similar services. As a result, 52 service sectors (subsectors) embedded into the common regulative framework represent 55 per cent (in value terms) of the total services provided in the EAEU (EDB 2019).

The EAEU states have also progressed in the creation of a common system of technical regulation. As of today, there are 41 EAEU technical regulations in force, 6 pending and 12 under discussion (EDB 2019). The EEC Council passed Agreement on EAEU Trademarks, Service Marks and Appellations of Origin, which is to simplify and facilitate the process of registration of trademarks in the EAEU. Further on, it is expected to come up with related Registers of Trademarks and Appellations of Origin. Besides, the EEC Board approved the Uniform Veterinary and Sanitary Requirements to implement uniform rules regulating the production, processing and storage of animal-derived products.

Work on the elimination of NTBs in the EAEU is also on the way. Under the framework of the 2016 White Paper on Barriers, Derogations and Restrictions in the EAEU, integrating states introduced the agreed-upon list of NTBs containing 60 obstacles (EEC 2017). Besides, almost 30 per cent of all of the decisions passed at the EEC platform in 2016 were devoted to removing the NTBs in the EAEU mutual trade.

In order to facilitate economic integration and lower administrative barriers, the EAEU states have introduced several digital initiatives and platforms. According to the Action Plan for the Development of an

Integrated EAEU Information System in 2019–2020, integrating states aim to create a uniform mechanism for cross-border electronic data exchange (EDB 2019). EAEU digital agenda under this Plan might also result in the implementation of the mutual recognition of electronic shipping documents within the EAEU as a basis for digital transport and digital traceability projects. Another digital initiative that could foster industrial cooperation and technology transfer within the EAEU is the Eurasian Network of Industrial Cooperation, Subcontracting and Technology Transfer. Designed for 2019–2020, it is expected to contribute to the development of industrial cooperation in the EAEU by putting small and medium enterprises into the game and digitalizing the whole process of contracting. This, in turn, could raise sustainability in business activities in the EAEU that is already on the way globally (Krivtsov 2020).

Overall, the EAEU format has generally allowed integrating states to collectively formulate and address common inbound and outbound economic agenda by focusing on economic modernization, raising global competitiveness and creating the framework of common regulation.

1.6 Integration in the EAEU: Major Challenges

Despite some progress achieved, Eurasian integration is still not without failing points, which mainly involve a relatively low level of intra-regional economic integration; an insufficient level of industry-wide supranational regulation; the presence of NTBs; an insufficient level of technological development and high deterioration rate of industrial assets and infrastructure; and the re-export of goods to Russia given the sanctions/countersanctions regime with the EU.

First, EAEU states display relatively low intra-regional economic integration. This is most vivid through the example of their low involvement into mutual trade. Objectively, this low level of intra-regional trade might be a consequence of integration asymmetry, when Russia secures 86 per cent of the EAEU GDP, 88 per cent of the EAEU industrial output, 65 per cent of the EAEU mutual trade and 80 per cent of the EAEU population (EEC 2018). Another reason for this comes from the dominance of inter-industry exchange within the EAEU and, thus, the low level of the overall industrial cooperation. Moreover, as far as the intra-industry exchange is concerned, almost 60 per cent of it accounts for intermediate goods with low value added (EEC 2018).

This generally insufficient degree of intra-regional integration also stems from multi-vector foreign economic policy of some of the EAEU states, that is, Kazakhstan. For instance, Italy, China and the Netherlands account for almost 40 per cent of the overall merchandise exports of Kazakhstan in 2018, whereas Russia is ranked fourth in related geography with a share of 8.4 per cent. In terms of FDI in stock, in 2018 the Netherlands, US, France and China together account for almost 75 per cent of the overall FDI stock in the economy of Kazakhstan—far ahead of Russia with its share 3.2 per cent (EEC 2018b).

A reasonable issue that leads to lower intra-regional economic integration in the EAEU comes from different conditions on which Russia and Kazakhstan entered the WTO in 2012 and 2015, respectively (Armenia and Kyrgyzstan were WTO members long before their joining the EAEU, and their foreign trade volumes do not exacerbate the problem). Overall, Kazakhstan joined the WTO on more preferential conditions than Russia, which raised the problem of the related re-exports of goods from Kazakhstan to Russia (Kheyfets 2019). This issue will be in place at least till 2025 when full harmonization of the EAEU members' tariffs with those with the WTO norms is expected

Second, integrating states have empowered the EEC to execute a common trade policy (incl. external with third economies), whereas investment, energy, transport, industrial, ecological and other issues are still being predominantly regulated at intergovernmental level. For instance, in the absence of a common market of oil, gas and petroleum, related areas remain one of the most challenging points when discussing the prospects of deepening Eurasian integration (e.g. in the case between Belarus and Russia). If limited to gas, the main obstacle comes from the frictions on setting the unified price on gas transit within the EAEU. Besides, a limited sphere of responsibility does not allow the EEC to negotiate with China on behalf of the EAEU when discussing the prospects of EAEU-BRI conjunction.

To some extent, the low level of common regulation achieved is a consequence of the desire integrating states and their elites maintain to retain national sovereignty (Laruelle 2015). Again, a vivid example comes from Kazakhstan with its first President N. Nazarbayev, who has been constantly stressing Kazakhstan's adherence only for the economic character of integration in the EAEU.

Third, another stumbling point of Eurasian integration comes from NTBs (e.g. import quotas, special licenses, subsidies, technical barriers, sanitary and phytosanitary measures, etc.) that limit the potential of the free movement of goods within the EAEU. According to EDB estimates (2019), NTBs substantially affect trade between Belarus and Russia as well as trade between Belarus and Kazakhstan. More specifically, NTBs are significantly present in mutual trade in chemicals, agricultural products, rubber and plastic products, textiles and garments and machine building. As the EEC (2017) quantifies it, should NTBs be eliminated, Belarus will benefit most of the EAEU states: its real GDP in medium term will increase by 2.8 per cent ahead of Kazakhstan (+0.7 per cent) and Russia (+0.2 per cent). In their turn, Vakulchuk and Knobel (2018) have empirically showed that a 1 per cent reduction of NTBs leads to a 1.6–1.7 per cent growth in mutual trade volumes. When viewing Belarus-Kazakhstan's mutual trade, a 50 per cent reduction of NTBs might result in 29–30 per cent growth, whereas full elimination of NTBs might lead to a 76 per cent rise in mutual trade.

Specifically, NTBs are also present in the area of public procurement. With the EAEU market of public procurement estimated at the level of $125 billion, this problem, for instance, prevents enterprises from Armenia, Belarus, Kazakhstan and Kyrgyzstan from participating in the process of import-substitution initiated in Russia (HSE 2019). This, in turn, limits the potential of the development of industrial cooperation within the EAEU.

Fourth, the low level of technological development also hampers deepening Eurasian integration. As for technological development, the share of high-technology exports as a percentage of manufactured exports of, for example, Russia is roughly two times lower than that of the world and equals to 10.9 per cent. In the case of Belarus, this figure is leveled at 4.0 per cent (World Bank 2019). Moreover, coupled with a predominantly resource-oriented economy, Russia and its partners to the EAEU are predominantly involved in upstream global value chains. Apart from that, EAEU members are facing a high deterioration rate of fixed assets and transport infrastructure. According to the EEC figures (2018), the deterioration rate of fixed assets in Belarus is equal to 37.8 per cent, in Kazakhstan 34.4 per cent and in Russia 48.1 per cent. As for transport infrastructure of the EAEU, its moral and technological deterioration rate is around 70 per cent. Overall, poor connectivity within the EAEU and via its territory hampers the overall rise of efficiency of Eurasian integration.

Finally, countersanctions imposed by Russia on European manufacturers of foodstuff in 2014 have led to the phenomenon of 'vanished transit' in the EAEU. Serious tensions on that exist between Russia and Belarus, with the latter accused of 'vanished transit': this means Belarusian cargo on paper channeled for consignees in Kazakhstan, Kyrgyzstan and Armenia in reality goes to Russia. It turns out to be a Belarusian re-export of EU-origin goods (i.e. dairy products, vegetables, fruits, fish, etc.) to Russia, yet, banned for import to Russia in accordance with the sanction's regime. For instance, in 2017, consignees in Kazakhstan, Kyrgyzstan and Armenia did not receive the shipments of 15 thousand tons of dairy products from Belarus (Kheyfets 2019).

Thus, it has been revealed that the EAEU is currently facing serious economic challenges, which on the one hand reveal its structural economic problems and on the other signal the existing integration-induced tensions between the EAEU members. However, all the abovementioned challenges (if not carefully approached by governments and businesses) in the medium and long run might undermine the attempts of the EAEU states to deepen Eurasian integration and create a full-fledged Common Market.

1.7 Promising Direction of the EAEU Outbound Development: Expanding the Set of Alliances for the EAEU

As of today, the existing global governance system is quite turbulent, as the centrality of global institutions is weakened and nation states are re-asserting their power. This, in turn, might be broadly conceptualized through the motion toward multipolarity (Simonia and Torkunov 2015). In this context, the intermediate layer of regionalism (between global institutions and nation states) has become one of the most prominent factors in changing the global governance system. At this stage, the trade policies of most developed economies, as well as some developing economies, have been delegated to the regional level. In the format of the EAEU, Armenia, Belarus, Kazakhstan, Kyrgyzstan and Russia all follow this tendency.

Thus, there are three potential gateways for the EAEU to strengthen its global competitiveness by forging alliances with other regional bodies: these are the BRICS+ circle, the pan-continental model and R20. Through such platforms for international cooperation the EAEU may accumulate the critical mass of alliances that elevates its 'diplomatic weight' in the regional network as an element of the emerging regional layer in global governance.

1.7.1 BRICS+ Circle

As argued before, syndicated regionalism could be neatly pursued in Eurasia with the EAEU in the front. However, when studied from the interregional perspective, a BRICS platform also suits the mission. Each BRICS state is, in turn, a party to the regional entity (i.e. Russia in the EAEU, Brazil in MERCOSUR, South Africa in the SADC, India in the South Asian Association for Regional Cooperation [SAARC], China in the Shanghai Cooperation Organization [SCO], China-ASEAN FTA and prospective RCEP). There are several regional development banks in which BRICS economies and their regional partners are members, such as the EDB, MERCOSUR Structural Convergence Fund (FOCEM) and Development Bank of South Africa (DBSA), with a coordinating role performed by the NDB.

More fundamentally, the uniqueness of BRICS is that each member is also a leading economy in its continent or sub-region within a regional integration arrangement. All countries that are partners of BRICS in these regional integration arrangements may form what might be termed as the BRICS+ circle; this becomes open to numerous flexible modes of economic cooperation on a bilateral or a regional basis (Lissovolik and Vinokurov 2019; Gu et al. 2016). Thus, the BRICS+ initiative seeks to create a new platform for forging regional and bilateral alliances across continents and aims at bringing together regional integration blocks, in which BRICS economies play a leading role. Accordingly, the main regional integration blocks that could form the BRICS+ platform include EAEU, MERCOSUR, SACU, SAARC and the China-ASEAN FTA. Altogether, in such a setting, 35 countries might form the BRICS+ circle.

The main modalities of the EAEU involvement into a BRICS+ format might involve greater trade and investment convergences, cooperation in an international organization (e.g. International Monetary Fund), cooperation between development banks of BRICS+ economies (e.g. AIIB, EDB, CDB and NDB) or the use of national currencies in mutual payments.

In effect, under the BRICS+ format, closer cooperation between the EAEU on the one hand and other regional blocks as well as development banks on the other is already taking place. In terms of cooperation between the regional blocks, the EAEU signed a memorandum of understanding with MERCOSUR in 2018 and henceforth continued discussions on a possible cooperation agreement between the two blocks. In terms of cooperation between the development banks of BRICS countries in 2016, the EDB, in collaboration with the NDB, Nord Hydro and the International Investment Bank (IIB), reached an agreement on the construction of small hydropower plants in the Republic of Karelia (Russia).

Thus, the BRICS+ network expands the EAEU's possibilities of forming alliances within and across continents on the basis of bilateral country-to-country alliances or via trade or investment deals between regional blocks.

1.7.2 Pan-Continental Alliances

Regionalism in the South-South dimension may take on multiple forms, but perhaps the most straightforward is a coordination framework between the pan-continental organizations for each of the continents representing the developing world, that is, Eurasia, South America and Africa (Lissovolik 2018). Importantly, these pan-continental agreements already exist and may serve as a foundation for a mega-alliance between the continental formats of developing economies—in the case of Africa it is the African Union (AU), in South America it is Community of Latin American and Caribbean States (CELAC) or UNASUR (Union of South American Nations), while in Eurasia the most comprehensive platform for South-South cooperation is the SCO+.

As of today, the SCO's priority is to reconcile cooperation (mainly regarding security) among the big three developing nations of Eurasia: Russia, China and India. A common SCO platform for economic cooperation among the respective regional organizations is on the way. For instance, the creation of a development bank for the SCO would potentially strengthen the institutional capacity of the organization for such coordination. In terms of its stature on the global scene, the SCO is perhaps the front-runner to representing what has been given the term Greater Eurasia. This, in turn, does not necessarily call for significant expansion in SCO membership—the SCO has several forms of association, including observer and dialogue partner status. A further extension could be an SCO+ framework that would seek to extend the remit of the organization's coverage to Greater Eurasia. The EAEU could become a key part of this wider Eurasian South-South framework linking some of the other regional integration projects in the CIS space.

As such, a cooperation mechanism represented by the developing economies of AU, SCO and CELAC (tentatively referred to here as the Trilateral Intercontinental Alliance, TRIA) could form the most extensive cross-regional platform for South-South cooperation in addition to other possible platforms such as the BRICS+ platform (McKinney 2017; Xing 2014). In fact, the TRIA framework could be viewed as an extension of the BRICS+ model that is to encompass a broader range of potential partners of BRICS economies.

Developing countries have recently undertaken important steps in the direction of strengthening cross-continental cooperation between the AU, CELAC/UNASUR and SCO. In particular, in its 2015 Declaration CELAC called for the promotion of bilateral ties with other regional groups and particularly with BRICS, the AU and the League of Arab States (LAS). As part of its regional outreach activities, during the 2014 BRICS summit Brazil invited leaders of UNASUR countries, while South Africa invited the AU members to attend the 2013 BRICS summit. In 2015 Russia held a BRICS-SCO Heads of State meeting in Ufa.

Thus, EAEU might explore pan-continental modalities being a party to the SCO+ platform (and further on to Greater Eurasia should it evolve). In doing so, the EAEU might also add economic features to the organization.

1.7.3 R20

Apart from being an integral element in the South-South platforms, another possibility for the EAEU to raise its global competitiveness is to become a part of a global platform for regional economic arrangements.

In this respect one of the key elements in the reform of global governance (e.g. considered by G-20 countries) may be greater coordination between regionalism and global institutions by introducing the global governance platform for regional arrangements (Lissovolik 2016). Indeed, the G-20 group itself comprises a set of regional integration blocks in which the respective G-20 members are leading economic powers. The resulting grouping may be designated as R20 ('Regional 20' as an offshoot of G-20) which could be represented by the following ten regional blocks: EU, United States-Mexico-Canada Agreement (USMCA) (US), SAARC or Bay of Bengal Initiative for Multi-Sectoral Technical and

Economic Cooperation (BIMSTEC) (India), ASEAN (Indonesia), EAEU (Russia), Gulf Cooperation Council (GCC) (Saudi Arabia), the planned RCEP (China, Japan, South Korea), SADC or SACU (South Africa), Australia-New Zealand Closer Economic Relations (CER) (Australia) and MERCOSUR (Brazil, Argentina). Incidentally, there is already a regional grouping that is part of the G-20 format, which is the EU.

The R20 platform may target the coordination of issues pertaining to regional integration, as well as the coordination of regional integration initiatives with global institutes such as the WTO. Apart from addressing the issues of trade liberalization via RTAs and FTAs, there may also be a 'connectivity track' within the R20 format (e.g. given Chinese BRI) from which the EAEU could also benefit. The latter initiatives could then be subject to greater coordination within the R20 framework and, hence, could address the lack of horizontal coordination among the regional development institutions and integration arrangements.

The mandate of R20 is not to challenge or override global institutions but to fill the voids in coordination among international institutions to the benefit of regional cooperation and the strength of global international institutions. The scope of the R20 initiative could also be expanded to cover not only regional integration arrangements and their respective development institutions, but also microregional agreements and alliances among sub-national constituencies, including national regions as well as the largest cities of G-20 countries.

Thus, participating in the R20 platform could provide the EAEU with an important global gateway for broadening its network of international cooperation. It could become an important element for the EAEU in overcoming the difficulties in advancing relations, for instance, with the EU.

1.8 Conclusions

The rise of regional formats for settling global economic, financial, security and political agenda is becoming more and more obvious. The process of regional economic integration is held on intra-regional, interregional and pan-continental bases.

Founded in 2015, the EAEU is the most successful integration body in the post-Soviet region. From the conceptual side, EU-centered theories of integration have generally failed to explain the dynamics of integration in the EAEU. Thus, the research has undertaken a comparative regionalism approach rooted in studying regional economic, historical, cultural, identity and security traditions through which Eurasian integration evolved. Such an approach has allowed the research to come up with the distinctive features of Eurasian integration.

The modest economic results achieved by the EAEU (low share of intra-regional trade) have made scholars view it as a political project. Nonetheless, Eurasian integration has overall contributed to the economic development of its integrating states in 2010–2019. For instance, in quantitative terms EAEU mutual trade and FDI volumes have increased; however, this has been adjusted to the adverse external shocks of 2014–2016. EAEU mutual trade experienced a relative non-energy shift with the rise of the intra-industry character of mutual trade in machine building. Integrating states have proportionally succeeded in creating a common regulative framework and harmonizing technical regulation within the EAEU. However, the existing degree of industry-wide common regulation limits any further development of Eurasian integration. Other serious challenges on the way to deepening Eurasian integration include a low level of the EAEU intra-regional economic integration, the presence of NTBs in mutual trade, an insufficient level of technological development of the EAEU economies and a high deterioration rate of transport infrastructure.

One of the promising outbound directions of the EAEU economic development is forging FTAs with states and trade alliances with other regional integration bodies. As of today, the EAEU runs FTAs with Vietnam, Singapore and interim one with Iran. EAEU's FTAs with other developing economies—that is, Egypt, Israel, India and Serbia—are on the way.

In raising its global competitiveness, the EAEU (which is fair for Eurasian integration as a conceptual basis of the EAEU as well) is also set to explore the modalities of syndicated regionalism involving greater cooperation between regional blocks and their institutions (including development banks). Such an approach overall addresses regional modernization and connectivity needs. Thus, there are three possible gateways for the EAEU to forge alliances with other regional blocks: BRICS+, the pan-continental model and R20.

In summary, despite all of its challenges, the EAEU is an established regional integration entity focused on economic and technological modernization as well as greater connectivity. In the EAEU format, integrating states are aimed at raising their inbound economic efficiency in trade, investments, energy, labor, transport and logistics, industrial, digital, ecological and humanitarian areas. By building an outbound system of FTAs and alliances the EAEU states might overcome the limitations of continental geography and sustain their growth potential through greater connectivity and a progressively more open regime for the flow of goods, services, capital and labor resources.

References

Acharya, A. (2014). *The End of American World Order*. Cambridge: Polity Press.

Acharya, A. (2016). Regionalism Beyond EU-Centrism. In T. Börzel & T. Risse (Eds.), *The Oxford Handbook of Comparative Regionalism*. Oxford: Oxford University Press.

Börzel, T., & Risse, T. (2019). Grand Theories of Integration and the Challenges of Comparative Regionalism. *Journal of European Public Policy, 26*(8), 1231–1252.

Diesen, G. (2019). *Russia's Geoeconomic Strategy for a Greater Eurasia (Rethinking Asia and International Relations)*. London: Routledge.

Dragneva, R., & Wolczuk, K. (2017). The Eurasian Economic Union. Deals, Rules and the Exercise of Power. *Clatham House Research Paper*. Retrieved from https://www.chathamhouse.org/sites/default/files/publications/research/2017-05-02-eurasian-economic-union-dragneva-wolczuk.pdf.

Eurasian Development Bank. (2017). *Eurasian Integration Barometer*. Retrieved from https://eabr.org/upload/iblock/3ef/EDB-Centre_2017_Report-46_EDB-Integration-Barometer_ENG_2.pdf.

Eurasian Development Bank. (2019). *Eurasian Economic Integration*. Retrieved from https://eabr.org/upload/iblock/211/EDB_Centre_Report_52_Eurasian_Economic_Integration_2019_eng.pdf.

Eurasian Economic Commission. (2017). *Barriers, Derogations and Restrictions in the Eurasian Economic Union*. Retrieved from http://www.eurasiancommission.org/ru/Documents/BARRIERS,%20DEROGATIONS%20AND%20RESTRICTIONS%20IN%20THE%20EURASIAN%20ECONOMIC%20UNION%20ANNUAL%20REPORT%202017.pdf.

Eurasian Economic Commission. (2018a). *EAEU Statistics Yearbook*. Retrieved from http://www.eurasiancommission.org/ru/act/integr_i_makroec/dep_stat/econstat/Documents/Stat_Yearbook_2018.pdf (In Russian).

Eurasian Economic Commission. (2018b). *Foreign Direct Investments in the EAEU*. Retrieved from http://www.eurasiancommission.org/ru/act/integr_i_makroec/dep_stat/fin_stat/statistical_publications/Documents/finstat_5/finstat_5_2018.pdf.

Fabbrini, S. (2008). *Compound Democracies: Why the United States and Europe are Becoming Similar*. Oxford: Oxford University Press.

Farrel, M., Hettne, B., & Van Langenhove, L. (2005). *Global Politics of Regionalism. Theory and Practice*. London: Pluto Press.

Gu, J., Shankland, A., & Chenoy, A. (2016). *The BRICS in International Development*. London: Palgrave Macmillan.

Hancock, K., & Libman, A. (2016). Eurasia. In T. Börzel & T. Risse (Eds.), *The Oxford Handbook of Comparative Regionalism*. Oxford: Oxford University Press.

Hettne, B. (2005). Beyond the 'New Regionalism. *New Political Economy, 10*(4), 543–571.

Higher School of Economics. (2019). *Eurasian Economic Integration: Promising Directions of Development and Strategic Interest of Russia*. Retrieved from https://conf.hse.ru/mirror/pubs/share/262128617 (In Russian).

Hooghe, L., Lenz, T., & Marks, G. (2019). *Community, Scale, and International Organization. A Postfunctionalist Theory of Governance*. Oxford: Oxford University Press.

Kazantsev, A. (2016). Five Scenarios for the Future Borders of Central Asia. In I. Ivanov (Ed.), *The World in 100 Years*. Moscow: NPMP RIAC. (in Russian).

Kelemen, D. (2006). Suing for Europe: Adversarial Legalism and European Governance. *Comparative Political Studies, 39*(1), 101–127.

Kheyfets, B. (2019). Eurasian Economic Union—Time for Modernization. *Outlines of Global Transformations, 12*(2), 29–50. (In Russian).

Kirkham, K. (2016). The Formation of the Eurasian Economic Union: How Successful Is the Russian Regional Hegemony? *Journal of Eurasian Studies, 7*, 111–128.

Knobel, A., Lipin, A., Malokostov, A., Tarr, D., & Turdyeva, N. (2019). Deep Integration in the Eurasian Economic Union: What Are the Benefits of Successful Implementation or Wider Liberalization? *Eurasian Geography and Economics, 60*(2), 177–210.

Krivtsov, A.I. (2020). Sustainable Development of Economic Entities: Key Objectives, Stages and Stakeholder Interests, in E. Popkova (Eds.), *Growth Poles of the Global Economy: Emergence, Changes and Future Perspectives. Lecture Notes in Networks and Systems*, Vol. 73. Cham: Springer. https://doi.org/10.1007/978-3-030-15160-7_34.

Lagutina, M. (2018). The Eurasian Economic Union in the Context of Transformation of the International Trade System. In A. Özer (Ed.), *Globalization and Trade Integration in Developing Countries*. Hershey: IGI Global.

Laruelle, M. (2015). Kazakhstan's Posture in the Eurasian Union: In Search of Serene Sovereignty. *Russian Analytical Digest*, No. 165. Retrieved from https://css.ethz.ch/content/dam/ethz/special-interest/gess/cis/center-for-securities-studies/pdfs/RAD-165-7-10.pdf.

Libman, A. (2007). Regionalization and Regionalism in the Post-Soviet Space: Current Status and Implications for Institutional Development. *Europe-Asia Studies, 59*(3), 401–430.

Libman, A., & Vinokurov, E. (2010). Is It Really Different? Patterns of Regionalization in the Post-Soviet Central Asia. *Frankfurt School of Finance and Management*, 155. Retrieved from https://www.econstor.eu/dspace/bitstream/10419/43711/1/641582641.pdf.

Lissovolik, Y. (2016). WTO: Lost in the Maze of Regionalism. *Valdai Discussion Club.* Retrieved from http://valdaiclub.com/a/highlights/wto-lost-in-the-maze-of-regionalism/.

Lissovolik, Y. (2018). Syndicated Regionalism: The Missing Link in Global Governance. *Valdai Discussion Club.* Retrieved from http://valdaiclub.com/a/highlights/syndicated-regionalism-the-missing-link-in-global/.

Lissovolik, Y., & Vinokurov, E. (2019). Extending BRICS to BRICS+: The Potential for Development Finance, Connectivity and Financial Stability. *Area Development and Policy, 4*(2), 117–133.

Lombaerde, P., Söderbaum, F., van Langenhove, L., & Baert, F. (2010). The Problem of Comparison in Comparative Regionalism. *Review of International Studies, 36*(3), 731–753.

McKinney, J. (2017). How Stalled Reform is Fueling Regionalism: China's Engagement with the G20. *Third World Quarterly, 38*(7), 709–726.

Michalopoulos, C., & Tarr, D. (1997). The Economics of Customs Union in the Commonwealth of Independent States. *Policy Research Paper*, No. 1786, World Bank. Retrieved from http://documents.worldbank.org/curated/en/428801468776749535/The-economics-of-customs-unions-in-the-Commonwealth-of-Independent-States.

Moravcsik, A. (1998). *The Choice for Europe: Social Purpose and State Power from Rome to Maastricht.* New York: Cornell University Press.

Pak, Y. (2020). Intra-Industry Trade in the EAEU: Case of Machine Building. *Adnances in Economics, Business and Management Research, 107*, 111–114. Retrieved from https://download.atlantis-press.com/article/125925179.pdf.

Popescu, N. (2014). Eurasian Union: The Real, the Imaginary and the Likely. *Chaillot Papers*, 132, European Union Institute for Security Studies. Retrieved from https://www.iss.europa.eu/sites/default/files/EUISSFiles/CP_132.pdf.

Risse, T. (2016). The Diffusion of Regionalism. In T. Börzel & T. Risse (Eds.), *The Oxford Handbook of Comparative Regionalism.* Oxford: Oxford University Press.

Roberts, S., & Moshes, A. (2016). The Eurasian Economic Union: A Case of Reproductive Integration? *Post-Soviet Affairs, 32*(6), 542–565.

Rotaru, V. (2018). The Eurasian Economic Union—A Sustainable Alternative for the Former Soviet Space? *Journal of Contemporary European Studies, 26*(4), 425–442.

Russkiy Mir Foundation. (2017). Russian Language in the CIS. Retrieved from https://russkiymir.ru/publications/266083/ (in Russian).
Sergi, B. (2018). Putin's and Russian-led Economic Union: A Hybrid Half-Economics and Half-Political 'Janus Bifrons. *Journal of Eurasian Studies, 9*, 52–60.
Shaw, T. (2018). Is the G20, Like the G7, an Endangered Species? *The Round Table, 107*(5), 601–611.
Shishkov, Y. (2007). The CIS—15 Years of Unavailing Efforts. *Voprosy Ekonomiki, 4*, 113–126. (In Russian).
Simonia, N., & Torkunov, A. (2015). New World Order: From Bipolarity to Multipolarity. *Polis. Political Studies, 3*, 27–37. (In Russian).
Söderbaum, F. (2015). Early, Old, New and Comparative Regionalism: The Scholarly Development of the Field. *KFG Working Paper*. Retrieved from https://www.polsoz.fu-berlin.de/en/v/transformeurope/publications/working_paper/wp/wp64/WP-64-Soederbaum.pdf.
Söderbaum, F., & Sbragia, A. (2010). EU Studies and 'New Regionalism': What Can Be Gained from Dialogue. *Journal of European Integration, 32*(6), 95–117.
The World Bank. (2019). World Bank Open Data. Retrieved from https://data.worldbank.org/.
Torkunov, A. (2018). Great Eurasian Power in the Stream of Changes. *International Trends, 1*(52), 6–13. (In Russian).
Vakulchuk, R., & Knobel, A. (2018). Impact of Non-Tariff Barriers on Trade within the Eurasian Economic Union. *Post-Communist Economies, 30*(4), 459–481.
Van Langenhove, L. (2011). *Building Regions. The Regionalization of the World Order*. Aldershot: Ashgate.
Vinokurov, E., & Libman, A. (2014). Do Economic Crises Impede or Advance Regional Economic Integration in the Post-Soviet Space? *Post-Communist Economies, 26*(2), 341–358.
Warleigh-Lack, A., Robinson, N., & Rosamond, B. (2010). *New Regionalism and the European Union: Dialogues, Comparisons, and New Research Directions*. London: Routledge.
Warleigh-Lack, A., & Rosamond, B. (2010). Across the EU Studies–New Regionalism Frontier: Invitation to a Dialogue. *Journal of Common Market Studies, 48*(4), 993–1013.
Warleigh-Lack, A., & Van Langenhove, L. (2010). Rethinking the EU Studies: The Contribution of Comparative Regionalism. *Journal of European Integration, 32*(6), 541–562.
World Trade Organization. (2019). Regional Trade Agreements Database. Retrieved from http://rtais.wto.org/UI/PublicMaintainRTAHome.aspx.
Xing, L. (2014). *The BRICS and Beyond: The International Political Economy of the Emergence of a New World Order*. Farnham: Ashgate.

CHAPTER 2

EAEU Intra-Regional Trade

Andrey N. Spartak

2.1 Introduction

The development and deepening of regional trade and economic cooperation was initially considered the main task of creating a Customs Union between Russia, Belarus and Kazakhstan in 2010, the formation of a single economic space of these countries in 2012, and the establishment of the Eurasian Economic Union (EAEU) in 2015.

According to the Treaty on the EAEU, free movement of goods, services, and factors of production is ensured in the internal market of the Union. Within the framework of the internal market, member-states do not apply import and export customs duties or non-tariff and trade defense measures (anti-dumping, countervailing, and safeguards) in mutual trade. Work is carried out to identify and eliminate existing barriers, exemptions, and restrictions that impede the functioning of the internal market. In March 2017, the Report ("White paper") "Barriers, Derogations and Restrictions in the Eurasian Economic Union" was officially published,

A. N. Spartak (✉)
All-Russian Market Research Institute, Russian Foreign Trade Academy of Ministry of Economic Development, Moscow, Russia
e-mail: spartak@vniki.msk.ru

N. A. Piskulova (ed.), *The Economic Dimension of Eurasian Integration*, https://doi.org/10.1007/978-3-030-59886-0_2

containing an agreed list of 60 consolidated obstacles to the full-scale functioning of the common market (Eurasian Economic Commission, 2017). As of early August 2019, the list included 71 obstacles and covered many regulatory areas, including technical, sanitary and phytosanitary regulation, tax, competition, energy, transport, industrial, agro-industrial, and migration policies.

By the time the EAEU was established in 2015, a common market for goods and a common labor market were mainly formed (since 2017, the common market regime has extended to such sensitive areas as medicines and medical articles). The key limitations on the free movement of goods in the EAEU are currently associated with incomplete work regarding the harmonization and unification of technical regulations, as well as with the actions of the parties being inconsistent with the principles of the Customs Union (Ivanova and Latyshov 2019). These inconsistencies include varying conditions of accession of its members to the WTO (primarily for Kazakhstan) which are currently undecided within the framework of the EAEU, Russia's unilateral so-called counter-sanctions against a wide range of imported goods from Western countries and Ukraine, the withdrawal of Russia and Ukraine from the free-trade regime, and the partial restoration of customs and other forms of control at the internal borders of the EAEU in response to the abuse by certain participants of the single customs territory regime.

The common services market started simultaneously with the creation of the EAEU in 2015, initially covering 43 service sectors, though as of August 2019 covers 49. Another 14 sectors will start operating in the common market mode in accordance with the liberalization plans by 2021. Patent attorneys, housing and communal services, education and media services, and a number of others have been withdrawn from the process of liberalization and formation of the common market of services.

It should be noted that, from the very beginning, special conditions and transition periods were established for Kazakhstan to join the common market in 29 service sectors (including services in the field of agriculture, forestry, and hunting, services for renting machinery and equipment without an operator, consulting services on architecture, management, market research, and public opinion, services for the development, application of software, photo services, services for entertainment, sports, etc.). In eight sectors (subsectors) Kazakhstan only plans to move to the common market of services in 2025 in order to protect the interests of national business, including construction, engineering, and urban design services. In another six sectors Kazakhstan refused to proceed with liberalization (i.e. maintenance and repair, auxiliary transport services). Thus, the common market of services is formed not in the full format of EAEU-5, but only where Kazakhstan participates (Spartak 2016).

The common electricity market of the EAEU is in the active stage of its formation. While the transition to the common market regime in such key areas as finance, oil, gas, and transport services is scheduled for 2025 (Eurasian Economic Commission 2018).

The declaration on further development of integration processes within the framework of the Eurasian Economic Union, adopted at the summit of the EAEU member-states in December 2018 (06.12.2018, St. Petersburg), named the first of the key directions of deepening integration as ensuring maximum efficiency of the EAEU single market and the realization of its opportunities for business and consumers. The priorities of the Union's activities in this area, which can support the development and diversification of intra-regional trade, are as follows:

- complete elimination of barriers and the maximum reduction of exemptions and restrictions for the free movement of goods, services, capital, and labor in the internal market of the EAEU;
- the formation of a favorable competitive environment for the development of entrepreneurship, small- and medium-sized businesses;
- improving the efficiency of the functioning of the goods market;
- the formation of a single market for services in more sectors;
- the formation of a common financial market of the EAEU;
- accelerated formation of common energy markets;
- the creation of an effective system of production cooperation, the stimulation of localization of production, and encouragement of projects forming regional production chains;
- the development of integration processes in the agricultural sector in order to increase agricultural production;
- joint implementation by EAEU countries of large-scale high-tech and infrastructure projects and the creation of transport corridors, including transcontinental and interstate;

- expanding the use of digital technologies (implementation of the digital agenda of the EAEU), creating favorable conditions for the development of cross-border e-Commerce;
- the creation of conditions for the interaction of national payment systems and expansion of the use of national currencies in mutual trade.

To date, not many studies have been published on the analysis of intra-regional trade in the EAEU or any assessment of its economic effects or the impact of non-tariff barriers on such trade. A number of works by authors from EAEU States are devoted to this topic; they reveal both economic and statistical aspects of intra-regional trade development, give estimates of ad valorem equivalents of non-tariff barriers in the Union, and make econometric calculations on their basis (Eurasian Development Bank: Centre for Integration Studies 2019, Report №52: Vinokurov 2017; Vinokurov et al. 2015a, b, 2017; Russian Foreign Trade Academy: Knobel 2015; Knobel et al. 2019; Vakulchuk and Knobel 2018; Spartak 2013, 2018a); Idrisova and Spartak 2014). Outside the EAEU, the problems of mutual trade and trade barriers within the EAEU, with some exceptions for the early EAEU (Tarr 2016; Jafari and Tarr 2015; Carneiro 2013), were practically not considered.

A small number of publications on trade-related aspects of Eurasian economic integration is due to the extremely insignificant role of mutual trade of member-states in international trade (0.3 per cent in 2018), the relatively recent emergence of quantitative assessments of non-tariff barriers within the EAEU, as well as the lack of recognition by many countries of the EAEU as a full-fledged and competent trading partner.

EAEU experts suggest that the role of integration factors in the development of mutual trade of EAEU countries will become significant only after a multiple reduction in the level of non-tariff barriers in the internal market of the Union. According to the Eurasian Development Bank study, the ad valorem equivalent of remaining non-tariff barriers at the time of the creation of the EAEU reached 15 per cent of the value of goods flows between the countries of the Union (Vinokurov et al. 2015a). In the meantime, the main role in shaping the dynamics and parameters of intra-regional trade is played by factors external to integration processes such as economic geography, economic and commodity markets situation, trade policy and geopolitics, geoeconomic competition, and so on.

2.2 Conditions for the Development of Intra-Regional Trade and the Interests of the Participants

The EAEU is fundamentally an economically highly unbalanced, geographically fragmented Union with an extremely high concentration of business activity and trade flows in Russia (RFTA Ed. by Dolgov and Spartak 2011). Russia's share in the EAEU PPP GDP accounted for 85 per cent in 2018 (87 per cent in GDP at market prices), in total foreign trade turnover of the Union 80 per cent, its per capita GDP exceeded the similar indicators for new members—Armenia and Kyrgyzstan—almost three and eight times, respectively (Table 2.1).

Almost the entire volume of mutual trade in goods in the EAEU is formed with the participation of Russia—about 97 per cent in 2012 and the same 97 per cent in 2018.[1] That is, over the years of the existence of the single economic space and the EAEU, there have been no significant changes in the geographical structure of intra-regional trade. Moreover, during this period, the mutual trade turnover of Belarus and Kazakhstan decreased and now makes only 1.35 per cent of intra-EAEU. Armenia practically does not trade with Kazakhstan and Kyrgyzstan and only has

Table 2.1 Indicators of Russia's economic leadership in the EAEU in 2018

Countries	*Share in total PPP GDP, per cent*	*GDP per capita as percentage of Russia's level*	*Share in total goods foreign trade turnover, per cent*
Total	100.0	–	100.0
Armenia	0.6	35	0.8
Belarus	3.8	68	8.3
Kazakhstan	10.2	94	10.8
Kyrgyzstan	0.5	13	0.8
Russia	84.8	100	79.3

Source: International Monetary Fund, World Economic Outlook Database, April 2019. Retrieved from: http://www.imf.org/external/pubs/ft/weo/2019/01/weodata. Foreign trade turnover data based on the EAEU countries national statistical sources

[1] Here and further, if no special indication is made, calculations were based on the data from national statistical bodies of the EAEU countries. For purposes of comparability of statistical data, if not specially mentioned, calculations were made for EAEU-5 for the whole analyzed period.

very small turnover with Belarus. Exchange of services and investment flows are also highly unbalanced as trade in goods.

Therefore, for all EAEU countries, the economic situation and the state of the Russian domestic market serve as key factors determining their attitude to the Eurasian integration project in general. There are, of course, other factors, including geopolitics and geoeconomics, but it is obvious that without the Russian economy developing sustainably the attractiveness of participation in the EAEU for partner countries is greatly reduced, and the prospects for integration become uncertain.

In particular, both experts and the leadership of Belarus recognize that the socio-economic development of the country is highly determined by the capabilities of the Russian economy: Belarusian GDP directly or indirectly depends on Russia by half (Snopkov 2017), and the fall in output in Russia by 1 per cent automatically reduces the GDP of Belarus by 0.8 per cent. According to Belstat and the National Bank of Belarus, Russia consistently accounts for half of the foreign trade turnover of Belarus (Table 2.2), and for the absolute majority of non-primary non-energy exports, Russia is a key and largely uncontested market for Belarusian suppliers, absorbing almost 80 per cent of all food exports (2018), 75 per cent of machinery and equipment, 68 per cent of clothing, textiles, and footwear, 64 per cent of vehicles, and 63 per cent of plastics and articles thereof (National Bank of Belarus 2019). Belarus is significantly involved in production cooperation with Russia: 70 per cent of all Belarusian exports of parts and components for engineering goods and more than 30 per cent of their imports are focused on the Russian Federation.

Table 2.2 Importance of Russia as a trade partner for the EAEU countries (share in total goods foreign trade turnover, per cent)

	2010	*2011*	*2012*	*2013*	*2014*	*2015*	*2016*	*2017*	*2018*
Armenia	20.6	20.4	23.5	23.2	24.1	24.7	26.7	27.1	26.1
Belarus	46.6	45.2	47.4	49.5	48.8	48.4	51.3	51.2	49.3
Kazakhstan	19.7	18.4	17.1	17.9	16.7	19.7	20.6	20.6	18.8
Kyrgyzstan	30.3	27.1	28.5	27.4	25.8	21.8	23.8	23.0	23.3
EAEU without Russia	30.1	29.3	29.1	29.5	28.9	31.4	33.7	33.6	31.5

Source: Compiled by the author based on the EAEU countries national statistical sources. Retrieved from: http://www.belstat.gov.by; http://www.customs.gov.by/; http://www.armstat.am; http://www.stat.kz; http://e.customs.kz/wps/portal/customs/; http://www.stat.kg; http://www.customs.ru

For Armenia, Russia is the first partner in trade turnover (26 per cent in 2018) and in exports. The latter has grown almost three times since 2015 and consists mainly of labor-intensive products (food, light industry goods, etc.), thus having a positive impact on employment in the country.

The foreign trade orientation of Kyrgyzstan on Russia is lower than that of Armenia and, especially, Belarus—23 per cent in the trade turnover, although supplies to the Russian market increased significantly in 2017–2018. Here we must take into account that a large part of Kyrgyz exports to Kazakhstan is actually intended for Russia. Mostly this applies to the supply of food and light industry products.

In addition to strong trade dependence there are other important benefits for the abovementioned three EAEU states from economic cooperation with Russia. Migration benefits are very high for Kyrgyzstan and high for Armenia, providing for a substantial part of their GDP. As a direct investor, Russia is most important for Belarus (over 55 per cent of all accumulated FDI at the beginning of 2018) and Armenia (32 per cent). However, Russia's presence in the investment field of Kyrgyzstan is more modest—about 22 per cent of accumulated FDI.

Russia also provides loans to Belarus, Armenia, and Kyrgyzstan in order to equalize the balance of payments, service and repay previously granted loans, and implement infrastructure and production projects. The share of the Russian Federation (including the Eurasian Fund for Stabilization and Development) in the external public debt of Belarus at the end of 2018 reached 46 per cent (on average for 2013–2018, 68 per cent), while in Armenia it reached 16 per cent. In the structure of Russia's official development assistance to foreign countries, the main recipient is Kyrgyzstan (along with Cuba), where significant funds were allocated before and after the country's accession to the EAEU—nearly $0.9 billion for the period 2014–2016 (OECD 2018). Armenia is also a recipient of such assistance, although in much smaller amounts (about $40 million per year).

According to the results of 2018, exports of goods and services to Russia, and direct investment and remittances by individuals from Russia amounted to the equivalent of 13.8 per cent of GDP of Armenia, 25.8 per cent of Belarus, and 31.3 per cent of Kyrgyzstan (Table 2.3).

In economic terms, Kazakhstan stands apart from other partners of Russia in the EAEU. Thanks to the oil and gas sector, this country has significant foreign currency reserves, enjoys a fairly strong financial position and high investment attractiveness for many non-regional players, and on the whole is less economically oriented to the Russian Federation.

Table 2.3 Importance of Russia for the EAEU countries as a source of currency and capital receipts in 2018

	GDP	*Exports of goods*	*Exports of services*	*Remittances, balance*	*FDI*	*Overall receipts from Russia*	
	Million $						*As per cent of GDP*
Armenia	12,411	636	339	647	91	1714	13.81
Belarus	59,643	12,410	2244	117	627	15,398	25.82
Kazakhstan	170,539	5349	1103	-696	367	6123	3.60
Kyrgyzstan	8093	251	245	1983	52	2531	31.27

Source: Compiled and calculated by the author based on Russian statistical sources and IMF data. Retrieved from: http://stat.customs.ru; http://www.cbr.ru; http://www.imf.org/external/pubs/ft/weo/2019/01/weodata/index.aspx

Note: For purposes of comparability of currency and capital receipts by EAEU members from Russia, respective indicators are taken according to Russian sources: goods and services—imports of goods and services in Russia; remittances and FDI—as reflected in Russian balance of payments statistics

Russia remains the main foreign trade partner of Kazakhstan (about 19 per cent of the country's foreign trade turnover in 2018), but is only in fourth place in terms of exports (8.5 per cent in total). Nevertheless, Kazakhstan's exports to Russia have demonstrated good dynamics lately (expanded from $3.5 billion in 2016 up to $5.2 billion in 2018) accompanied with diversification of foreign sales and increasing share of non-oil products. For Kazakhstan, the prospects of the Russian market are also important regarding eventual future sales of products planned for production in the framework of national modernization plans and joint industrial projects with China. In addition, as a supplier of oil to Europe, Kazakhstan is interested in ensuring the access of national operators to the energy transport infrastructure of Russia on the basis of common principles, conditions, and rules developed within the framework of the EAEU.

Of great importance is the joint formation with Russia and ensuring the effective functioning of international transit corridors in the East-West direction. Kazakhstan has invested and continues to invest heavily in the development of transit transport and logistics infrastructure. From an economic point of view, the Central Eurasian corridor linking China with Europe through Kazakhstan, Russia, and Belarus is the optimal route of the Chinese Belt and Road Initiative (BRI) among others passing through Kazakhstan.

The economic problems faced by Russia in recent years stimulated its EAEU partners to search for new markets and sources of financing; this strengthened multi-vector policy, but in general did not lead to a reorientation of integration preferences from the Russian direction and did not cause a significant weakening of economic ties with the Russian Federation. Many sources of development and income related to Russia are still uncontested for EAEU members.

At first glance, Russia itself is only focused on partners in the EAEU to a very small extent. According to the Federal customs service, the share of the EAEU in Russia's foreign trade turnover in goods is only 8–9 per cent, about the same in exports, and less than 8 per cent in imports. The growth of oil prices and recovery in the domestic economy usually leads to a decrease in these indicators. For comparison, the US, which dominates the North American Free Trade Area, directs over one-third of all commodity exports to partner countries—Canada and Mexico—and receives from them more than one-fourth of total imports; this is despite the almost sevenfold excess of the US foreign trade turnover over the Russian one. The share of the EAEU in Russia's foreign trade in services is 5.4–5.5 per cent and is especially small in imports (about 4 per cent). Accumulated direct investments from the EAEU States in the Russian economy at the beginning of 2019 were estimated by the CBR at $4.75 billion (over 60 per cent from Kazakhstan), or 1.17 per cent of all FDI.

At the same time, a more detailed examination of, for example, Russian commodity exports to the EAEU shows a significant advantage of its structure, compared with supplies to non-CIS countries. Thus, the share of non-primary non-energy goods in the total sales of Russia in the EAEU markets accounts for 60 per cent (2018), while in exports outside the CIS is less than 30 per cent. Accordingly, the contribution of EAEU partners to non-primary non-energy exports of the Russian Federation—15.2 per cent in 2018—is almost two times higher than total Russian exports (Russian Export Center 2019). This is more than the share of East Asia (14.2 per cent), which is seen as a top priority in Russia's foreign economic policy. The absolute increment of Russian non-primary non-energy exports to the EAEU in 2017–2018 exceeded $7 billion; Kazakhstan and Belarus today are entrenched on the second and third lines in the list of leading export markets for Russia's non-primary products, second only to China. Moreover, the nomenclature of Russian supplies of manufacturing and agricultural products to the EAEU is much wider than in trade with non-CIS countries.

EAEU countries, primarily Belarus and Kazakhstan, are important as buyers of Russian technologies (on average more than 10 per cent over the 2010s), while Kazakhstan is a supplier of many scarce non-energy mineral products in the Russian Federation (worth $1–2 billion annually).

A separate topic for Russia is the effective use of the international transit potential of a very big, advantageously located territory, which is extremely problematic without close cooperation in the field of transport and logistics within the EAEU. In the future, the entire set of international corridors "East-West" and "North-South" can bring substantial revenues to the country, qualitatively improve the transport and logistics infrastructure, and increase the connectivity of the integration space.

Thus, from an economic point of view, the Eurasian integration project is in demand, to a significant extent, by all its participants—this especially takes into account the numerous challenges faced by the EAEU countries and the proclaimed long-term strategies for their development.

2.3 Trends and Structural Parameters of Intra-Regional Trade

The value of mutual trade between EAEU countries (in the composition of five states) reached a peak in 2012 under favorable price conditions and the beginning of the full-scale functioning of the Customs Union, and then during 2013–2016 steadily declined, with a strong fall in 2015–2016. The reasons for such a downturn were the decrease in prices of commodities traded within the Union, as well as the slowdown and recession in the bigger economies of the EAEU, primarily Russia's. As a result, the indicator of mutual trade in 2016 was 39.4 per cent less than the level of 2012.

In 2017–2018, under the influence of rising commodity prices and improving macroeconomic dynamics in the EAEU region, the value of mutual trade showed a noticeable increase: the indicator of 2018 was 1.4 times higher than in 2016, but it was still 15 per cent lower than the peak level of 2012 (Fig. 2.1).

According to trends in 2019, a slight decrease in the value of mutual trade of the EAEU countries is expected. The main reason is the reduction in the physical volume of Russian energy supplies (oil and petroleum products) to Belarus. In principle, Russian energy exports to Belarus play a

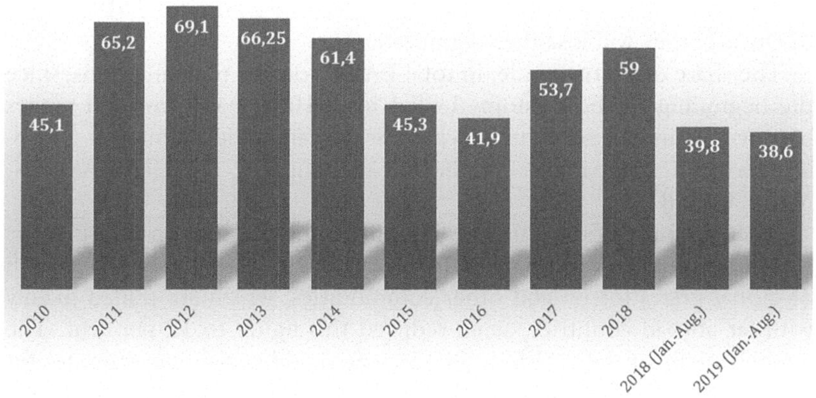

Fig. 2.1 Dynamics of the EAEU intra-regional exports of goods in 2010–2019 ($ billion). (Source: Calculated by the author based on the EAEU countries national statistical sources. Retrieved from: http://www.belstat.gov.by; http://www.customs.gov.by/; http://www.armstat.am; http://www.stat.kz; http://e.customs.kz/wps/portal/customs/; http://www.stat.kg; http://www.customs.ru)

significant role in the overall mutual trade of the Union (19 per cent in intra-regional exports in 2018); therefore, any fluctuations in this area—physical volumes and/or contract prices—affect the results of intra-regional trade.

Another important change in energy trade between Russia and Belarus is the restriction of Russian shipments of petroleum products from mid-2018 due to the use of incorrect schemes by Belarus when exporting such products outside the Union under other HS codes (more details later in the chapter). The export of oil from Russia to Belarus is now set at 18 million tons per year until 2024 (according to the bilateral indicative balance of supplies), but in May–June 2019 there were disruptions in supplies through the Druzhba pipeline, which sharply decreased due to oil pollution with organic chlorides. For these reasons, in January–August 2019 the export of Russian petroleum products to Belarus, according to the Federal customs service, decreased by 2.8 million tons (in value terms—by $1.04 billion) compared to the same period of the previous year, while oil shipments contracted by 0.9 million tons ($0.42 billion).

However, these are temporary factors of decline, typical for 2019, and in the future, they will lose their significance.

The share of mutual trade, in total EAEU foreign trade in goods, since the beginning of the Customs Union in 2010, remains low and ranges between 12 and 14 per cent, which is less than in foreign economic groupings with a comparable number of participants (NAFTA, ASEAN, MERCOSUR).

After the start of the Customs Union there was a slight increase in the share of mutual trade—up to 13.1 per cent in 2012—but then the growth of global prices for oil and other commodities, which are traded mainly with far abroad countries, again reduced this figure to 12 per cent. The establishment of the EAEU in 2015 created additional opportunities for intra-regional trade and coincided with the deterioration of the global commodity situation, so the share of intra-regional flows in total trade increased to about 14 per cent and remains at this level (Table 2.4).

On the whole, taking the decade of integration development, it is difficult to talk about any change in the importance of intra-regional trade: 13.1 per cent in 2009 (before the formation of the Customs Union) and less than 14 per cent in 2018–2019. This is especially because the value of mutual supplies is affected by the terms of energy trade (predictable and less predictable), commodity exchange schemes (including processing and return delivery), and so on. At the same time, for Armenia, which joined the Eurasian integration project in 2015, the increase in the role of trade with partners in the EAEU was quite obvious, being based on improved access to the capacious Russian market.

Table 2.4 Share of intra-regional trade in the total EAEU countries foreign trade in goods in 2010–2019 (per cent)

	2010	*2011*	*2012*	*2013*	*2014*	*2015*	*2016*	*2017*	*2018*	*Jan.–Aug. 2019*
Armenia	21.7	21.6	24.4	24.2	24.9	25.8	27.6	27.6	27.0	28.0
Belarus	48.3	46.1	48.7	50.9	50.2	49.5	52.3	52.6	50.8	50.0
Kazakhstan	11.5	20.0	18.5	19.2	18.3	21.3	22.2	22.4	20.4	21.4
Kyrgyzstan	45.0	39.0	41.3	39.8	41.1	29.8	37.2	38.2	39.3	39.0
Russia	7.3	7.6	8.0	7.3	7.4	8.1	8.5	8.8	8.2	8.5
EAEU	11.2	12.6	13.1	12.4	12.3	13.4	14.2	14.4	13.5	13.9

Source: Calculated by the author based on the EAEU countries national statistical sources. Retrieved from: http://www.belstat.gov.by; http://www.customs.gov.by/; http://www.armstat.am; http://www.stat.kz; http://e.customs.kz/wps/portal/customs/; http://www.stat.kg; http://www.customs.ru

Foreign trade flows of Belarus (50 per cent and more of the total merchandise trade turnover), as well as the small countries of the Union Kyrgyzstan (on average about 40 per cent) and Armenia (close to 30 per cent), are most concentrated on their EAEU partners. For Kazakhstan and Russia, who are focused on energy exports to far abroad, the importance of intra-regional trade is noticeably less—a little more than 20 per cent and about 8–9 per cent, respectively Eurasian Economic Commission 2019b).

When analyzing intra-regional trade, one should bear in mind that the value of even a slight increase in the role of such trade for the EAEU should be considered rather high. The actual state of mutual trade is still under the influence of the common past of the countries of the EAEU as part of the unified economic complex of the former USSR. Calculations based on the gravity model show that the states of the EAEU even over-trade with each other, against a situation where countries with similar GDP and distances between them form a Customs Union (Spartak 2018).

The value of intra-regional trade depends on two major groups of factors: basic economic factors (like economic growth and financial stability in the region, changes in the balance of supply and demand for certain goods, national and product competitiveness, etc.) and specific trade factors, which concern terms and conditions of trade, infrastructure, and market access. Among the latter, substantial impact on intra-EAEU trade has the following factors:

(1) Changes in global oil and other commodity prices, which are transferred—quickly or more slowly—to contract prices in mutual trade (both a plus and a minus for intra-regional trade).
(2) Politically motivated decisions to introduce/maintain preferential prices for Russian energy supplies (oil, petroleum products, natural gas) to other countries of the EAEU (minus for intra-regional trade, in case of cancelation of benefits—plus, with a jump in prices and, accordingly, the value of supplies).
(3) "Gray" schemes for the supply of goods to Russia via partner countries, bypassing import bans or violating Customs Union rules (controversial effects for intra-regional trade).
(4) Changes in the exchange rates (practically the Russian ruble) relative to the US dollar in cases of uses of national currencies when fixing prices in contracts (mostly minus for intra-regional trade).
(5) Developments of transport infrastructure and logistics, facilitating mutual supplies (plus for intra-regional trade).

(6) Any disruption of existing cooperation links (i.e. termination of processing and back delivery operations) or the creation of such links on a significant scale (like the construction of the Belarusian nuclear station with Russia's participation) (accordingly, a minus and a plus for intra-regional trade).
(7) The removal of barriers and restrictions for the free movement of goods (plus for intra-regional trade).

Due to the low dynamics of structural shifts in the economies of EAEU countries, the commodity composition of intra-regional exports changed insignificantly after the creation of the Union in 2015. The importance of trade in mineral products decreased by roughly 5 percentage points, mainly due to lower energy prices (a strong drop in 2019 was explained above), and the share of metals and machinery products slightly increased (Table 2.5).

Table 2.5 Commodity structure of the EAEU intra-regional exports by analytical groups (per cent of the total)

HS code	*Analytical commodity group*	*2014*	*2015*	*2016*	*2017*	*2018*	*Jan.–Aug. 2019*
	EAEU, total	100.0	100.0	100.0	100.0	100.0	100.0
01–24	Food products and agricultural raw materials (excluding textile)	14.5	15.6	16.5	15.2	14.6	15.5
25–27	Mineral products	33.3	33.3	27.0	27.5	28.7	25.5
28–40	Chemical products, rubber	10.3	11.6	12.3	12.1	11.6	12.5
41–43	Raw hides and skins, leather, fur skins and articles thereof	0.2	0.2	0.2	0.2	0.2	…[a]
44–49	Wood, pulp-and-paper products	2.5	2.4	2.8	2.7	2.7	…[a]
50–67	Textiles, textile articles, footwear	3.3	3.5	4.0	3.7	3.8	3.7
72–83	Base metals and articles of base metal	11.6	10.7	11.4	13.2	13.1	13.4
84–87, 90	Machinery, equipment, and land vehicles	18.8	16.7	17.9	18.5	19.0	19.8
68–71, 88, 89, 91–97	Other manufactured goods (including aircrafts and ships)	5.4	6.1	7.7	6.9	6.0	9.5

Source: Eurasian Economic Commission 2019a Retrieved from: http://www.eurasiancommission.org/

[a]Included in analytical group "Other manufactured goods"

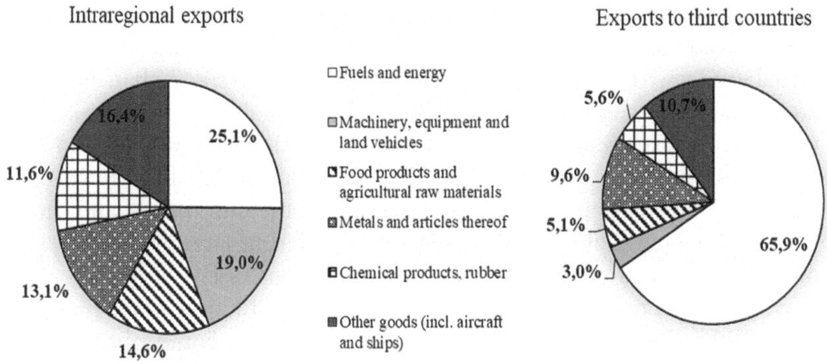

Fig. 2.2 Comparison of EAEU intra-regional exports and exports to third countries commodity structure in 2018 (per cent of the total). (Source: Calculated by the author based on the EAEU countries national statistical sources. Retrieved from: http://www.belstat.gov.by; http://www.customs.gov.by/; http://www.armstat.am; http://www.stat.kz; http://e.customs.kz/wps/portal/customs/; http://www.stat.kg; http://www.customs.ru)

In the structure of mutual trade, according to the Eurasian Economic Commission, currently 60–65 per cent falls on non-energy and non-metallurgical products, while in the export of the EAEU to third countries it is only 25–27 per cent—2–2.5 times less (Fig. 2.2). Thus, intra-regional trade is much more focused on the exchange of manufacturing and agricultural products than the supplies of the EAEU to third countries. If the share of mutual trade within the EAEU is about 13–14 per cent of the total foreign trade turnover of the Union, then in the group of machinery, equipment, and land vehicles (without aircrafts and ships), this figure in recent years exceeds 40 per cent (43.3 per cent in 2018), and for food supplies reaches 25–30 per cent.

Due to a more sophisticated structure of mutual trade for practically all of the EAEU countries, the share of their partners in the Union in non-primary non-energy exports is considerably bigger than in the overall exports. Respective figures for Armenia stand as 38 per cent and 27.9 per cent in 2018, for Belarus as 55 per cent and 41.3 per cent, for Kazakhstan as 22.9 per cent, and 9.7 per cent, and for Russia as 15.2 per cent and 8.45 per cent.

In addition to significant differences in the commodity content of intra-regional trade and trade of the EAEU with third countries, in principle, mutual trade within the Union is much more diversified than with far abroad, and the trend toward diversification is stable (Table 2.6). This intra-regional exchange involves a much wider range of industries and sectors, production activities of the EAEU States, and a much more diversified composition of participating companies and enterprises and small businesses, which makes it an important stimulating factor for the development of national economies and internal regions of the Union.

Existing data on industrial cooperation and production value chains in the EAEU is incomplete and fragmented. However, some observations can be made. One of the relevant studies was conducted for the EEC by Analytical Centre on Foreign Trade under the RF Ministry of Industry and Trade using 2013 statistics retrieved from Eora data base (Analytical Centre on Foreign Trade 2017). The authors of the study explored the origin of value added in various industrial activities in the EAEU countries (unfortunately without Belarus). The results show that Kazakhstan is mostly oriented on regional value chains, but for Russia respective figures

Table 2.6 Diversification levels of the EAEU countries merchandise exports to major trade partners (number of the four-digit HS codes actually traded in 2018)

Armenia (four-digit positions in total export—686)		*Belarus (four-digit positions in total export—1070)*		*Kazakhstan (four-digit positions in total export—997)*	
Russia	546	Russia	1031	Russia	841
Georgia	290	Ukraine	677	China	278
Germany	113	Germany	396	The Netherlands	147
Switzerland	46	United Kingdom	163	Italy	152
United Kingdom	42	The Netherlands	160	Switzerland	55

Kyrgyzstan (four-digit positions in total export—621)		*Russia (Four-digit positions in total export—1181)*			
Kazakhstan	313	Belarus	1121	China	652
Russia	228	Kazakhstan	1114	Italy	505
United Kingdom	21	Armenia	880	Turkey	487
Switzerland	19	Germany	758	Netherlands	482

Source: Calculated by the author based on the International Trade Centre data. Retrieved from: http://www.trademap.org/tradestat

are very small, while Armenia and Kyrgyzstan stay in the middle. Below are some estimates from this study:

- in manufacturing exports in 2013, for Kazakhstan 7.6 per cent of value added originated from EAEU partners, for Armenia 3.2 per cent (though it was not a member of the Union at that moment), and Russia only 0.7 per cent;
- in production of finished goods in the group "Metals and articles thereof" in 2013, for Kazakhstan 10.7 per cent of value added originated from the EAEU countries, and for Russia 1.3 per cent; respective figures in the group "Machinery and equipment (except transport)" stayed at 10.0 per cent for Kazakhstan and 0.8 per cent for Russia;
- in manufacturing gross value added the contribution of intra-EAEU production value chains, for Kazakhstan amounted to 7.5 per cent in 2010 and slightly over 8 per cent in 2013, for Kyrgyzstan stayed equal in 2010 and 2013 at around 6.5–6.6 per cent, for Armenia increased from 4.7 per cent in 2010 to 5.8 per cent in 2013, for Russia was the lowest and flat 2.2 per cent.

With the overall low level of development of intra-industry trade between EAEU countries and the low intensity of regional value chains, in the Russian-Belarusian exchange of engineering products the share of parts and components increased to 17 per cent in 2016—the maximum rate in the 2000s.

As in goods trade, the dominant share of all services trade in the EAEU is conducted with Russia's participation—about 91 per cent of total turnover in services in the Union in 2018. The share of intra-regional trade in total foreign trade in services of the EAEU countries amounted to 9.4 per cent in 2018, 11.7 per cent in total services exports, and 7.7 per cent in total imports (Fig. 2.3). For comparison, the contribution of intra-regional trade to the overall trade of the EAEU States in goods currently ranges between 13 and 14 per cent, including about 11–12 per cent in total exports and about 18 per cent in total imports. Different shares of intra-regional trade in the overall merchandise exchange and services trade can be explained to be quite narrow range of services traded within the EAEU (mostly transport, travel, and construction services), as well as by a different ratio of exports and imports in trade of goods and services (for goods a big surplus and for services a significant deficit). In contrast to mutual

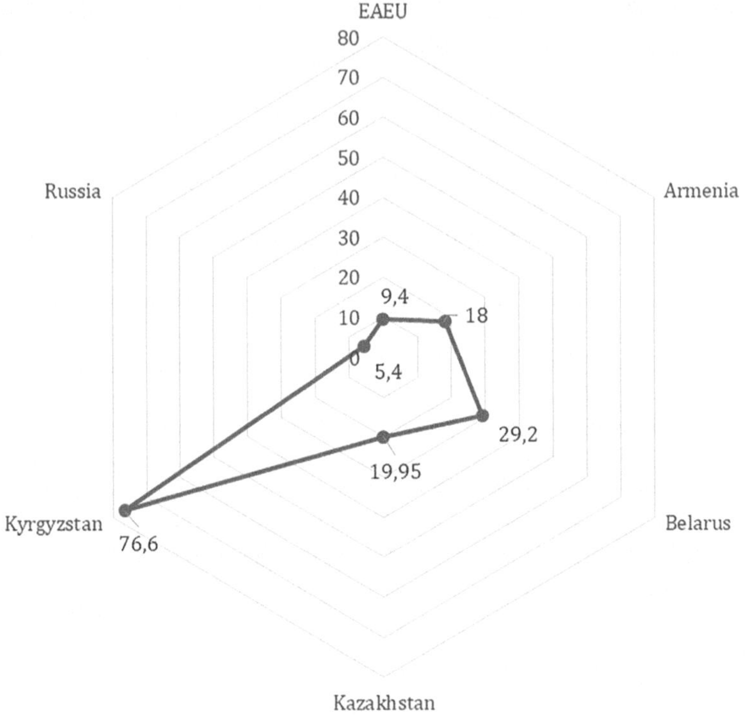

Fig. 2.3 Share of intra-regional trade in the overall foreign trade in services of the EAEU countries in 2018 (per cent). (Source: Calculated by the author based on the balance of payments statistics of the National/Central banks of the EAEU countries. Retrieved from: http://www.cbr.ru; http://www.nbrb.by; https://nationalbank.kz; https://www.nbkr.kg, https://www.cba.am)

trade in goods, Russia's share in intra-regional exports and imports of services is approximately the same and stays at the level of 44–46 per cent (for goods this figure in exports is almost twice as higher than in imports).

Closely related to the issue of intra-regional trade is the progress in the formation of a common market for goods. The latter is deemed to be mostly completed, but needs quantified economic proof. From this view, the results are not obvious enough.

Analysis of changes in the structure of supply for consumption in the internal market of the EAEU in the 2010s showed significant differences in supply trends by industry. However, at the level of two major economic sectors—agriculture and manufacturing—we can see a tendency, though still very weak, for the increasing importance of mutual trade against a reduction in the share of the component "supply of national products to national markets" and/or a decrease in the contribution of imports from third countries (in both cases the share of mutual trade increased by 1 percentage point in 2018 to 2011). Most noticeable shifts in supply in favor of intra-regional trade can be seen in such manufacturing industries as wood processing (plus 8.7 percentage points in the period 2011–2018), food production (plus 2.4 p.p.), textile and clothing production (plus 2.3 p.p.), electrical, electronic, and optical equipment (plus 2.0 p.p.), and chemical production (plus 1.7 p.p.). Improvement of the economic situation and the expansion of domestic demand in the EAEU in 2018 in most processing industries and in the manufacturing as a whole were not followed by the increase in the share of imports, which indicates the sustainability in the development of mutual trade and/or import substitution (Fig. 2.4).

Another quantifiable, though of course only indirect, measure of the degree of progress toward the common market is the price level indices (PLIs) obtained as a partial from dividing purchasing power parities by market exchange rates. Eurostat publishes a price convergence indicator calculated as the coefficient of variation of the PLIs (the ratio of standard deviation to average value) for a group of countries, such as the EU-28 or the Eurozone. A number of experts also suggest the use of PLIs at fixed exchange rates (to exclude the impact of exchange rate volatility) and in relation to actual individual consumption, which gives a more complete and more comparable picture of household consumption levels (Eurostat: Konijn 2014).

The analysis on the basis of the PLIs, showing differences in price levels in EAEU countries reduced to the common currency, indicates the absence of price convergence for the GDP of the member-states of the Union to date. Moreover, the divergence of price levels after the establishment of the EAEU has increased. However, the PLIs for GDP are not always indicative because of the sufficiently volatile PLIs for investment, exports, and imports.

In the sphere of the final consumption of households of the EAEU, after 2012, when the mechanisms of the Customs Union and single

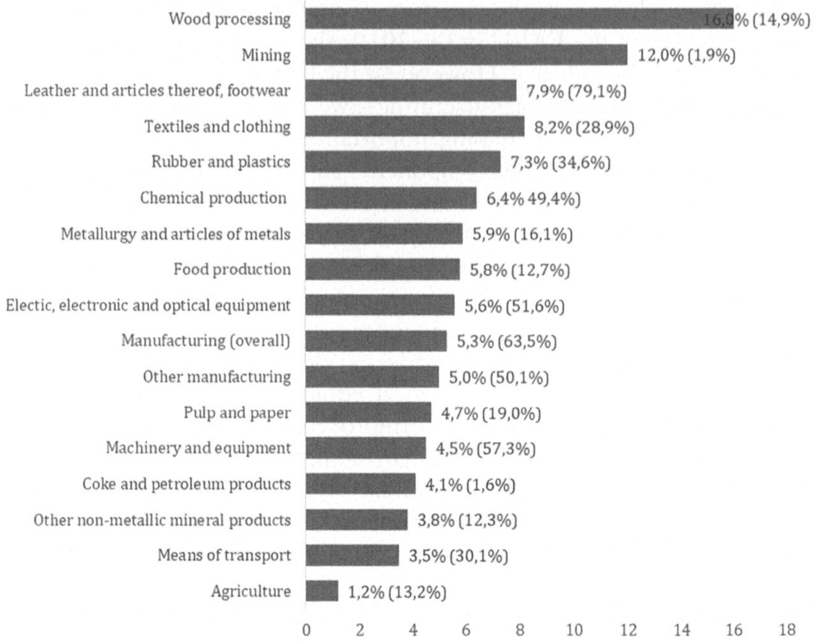

Fig. 2.4 Share of mutual trade in the structure of supply for the consumption on the EAEU internal market, by sector and industry in 2018 (per cent of the total supply*, in brackets—the share of imports). * Consists of three components: supply of national products to national markets, mutual trade, imports from third countries. (Source: Calculated by the author based on EEC data. Retrieved from: http://www.eurasiancommission.org/ru/act/integr_i_makroec/dep_stat/tradestat/Pages/default.aspx)

economic space, the CIS multilateral free trade area (important for Armenia and Kyrgyzstan) became operational, the most significant component of national markets (in contrast to calculations for the entire GDP) was a noticeable and fairly steady decline in the coefficient of variation, which means a convergence of price levels between the countries. Although not everything is clear, as the ratio of the Russian and EAEU partners' PLIs over different periods varied in different directions, plus the PLIs of final consumption are not quite comparable, since, for example, in EAEU countries the state participates differently in the provision of non-market services, such as healthcare and education.

Thus, based on the dynamics of the PLIs, it is impossible to draw an unambiguous conclusion about the convergence of prices within the EAEU, especially about the influence of the integration factor on the convergence of prices which, from the point of view of economic theory, should accompany the movement to the common market.

2.4 Trade Distortions Affecting Intra-Regional Trade

In the mutual trade of EAEU countries, serious statistical distortions arise in connection with their violations of the rules of the Customs Union and abuse of the single customs territory regime. This applies to unregistered imports from China by Kazakhstan and Kyrgyzstan for subsequent sales to Russia, "gray" supplies of fruits and vegetables from Uzbekistan through Kazakhstan to Russia, schemes used by Belarus for the actual re-export of Russian energy resources, transit supplies through Belarus to Russia of food produced by countries that fell under Russian counter-sanctions regime (Spartak 2019a, b).

In the mid-2000s, exports of textiles, clothing, and footwear from China to Russia increased significantly and also began to be realized in the form of overland transit through Kazakhstan and Kyrgyzstan. Deliveries of such products from China through Kazakhstan and Kyrgyzstan in the second half of the 2000s were comparable with direct exports to Russia and leading European countries. Furthermore, the bigger part of these goods was intended for sale in the Russian market. With some changes, the situation persisted in the 2010s, especially because following the formation of the Customs Union, which first included Kazakhstan and later Kyrgyzstan, the opportunities for "gray" transit supplies from China increased (Table 2.7).

In recent years, as shown in the above table, the estimated volume of smuggled Chinese textiles, clothing, and footwear through Kazakhstan and Kyrgyzstan to Russia—an average of about $5–6 billion in 2016–2018—became comparable to the gross output of light industry in Russia. As the order with Chinese imports on the Russian-Chinese border was established ("gray" supplies of textiles, clothing and footwear from China to Russia, according to "mirror" statistics, only for the period 2016–2018 decreased by $1.1 billion), the main routes of smuggling

Table 2.7 Difference between exports of textiles, clothing, and footwear from China to Kazakhstan and Kyrgyzstan and respective imports by Kazakhstan and Kyrgyzstan from China (based on mirror statistics, $ million)

HS code	*Description*	*Kazakhstan*				*Kyrgyzstan*			
		2015	*2016*	*2017*	*2018*	*2015*	*2016*	*2017*	*2018*
61	Knitted clothing	485.5	666.5	801.4	679.2	887.5	954.0	693.5	601.3
62	Sewing clothes	380.7	536.0	813.9	1007.6	552.0	1463.1	1704.0	1291.0
63	Textiles	278.3	436.3	556.6	527.5	116.4	76.3	92.1	193.9
64	Footwear	1144.5	1086.3	1520.8	694.9	569.8	676.5	712.6	717.5
Total		2289.0	2725.1	3692.7	2909.1	2125.8	2909.1	3202.2	2803.7

Source: Calculated by the author based on UN COMTRADE data. Retrieved from: https://comtrade.un.org/

predictably moved to Kazakhstan and Kyrgyzstan, which recorded a noticeable growth of "gray" imports from China after 2015.

Central Asian countries, especially Uzbekistan, have traditionally been major suppliers of fresh fruits and vegetables to Russia. In the 2010s, with the formation of the Customs Union, these commodity flows decreased significantly, but at the same time increased the scale of the flow of goods from Central Asia to Kazakhstan (today, according to the State Committee of the Republic of Uzbekistan on statistics, Kazakhstan is the main external market for Uzbek fruits and vegetables), which was previously virtually absent. Meanwhile, according to expert estimates, there was no significant decrease in physical supply of Central Asian fruits and vegetables on the Russian market, even in the Central regions (except Moscow), the most convenient for import from far abroad countries.

The bulk of Uzbek fruits and vegetables, which are actually sent to the Russian market, are not recorded by the Russian customs and tax authorities. Goods come from Uzbekistan to Kazakhstan and then disappear from the "radar". Only a small part is officially sold by Kazakhstan to Russia (in fact, re-export of Uzbek products). According to the author's assessment, the "gray" supplies from Uzbekistan via Kazakhstan to Russia in 2018 accounted for 45 per cent of total Russian imports (also including direct deliveries from Uzbekistan fixed by the Russian customs and re-exports through Kazakhstan) of Uzbek fruits and vegetables by physical volume and 58 per cent by value (in 2017, 65 per cent and over 70 per cent, respectively).

The high attractiveness of "gray" schemes for the supply of Uzbek food to Russia was due to the almost complete non-payment of taxes and fees in this business: neither when entering Kazakhstan (through shell companies), nor when importing and selling them in Russia, taking advantage of the "transparency" of borders in the Customs Union and the existence of a "shadow" market in the Russian Federation. Supply chains are long and include many intermediaries but are tax-free, cash-based, and quick-turn, as the Uzbek food brand is popular in Russia. This vision of the situation is shared by independent Kazakh and Kyrgyz experts.

To conceal the actual volume of export of petroleum products on which Russia and Belarus agreed on a return of export duties and energy balance, Belarus began, a decade ago, to practice the delivery of petroleum products to third countries under other commodity codes (solvents, lubricants, bitumen mixes, etc.). Through this scheme, for the period 2008–2018, the total amount of understating actual exports of petroleum products exceeded 15 million tons. Thus, Belarus exported all the volume of petroleum products it could produce from subsidized Russian oil, plus some hidden volume; to make this scheme work they imported additional quantities of petroleum products from Russia.

Since mid-2018 Russia has introduced a special regulatory regime for petroleum products exports to Belarus; however, the problem of unauthorized re-exports remains. In 2019, when Russia established a licensing procedure of coal exports to Ukraine, Belarus started buying this commodity in large quantities, further resaling Russian coal to Ukraine.

With the beginning of the sanctions confrontation and the introduction of counter-sanctions by Russia against Western countries (covering mainly food products), supplies of these goods to Belarus from third countries, primarily those that fell under the Russian counter-sanctions regime, have multiplied. The increase in sanctioned food supplies to Belarus from the countries under the counter-sanctions of the Russian Federation amounted to 3.5 times in 2016 against the pre-sanctions 2013 (in absolute terms the increase in purchases of such goods reached 1 million tons) and 3 times in 2017 (an increase of 0.8 million tons) (Table 2.8). A multiple increase in supplies was observed for almost all food items, especially for fruits and vegetables, and products made of flour or milk.

At the same time, in 2016–2017, the statistically recorded deliveries of the same food assortment from Belarus to Russia also significantly increased. Russia's official imports of sanctioned food from Belarus

Table 2.8 Volume of violation by Belarus of the Russian counter-sanctions regime in 2016–2017 (thousand tons)

	2013	*2016*		*2017*	
		Total	*Growth to 2013*	*Total*	*Growth to 2013*
Russian official imports from Belarus of sanctioned food	496.3	1034.8	538.5	1051.9	555.6
Supplies to Belarus of sanctioned food from countries that fell under Russia's counter-sanctions regime	395.3	1373.4	978.1	1198.0	802.7
Excess of imports growth of Belarus from sanctioned countries over imports growth of sanctioned food by Russia from Belarus	–	–	439.6	–	247.1

Sum of the following HS codes: 0207, 0302, 0401, 0702–0705, 0709, 0710, 0712, 0808–0811, 190190

Source: Calculated by the author based on UN COMTRADE data and Russian customs statistics. Retrieved from: https://comtrade.un.org/ and http://customs.ru/statistic

augmented by more than two times in physical volume in 2016–2017 compared to 2013 or in absolute terms by an average of 0.54–0.55 million tons. However, this increase was still 1.5–2 times less than the growth in purchases of the same range of goods in the sanctioned countries. Thus, in addition to large-scale violations in determining the origin of goods, from 300 to 400 thousand tons of sanctioned food came to Russia from Belarus using "gray" schemes, including direct smuggling, pseudo-transit of sanctioned food through the territory of the Russian Federation, and so on. In fact, the actual smuggling component was much larger, if we take into account the mobilization of Belarusian own agricultural sector to provide Russian market with sanctioned food.

In 2018, supplies of sanctioned food to Belarus from third countries, primarily from countries that fell under the Russian counter-sanctions regime, decreased by almost half. As a result, the volume of sanctioned food supplies approached the level of pre-sanctions 2013. Purchases of sanctioned food significantly declined over practically the whole traded range, which was the result of increased control over transit deliveries of such products to Russia.

The total amount of distortions in the statistics of mutual trade—due to various violations of the rules of the Customs Union, the use of "gray" schemes and direct smuggling—is quite large throughout the entire period of operation of the Customs Union and then the EAEU. This is due to the still low level of integration solidarity of EAEU participants and a significant volume of the shadow economy in member-states.[2]

2.5 Prospects for Intra-Regional Trade in the EAEU

In the future, trade within the EAEU will be influenced by a large number of factors and often in different directions. The most important of these factors include the economic situation in EAEU countries; progress in the formation of common markets and support of mutual trade by governments and regional financial institutions; the prospect of rising import intensity of the Russian market for the supplies from other EAEU countries; terms and conditions for energy trade in the Union; the extent of trade distortions in connection with the use of "gray" schemes in regional commerce; the degree of trade liberalization of the EAEU with third countries; and the influence of major non-regional players, especially China and the EU, on economic processes in the EAEU. The value of intra-regional trade, as we noted above, also strongly depends on the dynamics of world commodity prices.

According to the IMF forecasts, the main market of the EAEU—Russian in the medium term—will develop at a rate of no more than 2 per cent per year (IMF World Economic Outlook 2019). This means that domestic demand will actually stagnate. The Belarusian economy will be teetering on the brink of recession, which will further limit its purchasing power, but at the same time may stimulate exports to EAEU countries in an attempt to prevent a fall in GDP. Kazakhstan's economic performance looks better, but GDP growth is expected to slow after 2020.

The forecast for Armenia and Kyrgyzstan is quite favorable, but their contribution to intra-regional trade is extremely small. Therefore, we can assume that macroeconomic factors will not be able to provide any positive impulses for the development of mutual trade in the EAEU, especially when the phenomenon of overtrading between Russia and partners in the EAEU exists.

[2] According to the CIS Statistical Committee, the share of shadow economy in the GDP of Kazakhstan reached 20.3 per cent in 2017 (in gross value-added in the wholesale and retail trade—50.5 per cent), in the GDP of Kyrgyzstan—3.5 per cent (16 per cent), Russia's GDP—4.4 per cent (9.5 per cent).

Currently, the formation of the common market of goods in the EAEU is deemed to be completed, although a significant number of barriers, exemptions, and restrictions remain, which are monitored and discussed within the framework of the EEC. At the moment there is no statistically significant evidence of the influence of the functioning of the common market of goods on the volume of mutual commodity flows in the EAEU. Rather, thanks to the common market regime, it is possible to maintain a fairly high intensity of mutual trade of the EAEU countries, despite the strong trade deviation impulses generated by China and the EU.

Nevertheless, the calculations of RFTA experts based on the CGE-model, which were made for the moment of the EAEU creation in 2015, indicate a vast potential for increasing intra-regional trade in the EAEU if the remaining non-tariff barriers and restrictions are completely eliminated. The total volume of mutual trade of the EAEU countries can grow almost twice, and the most noticeable increase will take place in exports from Belarus to other EAEU States and from the EAEU to Kazakhstan—in both cases by 2.3 times (Table 2.9). The most dynamic trading pair will be Belarus-Kazakhstan.

However, the complete elimination of non-tariff barriers in the EAEU is highly unlikely due to the different structures of their economies and conflicting economic interests, the prevailing low share of intra-industry trade as an incentive for further liberalization, and the projected weak economic dynamics of the EAEU countries, which encourages restrictive import policies.

Under existing financial and economic limitations, it is difficult to expect that EAEU States will use significant resources to stimulate mutual trade. Meanwhile, the largest export credit agency in the EAEU—the Russian export center—has a relatively high percentage of CIS countries, including the EAEU, in the total insurance and credit portfolio of export support—about 25 per cent in 2017 (Russian Export Center 2018). In 2015, a representative office of REC group was opened in Belarus. VEB.RF (former Vnesheconombank) provides significant support to joint projects and bilateral trade through its affiliate in Belarus "Bank BelVEB". To facilitate mutual trade and settlements in national currencies, the Interstate Bank was established (founded by five members of the EAEU and three other CIS countries—Moldova, Tajikistan, and Turkmenistan).

As a result of the interaction of National/Central banks and the activities of Interstate Bank, the share of payments in national currencies in mutual trade in goods and services of the EAEU countries has significantly

Table 2.9 Assessment of intra-EAEU trade growth due to full elimination of non-tariff barriers (based on 2015 values)

Exporting region	*Importing region*	*Growth, per cent*
Armenia	EAEU	97.6
EAEU	Armenia	29.5
Belarus	EAEU	126.0
EAEU	Belarus	112.7
Kazakhstan	EAEU	110.0
EAEU	Kazakhstan	125.9
Kyrgyzstan	EAEU	88.1
EAEU	Kyrgyzstan	18.8
Russia	EAEU	82.6
EAEU	Russia	71.8
	EAEU total	96.0

Source: RFTA (Knobel, A.) calculations based on CGE-model (2018). Unpublished

increased over the last years—from 63 per cent in 2013 to 74–76 per cent on average in 2016–2018. Of the total amount of payments in national currencies, more than 98 per cent is accounted for by the Russian ruble (Fig. 2.5).

The level of settlements in national currencies in mutual trade of EAEU countries has stabilized recently, which apparently reflects the achieved balance of interests of economic operators. Therefore, it is hardly possible to talk about the stimulating influence of this factor on the further development of intra-regional trade.

Real and significant support for intra-regional trade in the EAEU through supranational programs and projects is very unlikely in the foreseeable future. The EAEU does not have its own budget, and even if it does, it will not be enough to effectively stimulate integration and mutual trade. The current budget of the Union State of Russia and Belarus for the implementation of bilateral programs is about $80 million. According to our estimates, for a statistically significant impact on integration and intra-regional trade the EAEU budget should reach $13–14 billion. This is now an absolutely unaffordable value for EAEU countries.

Significant trade imbalances in favor of Russia are a serious economic constraint on Eurasian integration and intra-regional trade. With the share of the Russian Federation in mutual exports of the EAEU at 64 per cent in 2018, its position in mutual imports is twice as weak—only 32 per cent

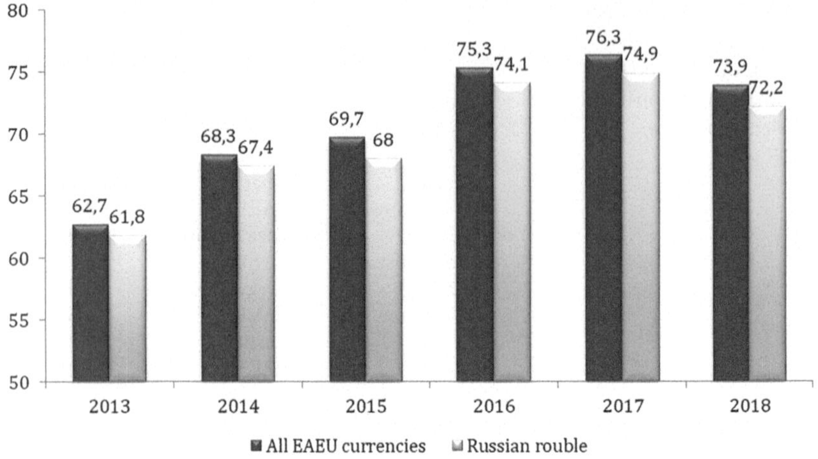

Fig. 2.5 Share of receipts (payments) in national currencies in the EAEU mutual trade in goods and services (per cent). (Source: Compiled by the author based on data from Eurasian Economic Commission. Retrieved from: http://www.eurasiancommission.org/ru/act/integr_i_makroec/dep_stat/fin_stat/express_information/Pages/express_payments.aspx)

(in 2012 even slightly more—33 per cent). Belarus, whose economy is about 4 per cent of Russia's, has a larger volume of intra-regional imports than Russia (39.4 per cent in 2018).

The total positive balance for Russia in merchandise trade with the EAEU increased to $19.4 billion in 2018 ($12 billion in 2016), the coefficient of trade turnover imbalance in favor of Russia was 34 per cent (with Kyrgyzstan 73 per cent, Kazakhstan 42 per cent, Armenia 36 per cent, and Belarus 28 per cent). That is, Russia has significant imbalances with each country (Table 2.10).

The situation with trade imbalances is explained by large (relative to the size of trade turnover) energy supplies from the Russian Federation, a more powerful Russian export sector, but most importantly by the prevailing low competitiveness and limited export supply from the EAEU partners, especially given the growing complexity and technological intensity of Russian imports. An increase in the capacity of the Russian market for products from EAEU countries could be expected, all other things being equal, if the EAEU implements a coordinated industrial policy aimed at creating complementary industries and new regional value chains, but this is not happening.

Table 2.10 Shares of the EAEU countries in mutual trade in goods and trade imbalances in 2018

Countries	*Share in mutual exports, per cent*	*Share in mutual imports, per cent*	*Balance in trade with Russia, $ billion*	*Coefficient of trade turnover imbalance with Russia*[a], *per cent*
EAEU	100.0	100.0	-19.35	34
Armenia	1.2	2.3	-0.71	36
Belarus	23.5	39.4	-9.55	28
Kazakhstan	10.0	22.9	-7.69	42
Kyrgyzstan	1.0	3.1	-1.39	73
Russia	64.4	32.3	–	–

Source: Compiled and calculated by the author based on the EAEU countries national statistical sources. Retrieved from: http://www.belstat.gov.by; http://www.customs.gov.by/; http://www.armstat.am; http://www.stat.kz; http://e.customs.kz/wps/portal/customs/; http://www.stat.kg; http://www.customs.ru

[a]Ratio of net balance to trade turnover

Taken the considerable modernization and innovation efforts of the EAEU countries, their intra-regional exports became less consistent with prevailing import demand trends. This is illustrated by the index of commodity complementarity of regional trade,[3] which for all countries of the Union, without exception, decreased in comparison with the beginning of the 2000s and was in 2018 at the level of two-digit groups: 0.27 for Armenia (0.33 in 2001), 0.54 for Belarus (0.60), 0.17 for Kazakhstan (0.26), 0.33 for Kyrgyzstan (0.39), and 0.28 for Russia (0.39). Massive imports of finished industrial products, components, and technological equipment from outside the EAEU, the creation of joint (assembly) enterprises with partners from the far abroad and formation of cross-border production chains with them are all factors which accelerate the modernization and development of relevant domestic industries and sectors, but at the same time reduces the incentives for deepening integration and cooperation between the EAEU members.

The terms of Russian energy supplies to the EAEU partners will change significantly in the near future due to the implementation of a tax

[3] Index of commodity complementarity in regional trade assesses similarity of country's export structure to the world and the targeted region (EAEU) import structure from the world. If this index is 1 then there is complete coincidence of country's export and region's import structure, if 0—complete mismatch.

Table 2.11 Assessment of the size of Russia's oil and gas transfer to Belarus in 2010–2018

	2010	*2011*	*2012*	*2013*	*2014*	*2015*	*2016*	*2017*	*2018*
Transfer, total, $ billion	4.3	6.1	9.4	9.3	9.8	4.9	2.0	2.9	4.9
as per cent of total merchandise imports of Belarus	12.2	13.2	20.2	21.6	24.3	16.3	7.2	8.5	12.8
as per cent of Belarusian GDP	7.5	9.9	14.3	12.3	12.5	8.7	4.1	5.3	8.2
as per cent of Russian GDP	0.26	0.30	0.42	0.40	0.48	0.36	0.16	0.19	0.30

The sum of Russian subsidies to Belarus through preferential contract prices for oil and gas

Source: Calculated by the author based on the Russian and Belarusian statistical sources. Retrieved from: http://www.customs.ru/; http://www.gks.ru/; http://www.belstat.gov.by; http://www.nbrb.by

maneuver in Russia (transfer of export duties on fuels to internal taxation), which leads to a substantial rise in fuel prices in the internal market of the EAEU and thus will have an increasing effect on the importers of Russian energy resources in the region.

Until recently, the volume and attractiveness of the annual Russian oil and gas transfer (i.e. preferential component of supplies due to lower prices) for EAEU partners—Belarus, Armenia, and Kyrgyzstan[4]—remained quite high. According to the calculations of RFTA experts, the size of such a transfer in favor of the current members of the Union reached $11.8 billion in 2012, or 0.53 per cent of Russia's GDP (Knobel 2015). In the subsequent period, the size of the transfer decreased due to the fall in global oil prices, the reduction of marginal rates of export duties on oil, and the calculated coefficients of export duties on petroleum products. However, in 2018 the size of such a transfer amounted to $5 billion only for Belarus (it accounts for about 90 per cent of the total Russian oil and gas transfer to partners in the EAEU) (Table 2.11).

Largely due to a tax maneuver in Russia, which bears serious and accelerating negative effects on the economy of Belarus through higher energy

[4] Includes Russian gas supplies on preferential price terms to Belarus and Armenia, oil supplies on preferential price terms within established limits to Belarus, petroleum products supplies without paying export duties within established limits to Armenia and Kyrgyzstan, and unlimited (until mid-2018) to Belarus.

prices, during 2019 additional efforts were taken and sectoral "roadmaps" were elaborated to promote comprehensive implementation of the basic ideas of the Treaty on Union State of Russia and Belarus (signed in 1999). Parties intend to make decisive steps toward the creation of an Economic Union, deepening cooperation in the areas of finance, tax regulation, and monetary policy. In practice these activities mainly focus on elaborating mutually acceptable compensatory economic measures for Belarus against expected growth of prices on imported Russian fuels.

As noted above, various trade distortions arising from the violation of the Customs Union rules by EAEU countries have a significant multidirectional impact on the parameters of intra-regional trade. The tendency to reduce the volume of such distortions will take place, but at this stage of the integration process, characterized by sufficiently strong centrifugal manifestations, new "gray" schemes and other violations affecting mutual trade may appear.

A serious non-economic factor affecting the economic prospects of the EAEU and intra-regional trade, however, is the sanctions confrontation between Russia and the West, as well as the acute conflict situation in Russia's relations with Ukraine. Under these circumstances, participants of the EAEU have actually turned to using different regimes of trade and economic cooperation with third countries. Russia imposed an embargo on the supply of food and a number of other goods from Western countries and Ukraine, established MFN regime (instead of free trade) with Ukraine, and imposed restrictions on the supply of goods from Turkey, while the partners in the EAEU did not take any such action.

The whole situation with different regimes of trade and economic cooperation of EAEU States with third countries (including the EU, varying obligations under the WTO, etc.) leads to significant specific costs of functioning of the Customs Union and the single customs territory instead of facilitating trade, not so much creating new trade flows but redistributing them, and often in the "gray" zone. These developments call into question the economic feasibility of the chosen supranational model of integration and undermine the very foundations of the Eurasian integration project.

The conclusion of free-trade agreements with third countries may have a sensitive impact on intra-regional trade (Knobel and Chokaev 2014). Everything, of course, depends on the composition of the participants and the terms of such agreements. To date, the EAEU concluded FTAs with Vietnam, Singapore, Serbia, and Iran—little cause for concern yet, with negotiations with Egypt and Israel are on the agenda. The Indian track seems to be frozen, so in a medium-term period any substantial effects from FTAs on intra-regional trade are not expected.

One important aspect of Eurasian economic integration is that, according to the estimated economic effects of the implementation of the internal and external integration agenda, the EAEU members are divided into two groups.

On the one hand, RFTA calculations (based on the CGE-model) show that there is a serious asymmetry in the potential effects of deepening integration within the EAEU for different participants. Smaller countries of the Union—Armenia, Belarus, and Kyrgyzstan—are most interested in reducing (completely eliminating) non-tariff barriers within the EAEU. This is due, primarily, to the structure of trade of EAEU countries with greater orientation of Armenia, Belarus, and Kyrgyzstan on the internal market of the Union, while Russia and Kazakhstan direct dominant trade volumes to far abroad and thus have relatively low dependence on the EAEU market.

On the other hand, the RFTA calculations show an inverse asymmetry in the distribution of effects between the EAEU partners from integration with third countries by concluding free-trade agreements. In this case, Russia and, to a lesser extent, Kazakhstan are the main winners, while smaller EAEU countries may even suffer losses due to their export structure and focus on the Russian market, which will become more competitive after the emergence of new categories of preferential suppliers.

The expansion of the membership of the EAEU may significantly affect the parameters of intra-regional trade, if a potential candidate is large enough (Spartak and Voronova 2018). Until the middle of 2019, the possibility of new members joining the EAEU was not considered as a near-future task, but then the issue of Uzbekistan's rapprochement with the EAEU arose. Uzbekistan is a large and dynamic partner with a large economic and trade potential, and the calculations of the effects of its accession to the EAEU, based on the CGE-model, indicate the stimulating effect of this step on intra-regional commodity flows. According to RFTA assessments, Uzbekistan's exports to EAEU countries may grow by \$2 billion with a decrease in intra-regional exports of the EAEU countries by only \$0.12 billion; Uzbekistan's imports from the EAEU may increase by \$0.4 billion with the reduction of intra-regional imports of the EAEU countries by \$0.13 billion.

Strong trade reorientation effects in the EAEU area are due to the powerful gravitational influence of two major external players—China and the EU.

Launched in the mid-2010s, the initiative of conjugation of building the Eurasian Economic Union and the Economic belt of the Silk Road (in fact, this format serves for the inclusion of the EAEU in the Chinese Belt and Road Initiative) contributed to boosting the bilateral economic ties of EAEU participants with China, accelerating the growth of mutual trade and Chinese investment in partner countries, as well as the entry of Chinese capital into strategic assets in Russia and other EAEU members. The institutional and legal framework of the conjugation today is determined by the non-preferential Agreement on trade and economic cooperation between the EAEU and China, signed in May 2018.

Positively assessing the overall initiative of conjugation, it is necessary to pay attention to the following points. Despite the initial integration and multilateral vision of conjugation, this initiative has, in fact, resulted almost entirely in bilateral projects with a primary focus on the countries of Central Asia (Spartak 2017). In these countries the main infrastructure and production projects of the PRC are being implemented, including the transfer of environmentally disadvantaged enterprises from China. At the moment the conjugation initiative has led to a growing orientation of the economies of the EAEU on China, especially the Central Asian ones (both members and not members of the EAEU), the latter having elaborated or currently elaborating their own programs and plans of pairing the development of national economies with Chinese BRI. Such multi-level interaction with the PRC generates differences within the EAEU in the formation of common markets (in particular, Kazakhstan retains exemptions and postponements for the liberalization of services sectors serving infrastructure and other projects of the PRC in the country) (Spartak 2018a).

The role and influence of China on Eurasian economic integration is a very difficult topic. Chinese-style globalization and traditional regional integration are at least of very low compatibility. In our opinion, the Chinese factor (of course, not only because of it) is slowing down integration processes around the world. The EAEU is no exception.

The PRC share in the merchandise trade turnover of the EAEU with third countries, according to the EEC, approached 17 per cent in 2018 (which is more than the following Germany and the Netherlands taken together) and in absolute terms exceeded $126 billion, an increase by

Table 2.12 Ranking merchandise trade partners of the EAEU countries in 2018 (per cent of the total foreign trade turnover)

EAEU countries	*Rank*				
	1	*2*	*3*	*4*	*5*
Armenia	EAEU (27.0 per cent)	EU (24.8 per cent)	China (10.3 per cent)	Switzerland (6.3 per cent)	Iran (4.9 per cent)
Belarus	EAEU (50.8 per cent)	EU (24.0 per cent)	Ukraine (7.6 per cent)	China (5.0 per cent)	Turkey (1.4 per cent)
Kazakhstan	EU (40.3 per cent)	EAEU (20.4 per cent)	China (12.5 per cent)	Korea Rep. (4.2 per cent)	Switzerland (3.3 per cent)
Kyrgyzstan	EAEU (39.3 per cent)	China (30.0 per cent)	EU (16.1 per cent)	Turkey (5.9 per cent)	Uzbekistan (5.2 per cent)
Russia	EU (42.7 per cent)	China (15.7 per cent)	EAEU (8.2 per cent)	Turkey (3.7 per cent)	US (3.6 per cent)

Source: Compiled by the author based on the EAEU countries national statistical sources. Retrieved from: http://www.belstat.gov.by; http://www.customs.gov.by/; http://www.armstat.am; http://www.stat.kz; http://e.customs.kz/wps/portal/customs/; http://www.stat.kg; http://www.customs.ru

$24 billion in 2018 alone (for EAEU member states see Table 2.12). The Chinese contribution to EAEU imports from third countries is substantially higher and increased by almost 10 percentage points during the first four years of operation of the EAEU: from 14.6 per cent in 2014 to 24.1 per cent in 2018. The available data for 2019 show further enhancement of Chinese trade positions in the EAEU region. In fact, through massive supplies to the EAEU of all possible range of manufacturing products, China devalues and makes the efforts of the EAEU countries to establish industrial cooperation unnecessary (and more costly) and reduces the potential and need for the development of intra-industry trade within the Union. Moreover, the financial conditions of Chinese supplies are the most favorable.

The investment and project component of Chinese business activity in the EAEU also poses a serious challenge to Eurasian integration. As a result, of the expansion of Chinese capital, the value chains and business processes are increasingly closed to the Chinese economy, the elements of competition in the economic specialization of the EAEU countries are increasing (Spartak 2019b).

Of course, cooperation with China may support intra-EAEU trade flows in some areas: for example, through the creation on the EAEU territory of assembly plants and other businesses focused on the supply of goods to Russia, or through the construction of transport corridors in the East-West direction, which can increase connectivity between the regions of the EAEU. Nonetheless, the overall Chinese influence on intra-regional trade in the EAEU should be considered as restraining for its development.

A new factor that must be taken into account for any integration undertaking is the Fourth industrial revolution, including its consequences for the economy and international trade (Schwab 2017). We will highlight only one of the expected effects, which in our opinion is significant for Eurasian integration.

This is the concept of distributed/decentralized manufacturing, which is an alternative to traditional economic globalization and the principles on which it was based, including the international division of labor, based on national comparative and competitive advantages. The main idea, backed by the newest digital, additive, cognitive, and further advanced technologies, is to place production closer to the buyer/consumer, with more effective integration of the latter into the process of value creation through participation in the development of design, other product parameters, considering own preferences and local conditions. This reduces the time and cost of production, and significantly increases its adaptability to customer needs. In this model, physical supply chains will increasingly be replaced by electronic communications and data exchange, that is, they will be increasingly dematerialized (Impact of the Fourth Industrial Revolution on Supply Chains 2017).

Trade will tend to be more local or regional, with a significant reduction in long-distance deliveries. The role of border and coastal trade between neighboring regions in partner countries is likely to increase. For geographically separated integrations, such as the Eurasian Economic Union, the formation of a new production and technological configuration is likely to mean a reduction in the role of intra-industry trade and industrial cooperation as factors of integration cohesion and the need to search for new integration drivers, most likely in the digital, innovative, and socio-humanitarian spheres. So far, these areas are practically not covered by the Treaty on the EAEU.

2.6 Conclusions

We consider the following points as important characteristics and conclusions for understanding the development of intra-regional trade in the EAEU:

(1) Russia dominates the economy and intra-regional trade of the EAEU.
(2) The current levels and structures of intra-regional trade are rooted in the common past of the EAEU as part of the unified economic complex of the former USSR.
(3) Before the creation of the Customs Union and the single customs territory, the participating countries had passed a long way of integration convergence within the framework of the Union State of Russia and Belarus, the Eurasian Economic Community, and other formats.
(4) The real value added of deepening Eurasian economic integration was obtained in the early stages of functioning of the Customs Union and single customs territory—mainly in 2011–2013, when the common market of goods was launched, which stimulated the expansion of intra-regional, but also import, trade flows, and was supported by favorable economic situation in the participating countries.
(5) In the period 2014–2019, intra-regional trade mostly stagnated and there was a redistribution of market niches in favor of more active integration partners (first of all, Belarus in the Russian market, which was facilitated by the introduced counter-sanctions against Western countries and restrictions in trade between Russia and Ukraine).
(6) The dynamics and volumes of mutual trade of EAEU countries, where the share of energy and other primary resources is relatively high, remain under strong pressure of the situation on global commodity markets, which determines the price level of mutually supplied goods; as a result, the value of intra-regional trade is subject to significant fluctuations.
(7) Trade within the EAEU is dominated by inter-industry exchange; the levels of intra-industry trade and production and technological cooperation in international comparison are very low, with the exception of the pairing of Russia-Belarus for certain sectors of mechanical engineering.

(8) A very strong and growing influence on trade flows within the EAEU is exerted by the largest non-regional centers of attraction—the European Union and China, implementing their own large-scale programs of strategic cooperation with the EAEU member-states (the Eastern partnership project and the Strategy of the new partnership with the Central Asian countries on part of the EU, the Chinese Belt and Road Initiative, and bilateral programs of pairing the economic development plans of the PRC and individual EAEU countries, primarily with Kazakhstan and Kyrgyzstan).
(9) To date, the phenomenon of intra-regional trade has different significance for the individual states of the EAEU and their economic development. The main beneficiaries in the case of the complete elimination of non-tariff barriers on the common market will be smaller countries of the EAEU—Belarus, Armenia, and Kyrgyzstan—due to their strong orientation on intra-EAEU trade.
(10) So far, the impact of integration factors on the dynamics and parameters of mutual trade was secondary to the influence of exogenous factors (economic geography, market situation, currency exchange rates, trade policy and geopolitical trends, geoeconomic competition, and strong gravity waves from the largest non-regional powers—the EU and China, as well as a number of others).
(11) On the positive side, the structure of trade within the EAEU is significantly different from the trade of the Union members with third countries. In mutual merchandise exchange the share of manufacturing and agricultural products, goods with higher value added, is substantially bigger. The product and business structure of trade is much more diversified. This is a consequence of the preservation of a certain amount of inter- and intra-industry trade, cooperation-type relations that existed in the former Soviet Union, which since the early 1990s were supported by the free-trade regime, as well as the result of the high adaptation of the EAEU national markets to each other's products due to the same historical reasons, technological compatibility, and a number of other factors.
(12) On the whole, the analysis shows that the contribution of the integration factors to the development of intra-regional trade is not yet obvious. There are numerous formal and informal restrictions in mutual trade, which are aggravated by violations of the basic principles of the Customs Union and abuse of the single customs territory regime by member-states. The deviation of trade flows in favor of

intra-regional trade does not occur due to the absence of significant barriers for trading with third countries and the lack of integration incentives for mutual supplies, except for the situation with Russian counter-sanctions, which switched market operators to purchase food from partners in the EAEU and the CIS. However, the latter has nothing to do with integration.

References

Analytical Centre on Foreign Trade. (2017, Unpublished, October 11). *Promyshlennaya kooperaciya i proizvodstvennye cepochki v EAES.* Moscow: Presentation at the Meeting of the RF CCI Committee on the Economic Integration and Foreign Economic Activity.

Carneiro, F. (2013). *What Promises Does the Eurasian Customs Union Hold for the Future? Economic Premise, 108, Poverty Reduction and Economic Management Network (PREM).* Washington, DC: World Bank.

Dolgov, S., & Spartak, A. (Eds.). (2011). *Integracionnye processy v mire i na prostranstve SNG: nakoplennyj opyt, sovremennye tendencii i perspektivy.* Moscow: Russian Foreign Trade Academy.

Eurasian Development Bank, Centre for Integration Studies. (2019, Report № 52). *Evrazijskaya ekonomicheskaya integraciya—2019.* Retrieved from http://www.eabr.org/r/research/centre.projectsCII/.

Eurasian Economic Commission. (2018). *Eurasian Economic Union: Facts and Figures.* Library of the Eurasian Integration. Retrieved from http://www.eurasiancommission.org.

Eurasian Economic Commission. (2019a). *Doklad o realizacii osnovnyh napravlenij integracii v ramkah Evrazijskogo ekonomicheskogo soyuza. 2018 god.* Retrieved from: https://www.eurasiancommission.org.

Eurasian Economic Commission, "White Paper". (2017). *Barriers, Derogations and Restrictions in the Eurasian Economic Union.* Report. Retrieved from http://www.eurasiancommission.org.

Eurasian Economic Commission. *Monitoring-2018.* (2019b). *Osnovnye pokazateli urovnya i dinamiki razvitiya vnutrennego i vneshnego rynkov EAES. Mirovaya torgovlya.* Retrieved from http://www.eurasiancommission.org.

Idrisova, V., & Spartak, A. (2014). Analiz i ocenka tekushchih rezul'tatov integracii v ramkah Tamozhennogo soyuza i Edinogo ekonomicheskogo prostranstva, opredelenie neobhodimyh mer po sozdaniyu na ih osnove Evrazijskogo ekonomicheskogo soyuza. *Gosudarstvennyj audit. Pravo. Ekonomika, 1–2,* 120–127.

IMF. (2019, October). *World Economic Outlook: Global Manufacturing Downturn, Rising Trade Barriers.*

Impact of the Fourth Industrial Revolution on Supply Chains. (2017). *System Initiative on Shaping the Future of Production. Geneva: World Economic Forum.* Retrieved from http://www.weforum.org/docs/WEF_Impact_of_the_Fourth_Industrial_Revolution_on_Supply_Chains_pdf.

Ivanova, S., & Latyshov, A. (2019). Torgovlya stran EAES agroprodovol'stvennoj produkciej: tendencii, kollizii, faktory. *Mezhdunarodnaya torgovlya i torgovaya politika, 4*(20), 109–123.

Jafari, Y., & Tarr, D. (2015). Estimates of Ad Valorem Equivalents of Barriers Against Foreign Suppliers of Services in Eleven Services Sectors and 103 Countries. *The World Economy, 40*(3), 544–573. https://doi.org/10.1111/twec.12329.

Knobel, A. (2015). Evrazijskij ekonomicheskij soyuz: perspektivy razvitiya i vozmozhnye prepyatstviya. *Voprosy ekonomiki, 3*, 87–108.

Knobel, A., & Chokaev, B. (2014). Vozmozhnye ekonomicheskie posledstviya torgovogo soglasheniya mezhdu Tamozhennym i evropejskim soyuzami. *Voprosy ekonomiki, 2*, 68–87.

Knobel, A., Lipin, A., Malokostov, A., Tarr, D., & Turdyeva, N. (2019). Deep Integration of the Eurasian Economic Union: What Are the Benefits of Successful Implementation of Wider Liberalization? *Eurasian Geography and Economics, 60*(2), 177–210.

Konijn, P. E. (2014). *Purchasing Power Parities in Europe—Reflections on Uses, Recent Developments and the Future of ICP.* In Paper Presented at the Workshop on Inter-Country and Intra-Country Comparisons of Prices and Standards of Living. Aresso. Retrieved from http://www.polo-uniar.it.

National Bank of Belarus (2019). *Platezhnyj balans Respubliki Belarus' s Rossijskoj Federaciej.* Retrieved from http://www.nbrb.by

OECD, Development Assistance Committee. (2018). *Geographical Distribution of Financial Flows to Developing Countries. Disbursements, Commitments, Country Indicators: 2012–2016.* Paris: OECD.

Russian Export Centre. (2018). *Godovoj otchet Akcionernogo Obshchestva «Rossijskij eksportnyj centr» za 2017 god.* Retrieved from https://2017.exportcenter.ru/?_ga=2.237640192.1651426857.1577643474-1993794410.1577643474.

Russian Export Centre (2019). *Analiticheskaya spravka. Razvitie obshchego i nesyr'evogo eksporta Rossii v yanvare-dekabre 2018 goda.* Retrieved from https://www.exportcenter.ru.

Schwab, K. (2017). The Fourth Industrial Revolution. Geneva:World Economic Forum.Snopkov, N. (2014). *VVP Belorussii napolovinu zavisit ot Rossii.* Retrieved from https://https://belaruspartisan.by/economic/288865/

Spartak, A. (2013). Perspektivy Evrazijskoj ekonomicheskoj integracii. *Mezhdunarodnaya ekonomika, 3*, 9–22.

Spartak, A. (Ed.). (2016). *Mezhdunarodnaya torgovlya uslugami: novye tendencii razvitiya i regulirovaniya, rol' v integracionnyh processah.* Moscow: Russian Academy of Foreign Trade.

Spartak, A. (2017). Sopryazhenie EAES i Ekonomicheskogo poyasa Shelkovogo puti: koncepcii i real'nost'. *Mezhdunarodnaya ekonomika, 4*, 8–24.

Spartak, A. (2018a). *Sovremennye transformacionnye processy v mezhdunarodnoj torgovle i interesy Rossii.* Moscow: Russian Academy of Foreign Trade.

Spartak, A. (2019a). *Topical Issues of Russia's Positioning in the Polycentric World Order.* Proceedings of the External Challenged and Risks for Russia in the Context of the World Community's Transition to Polycentrism: Economics, Finance and Business (ICEFB 2019). Retrieved from http://www.atlantis-press.com/proceedings/icefb-19/125925194.

Spartak, A. (2019b) *Sovremennyj masshtab rossijsko-kitajskogo torgovo-ekonomicheskogo sotrudnichestva i perspektivy udvoeniya vzaimnoj torgovli k 2024 godu.* Trudy VEO Rossii, 220 tom, 83–108.

Spartak, A., & Voronova, T. (2018b). Perspektivy i ogranicheniya Evrazijskoj politiki sosedstva. *Mezhdunarodnaya torgovlya i torgovaya politika, 4*(16), 5–20.

Tarr, D. (2016). The Eurasian Economic Union among Russia, Belarus, Kazakhstan, Armenia and the Kyrgyz Republic: Can It Succeed Where Its Predecessor Failed? *Eastern European Economics, 54*(1), 1–22. https://doi.org/10.1080/00128775.2015.1105672.

Vakulchuk, R., & Knobel, A. (2018). Impact of Non-Tariff Barriers on Trade Within the Eurasian Economic Union. *Post-Communist Economies, 30*(4), 459–481.

Vinokurov, E. (2017). Eurasian Economic Union: Current State and Preliminary Results. *Russian Journal of Economics, 3*, 54–70.

Vinokurov, E., Demidenko, M., Movchan, V., Pelipas, I., Tochitskaya, I., Shimanovich, G., & Lipin, A. (2015a). *Estimating the Economic Effects of Reducing Non-Tariff Barriers in the EEU.* EDB Centre for Integration Studies Report no. 29. St Petersburg: Eurasian Development Bank.

Vinokurov, E., Demidenko, M., Pelipas, I., Tochitskaya, I., Shimanovich, G., & Lipin, A. (2015b). *Assessing the Impact of Non-Tariff Barriers in the EEU: Results of Enterprise Surveys.* Eurasian Development Bank (EDB) Centre for Integration Studies Report no. 30. St Petersburg: Eurasian Development Bank.

Vinokurov, E., Demidenko, M., Korshunov, D., Pereboev, V., Tsukarev, T., Gubenko, R., & Khmarenko, E. (2017). *Eurasian Economic Integration.* EDB Centre for Integration Studies Report no. 43. St Petersburg: Eurasian Development Bank.

CHAPTER 3

Foreign Direct Investments in the EAEU

Galina M. Kostyunina

3.1 Introduction

Under UNCTAD' methodology, Foreign Direct Investment (FDI) can be defined as an investment reflecting a lasting interest and control by a foreign direct investor resident in one economy in an enterprise resident in another economy (foreign affiliate).

According to research findings, there are prospective benefits from FDI, among which are new or updated technologies' transfer, as well as the transfer of skills and knowledge, a positive impact on a host country's economic growth and exports, and jobs. Apart from traditional FDI determinants, regional trade agreements (RTA) such as the Eurasian Economic Union can change FDI inflows. The RTA can affect not only trade flows, but also FDI flow pattern of the region.

Investment regulation is carried out at several levels: national, bilateral, regional, and international, with a large number of interstate agreements. Previous studies on the topic (Altomonte 2000; Berger et al. 2013; Blomström and Kokko 1997; Heifetz 2016; Kindleberger 1966) suggest the following key explanations of the effect of a country's

G. M. Kostyunina (✉)
MGIMO University, Moscow, Russia

N. A. Piskulova (ed.), *The Economic Dimension of Eurasian Integration*, https://doi.org/10.1007/978-3-030-59886-0_3

participation in RTA on attracting FDI. First, the national investment legislation must be in accordance with international standards and provide transparency and efficiency. Second, liberal admission for foreign investors has a significant stimulating effect on bilateral and regional FDI flows. Third, in accordance with the theory of C. Kindleberger, the country's participation in the regional trade agreement has a static and dynamic effect on investment flows. The static effect is associated with the influence of trade and investment liberalization and is manifested as the effect of investment diversion and the effect of investment creation. The effect achieved depends on factors such as the level of economic development of member countries, the volume of mutual investment and their significance for each country, the nature of changes in mutual investments, the level of competitiveness, the level of openness of the economy, and a form of economic integration. The dynamic effect is manifested in the long term in the form of increasing the region's investment attractiveness for FDI (Kindleberger 1966).

The main purpose of this chapter is to identify the peculiarities of investment regulation of the Eurasian Economic Union's member countries and the main FDI trends in the economies of participating states, with an emphasis on mutual investments. The hypothesis that must be solved within the framework of the study is that participation in an integration block provides countries with an economic effect in the medium- and long-term perspective, as a result of FDI inflows into their economy thanks to gradual investment liberalization. This chapter will first concentrate on the analysis of national, bilateral, regional, and international investment regulation in EAEU. It will also discuss the dynamics of FDI inflow into Eurasian economies and their geography and sector structures, as well as problems and perspectives of FDI.

The chapter is organized as follows. After the introduction, the second part concentrates on national and bilateral investment regulation; the third part briefly outlines the regional and the international level of investment regulation in accordance with obligations between international economic organizations. The fourth part concentrates on the main trends of FDI inflow in the EAEU. The fifth part analyses the mutual FDI in the EAEU as well as problems and perspectives. The sixth part concludes the chapter.

3.2 National and Bilateral Investment Regulation in the EAEU

At the national level, there are both special investment laws and general laws relating, inter alia, to foreign investment, including the Constitution, the Tax Code, the Civil Code, the Law on Foreign Exchange Regulation, and so on.

In three countries of the EAEU, there is a general investment law for national and foreign investors. In Kazakhstan, this is the Entrepreneur Code of the Republic of Kazakhstan of October 29, 2015, No. 375-(Entrepreneur Code 2015); in Belarus it is the Law of July 12, 2013, No. 53–3 "On Investments" (Law 2013); and in Kyrgyzstan, it is the Law of March 27 2003, No. 66 "On Investments in Kyrgyz Republic" (Law 2003a). In the other two countries, there is special legislation for foreign investors. In Russia, this is the Federal Law of 09.07.1999 No. 160-FZ "On Foreign Investments in the Russian Federation" (1999) (Federal law 1999), and in Armenia the Law of July 31, 1994, No. ZR-115 "On Foreign Investments in the Republic of Armenia" (Law 1994). In the countries with special legislation for foreign investors, there can be no full equalization in the rights of foreign and national investors, as seizures remain to protect national security, the country's defense, public morality, the health of the nation, and the lives of animals and plants, as well as sectoral seizures.

The main objective of these basic legislative acts is to regulate relations connected with guaranteeing the protection of investors' rights and interests. In the legislative practice of EAEU countries, with the exception of Belarus, a national treatment can be defined as a principle whereby a host country extends treatment to foreign investors that is at least as favorable as the treatment that it accords to national investors in circumstances (UNCTAD), but with general and sectoral exceptions. In Russia, there are not only restrictive, but also stimulating, exceptions. In the latter case, a foreign investor may be granted a greater volume of preferences if he participates in a priority investment project. The Law of the Republic of Armenia "On Foreign Investments" (Law 1994) restricts the activities of foreign investors in certain territories in order to protect national security. The second mode—the most-favored-nation-treatment as a treatment for a foreign investor—is no less favorable than for other foreign investors, enshrined in the law of Kyrgyzstan (Law 2003a).

One of the most important forms of state guarantees for foreign investors is the guarantee of compensation for the nationalization of property with the payment of prompt, effective, and adequate compensation. It is installed in EAEU countries. The calculation of compensation is based on the market value of the property being nationalized. The problem of compensating the investor for losses related to loss of profits is solved differently. Loss of profits is taken into account in the practice of only Armenia and Kyrgyzstan.

Another important guarantee for the investor is the grandfather clause—a stabilization clause as a guarantee against unfavorable changes for a foreign investor's legislation in the EAEU countries, with the exception of Belarus. Its duration is equal to the payback period of the investment project, but not more than five years in Armenia (Law 1994), seven years in Russia (Federal law 1999), and ten years in Kyrgyzstan (Law 2003a). The investor must meet the established criteria in accordance with national legislation.

Another important guarantee is a proper resolution of investment disputes, which is determined in all countries of EAEU except Kazakhstan. The main way is to conduct negotiations, but if it is impossible to reach a consensus within, as a rule, three months, the parties have the right to appeal to the national court or to the ICIDS.

The guarantee of use in the territory of the country or transfer of incomes outside of its limits and other lawfully received monetary sums is also fixed in the national investment legislation in EAEU states.

Russian legislation has more numerous forms of guarantees for investors. They are (1) the guarantee of legal protection of foreign investors; (2) the guarantee of use for foreign investors of various forms of investment; (3) the guarantee of the transfer of rights and obligations of a foreign investor to another person; (4) the guarantee for participation in privatization; (5) the guarantee for the purchase of securities; (6) the guarantee of the right to land and other non-movable property; (7) the guarantee of payment benefits; and (8) the guarantee of the use of benefits and guarantees provided to a foreign investor by subjects of the Russian Federation and local governments (Federal law 1999).

In Kazakhstan they are (1) the guarantee of the right to compensation for harm caused as a result of issuing by-laws by state bodies that do not comply with Kazakh laws; (2) the guarantee of the stability of contracts between the investor and the state bodies of the Republic of Kazakhstan; and (3) the guarantee of the transfer of the investor's rights to another person in the event that the investor makes investments in the Kazakh economy and fulfills his contractual obligations (Entrepreneur Code 2015).

In Kyrgyz legislation, the other forms of guarantees include (1) the guarantee of free employment of persons who are not citizens of Kyrgyzstan, (2) their right to transfer received wages abroad, and investors' entitlement to transfer funds under established forms of social insurance to authorized bodies, and (3) investment disputes are resolved in a judicial order in accordance with Kyrgyz legislation, as well as within the framework of ICIDS (Law 2003a).

In the EAEU, different forms of tax and financial preferences are also determined for investors. To obtain them, the investor must meet a number of criteria: if the share of foreign capital is not less than 30 per cent under Armenian law (Law 1994).

In national legal practice, there are other investment laws. For instance, in Russia there is the Federal Law of April 29, 2008, No. 57-FZ "On the Procedure for Making Foreign Investments in Business Companies of Strategic Importance to Ensure the Defense of the Country and the Security of the State". Its norms limit exceptions on the participation of foreigners in the authorized capital of business societies in relation to establishing control and determine the rules for foreign investors to enter into transactions with shares. Foreign investors are required to go through a preliminary approval procedure if more than 25 per cent of the total votes of the authorized capital of business entities of strategic importance is under their control. Forty-two strategic sectors have been identified, such as telecommunications, hydrometeorology, aviation security, weapons production, and so on. Control is exercised by a government commission to monitor the implementation of foreign investment in the Russian Federation, authorized to conduct assessment and coordination of foreign investment in such societies (Federal law 1999). The decision is made within 30 days. According to the government of the Russian Federation, as of June 2019, 85 applications were received from foreign investors with a cumulative amount of potential investments of $1 trillion. In just ten years of activity, 229 applications were considered, with only a small percentage of failures of 5 per cent. Over the past three years, $16 billion has been invested in the Russian economy (Government 2019).

Legal regulation of foreign investment in defense, as well as other areas related to state security, always has at least two components: the military-political threat (i.e. secrets leaking) and military-technical threat (i.e. industrial espionage leading to more military-technical cooperation markets). However, this, as a rule, is not openly spoken about. Exceptions are rare. As an example, one can cite Ukraine, which has almost completely sold off the military-technical secrets of the former USSR.

In Kazakhstan the Law of November 4, 2003, No. 490-II "On State Monitoring of Property in Strategic Economic Sectors" regulates foreign investments in strategic sectors of the national economy, such as the mining and processing of coal, oil, natural gas, uranium and metal ores, engineering, chemical industry, military industrial complex, transport and communications, and the production and distribution of electricity (Law 2003b).

Thus, from the point of view of the specifics of the investment legislation of EAEU countries, it can be divided into two groups: the first group of states that have general investment legislation in relation to national and foreign investors (Kazakhstan, Belarus, Kyrgyzstan) and the second group of countries that maintain special legislation regulating the activities of foreign investors (Russia and Armenia).

In all EAEU countries, the national treatment is guaranteed to investors, as the treatment is no less favorable for foreign investments as for national entrepreneurs. The main reason for the impossibility of full equalization in the rights of foreign and national investors is associated with differences between foreign private property and the property of the national legal and physical persons of the recipient country. This is proven by the global investment practice of different countries, both developed and developing, in which the national treatment is combined with the preservation of such differences. Any state strives to enjoy political and economic independence and national sovereignty, as well as to attract as much foreign investment as possible, including through incentive instruments. For this, foreign investors can be granted great benefits in the framework of incentive exemptions from the national treatment, which is recorded, for example, in Russian investment legislation. On the other hand, a different approach is regulation of foreign investments in strategic sectors of the national economy such as in Russia and Kazakhstan.

The national investment legislation of EAEU countries has many common rules, but there are differences. Of these, the following should be highlighted: (1) general investment legislation for national and foreign investors in Kazakhstan, Belarus, and Kyrgyzstan, and the preservation of special investment legislation for foreign investors in Russia and Armenia; (2) differentiation of the term for granting a "grandfather clause" from five to ten years; (3) the inclusion of lost profits in the calculation of the amount of compensation for the nationalization of foreign ownership, which is recorded in the legislative practice of only Kyrgyzstan and Armenia; and (4) the concept of direct investment under Kyrgyz law (at least 1/3) differs from the recommendations of the IMF and the OECD. In the national laws of other EAEU countries FDI is at least 10 per cent.

Thus, the investment legislation of EAEU countries as a whole complies with international standards and gradually evolves toward the regulation of investment activities without regard to the nationality of the investor, while preserving exemptions from the national treatment. At the same time, protectionist tendencies remain in relation to the support of national companies, which manifests itself in the demand for licensing certain types of entrepreneurial activities, in establishing minimum investment volumes in the implementation of joint investment projects, and in preserving a large number of controlling state structures.

In accordance with established international practice at the bilateral level, EAEU countries have signed the interstate agreements on mutual protection and promotion of foreign investments, or BITs. Such agreements detail the investment relations between the two contracting countries, including such issues as investment treatment with common and sectoral exemptions, protection of the rights of investors' interests from possible nationalization by a foreign property, guaranteeing the unimpeded transfer of investment income abroad, and the determination of the order of resolving investment disputes. In total, the EAEU countries signed 284 BITs, of which 214 are in force (UNCTAD 2019).

Thus, the main purpose of BITs is to detail the conditions for the activities of foreign investors, including those from the EAEU member countries.

3.3 Regional and Multilateral Investment Regulation in the EAEU

The main trend in the sphere of regulation is the current treaty on the EAEU, which aims to liberalize mutual investments, and takes into account international standards in the sphere of investment regulation. A single detailed supranational regulation on the model of the European Union does not yet exist in the EAEU. At the same time, it should be noted that the introduction of a single investment policy in the EU began to take place only ten years after the formation of a single market.

EAEU states have signed investment agreements in accordance with their participation in regional economic organizations. They are the CIS Investor Rights Convention (CIS 1997), the EU-Armenia Partnership and cooperation agreement (Partnership 1999), the EU-Kazakhstan Enhanced Partnership and Cooperation Agreement (EU 2017), the EU-Kyrgyzstan Comprehensive Agreement (EU 2019), the US-Central Asia Trade and Investment Facilitation Agreement (US 2013), the OIC Investment Agreement (OIC 1981), the Energy Charter Treaty (The Energy 1994), the APEC Non-binding investment principles (APEC 1994), the Pacific Basin Charter on International Investments (Pacific 1995), and so on.

The EAEU countries in the Treaty on the EAEU (05/29/2014, ed. 04/11/2017) set goals to form an internal market based on the free movement of goods, services, investments, and individuals. Thus, in the investment sphere, the formation of a free investment zone is provided by eliminating barriers to mutual capital flows, guaranteeing the protection of investors' rights and harmonizing the national investment law (Treaty 2014).

The agreement defines investment regulation issues in Articles 65–69 and in more detail in the Appendix—the Protocol on Trade in Services, Establishment, Activity and Investment. Investors of the participating countries are guaranteed three investment treatments: (1) national treatment; (2) the most-favored-nation treatment (MFN), and (3) a fair and equitable treatment. An investor has the right to choose a more favorable treatment for oneself—national or MFN. The admission of investments is made in accordance with the national legislation of the host country, including exemptions from the national treatment and the MFN. After the fulfillment of tax obligations, an investor has the right to use and dispose of lawfully received investment incomes, as well as export them abroad.

Protection of the rights of foreign investors is carried out in accordance with the national legislation of the host country. The following are guaranteed: (1) damages in the event of civil unrest, hostilities, or a state of emergency under a national or most-favored-nation treatment; (2) protection against direct or indirect expropriation or nationalization on the basis of the payment of prompt and adequate compensation is paid no later than three months from the date of nationalization; (3) the possibility of transferring the rights of investors; (4) in the procedure for resolving disputes based on negotiations, if the dispute is not resolved within six months from the date of the written notice, the parties are entitled to apply to the court of the host country, or to international commercial arbitration, or to arbitration of the court ad hoc, or the ICIDS. The award is binding and the parties to the investment dispute are obliged to ensure its implementation.

At the international level, EAEU countries have obligations to international organizations that are involved in investment regulation and of which they are members. This applies to the World Bank, under which EAEU states have signed the Convention of the MIGA, the Convention of the ICIDS, and the Investment Principles of the World Bank.

Russia, Armenia, and Kyrgyzstan, as WTO member countries, have obligations to WTO investment agreements, such as the GATS, the Fourth Protocol on GATS, the Fifth Protocol on GATS, the TRIPs, and the TRIMs.

As a result, it can be stated that the multilateral regulation of the admission of foreign investment in EAEU economies generally conforms to international standards for the protection of the rights and interests of investors, but sometimes contradicts the national regulation. In order to improve the issues under consideration, it is necessary to harmonize the national legislation of EAEU countries and bring it in line with the norms of the Treaty on the EAEU. Another important task is to form a single conceptual apparatus, in particular the concepts of an investment agreement. One of the reasons is related to the inconsistency of the very concept of "investment" between the national laws and the EAEU Treaty, which is the cornerstone of the investment legislation of any country.

3.4 Main Trends of FDI Inflow in EAEU Economies

EAEU countries are not significant recipients of FDI. The main reasons include the problems of economic development of EAEU countries, in particular, sluggish GDP growth, high political risk, an unfavorable investment climate, and the unfavorable situation in the global economy.

It should be noted that these countries are sufficiently open to the outside world: indicators of trade openness exceed the global average (29.4 per cent), making up 70.2 per cent in Belarus, 37.5 per cent in Armenia, 34.4 per cent in Kazakhstan, 32.7 per cent in Kyrgyzstan, and 30.7 per cent in Russia (World Bank 2020). This is a favorable factor for mutual investments.

EAEU countries suffer from non-high level of international competitiveness. According to the World Economic Forum, Russia is 43rd in the world from among 140 countries, Kazakhstan 59th, Armenia 70th, and Kyrgyzstan 97th (Global 2018). The share of accumulated FDI in the GDP of the economies of the EAEU is quite substantial and amounts to more than 34 per cent. All EAEU countries are net importers of FDI.

The value of accumulated FDI in EAEU countries as a whole increased from $31,870 million to $34,630 million from 2014 to 2017. Between 2014 and 2017, the share of accumulated FDI in the EAEU countries' GDP increased significantly from 36 per cent to 41 per cent in Armenia, from 23 per cent to 36 per cent in Belarus, from 62 per cent to 99 per cent in Kazakhstan, from 49 per cent to 70 per cent in Kyrgyzstan, and from 18 per cent up to 34 per cent in Russia.

The growth was achieved due to FDI from non-member countries, the volume of which increased from $30,110 million to $33,508 million (see Table 3.1).

As can be seen from Table 3.1, the maximum total accumulated FDI was reached in 2016, due to the favorable investment situation in the global economy and the growth of global FDI. The mutual accumulated FDI of EAEU countries decreased from $1760 million to $1122 million between 2014 and 2017. The main reasons include weak mutual economic cooperation and a lack of sectors that are attractive for investment. As a result, the share of mutual direct investments in total FDI decreased from 5.5 per cent to 3.2 per cent, respectively.

The situation in each of the EAEU countries differs: if Russia and Kazakhstan are fairly large recipients of global FDI, then Belarus, Armenia, and Kyrgyzstan are not.

According to the accumulated FDI in the EAEU economies, Russia is a leading investor. The total FDI amounted to $529.6 billion at the end

Table 3.1 Accumulated FDI inflow into EAEU ($ million)

Country	*2014*	*2015*	*2016*	*2017*
Total accumulated FDI	31,870	16,204	51,641	34,630
Mutual accumulated FDI	1760	2139	1434	1122
Accumulated FDI from non-participating countries	30,110	14,065	50,207	33,508

Source: Direct investment (2018). P. 7

of 2017, of which $5.4 billion accounted for investments of the EAEU countries, or 1.0 per cent.

The amount of FDI in Russia declined from $43,168 million in 2010 to $8816 million in 2018, or five times. The main investors are the Netherlands, the United Kingdom, Switzerland, and the British Virgin Islands, which are considered (with the exception of the United Kingdom) as well-known offshore zones. This list does not include such famous offshore zones as Cyprus, Ireland, and Luxemburg, which are the other major investors in the Russian economy. However, by the end of 2018, the volume of direct investment taken out by them exceeded the amount of FDI invested. FDI from offshore zones are of Russian origin and mean the return of previously exported funds to the Russian economy. This phenomenon was called "capital turnover".

Between 2010 and 2018, the total volume of FDI inflows from EAEU states into the Russian economy increased from $68 million to $177 million, or 2.6 times (see Table 3.2). The trend is relatively upward with the exception of 2014. The share of the EAEU, although it increased from 0.2 per cent to 2.0 per cent in the total FDI, continues to remain at a low

Table 3.2 FDI inflow into Russia ($ million)

Country	*2010*	*2011*	*2012*	*2013*	*2014*	*2015*	*2016*	*2017*	*2018*
Total	43,168	55,084	50,588	69,219	22,031	6853	32,539	28,557	8816
The Netherlands	3733	7383	10,330	5716	1102	-246	654	-1427	7910
Kazakhstan	46	56	277	208	357	433	130	205	148
The United Kingdom	1142	2007	46	18,927	120	1112	422	2076	2511
Switzerland	-1	741	401	1086	2472	203	1010	1511	1690
The British Virgin Islands	2139	7225	2474	9379	3123	2374	-798	-827	1491
Belarus	34	121	110	219	59	42	4	48	53
Armenia	-24	-7	48	52	38	56	21	-142	-1
Kyrgyzstan	12	23	21	28	6	-18	-1	-20	-24
EAEU, total	68	194	576	507	311	535	414	91	177
Share of EAEU, per cent	0.2	0.4	1.1	0.7	1.4	7.8	1.3	0.3	2.0

Source: Compiled on the basis of data from the Central Bank of Russia. Retrieved from: http://www.cbr.ru/statistics/?PrtId=svs

level. It should be noted that over the period of the EAEU being in force (since 2015), FDI inflow of the member-states into Russia have been characterized by a more dynamic growth rate than the total FDI.

The geographical distribution of FDI in Russia from the EAEU countries is characterized by the dominant position of two states—Kazakhstan and Belarus. Kazakh direct investment increased 3.2 times and Belarusian direct investment increased 1.5 times in 2010–2018. FDI from Armenia and Kyrgyzstan is minimal. In general, the share of the EAEU in total FDI in the Russian economy is extremely low (2.0 per cent). The main reasons include the predominance of investment from Western countries, the large capacity of the domestic market, and the lack of investment in the EAEU countries. It should be noted that within the EAEU, Russia is not only the main importer, but also the main exporter of investments, "which is explained by objective factors, such as historically established production and investment ties, cultural and linguistic community, a higher level of economic development, the capacity of the domestic market, and a diversified economic structure" (Kostyunina 2019). The most attractive sectors for FDI in the Russian economy include mining (29.1 per cent), financial and insurance activities (24.9 per cent), manufacturing (10.0 per cent), research and development (8.8 per cent), and construction (7.1 per cent).

Since 2008, the growth rate of foreign investment in Russia has slowed down and over the course of almost all ten years, there has been a decrease in their volume, with some exceptions. This is due to factors such as fluctuations in the ruble exchange rate (with a weakening national currency exchange rate, investors are aimed at obtaining super-profits in exporting products, i.e. currency dumping), the sanctions of several Western states due to the annexation of Crimea, complication of relations with Ukraine, and deterioration of the Russian economy. With such factors, any investor is aimed at preserving his investment project, but not closing.

The Russian investment climate is not quite favorable which is caused by aggravation of economic situation from 2014. It was affected by the fall in oil prices, an increase in the number of measures to regulate foreign FDI, a decrease in GDP growth, and a decrease in investment attractiveness.

In accordance with a survey of leading foreign investors, 77 per cent of their number are concerned about the investment regulation measures taken and advocate a moratorium on new legislation introduced that destabilizes Russia's investment attractiveness. At the same time, there remains a favorable factor from the point of view of investors, as a huge economic potential (90 per cent of respondents), and 50 per cent of respondents declared their readiness to expand business in Russia and also improve the investment climate in many regions of the country (the Investment Climate 2015).

Another problem in attracting foreign investment is a high political risk for foreign investors, which is associated with a weak enforcement mechanism of investment legislation, namely, with a low level of protection of the rights and interests of foreign investors in practice. Thus, according to the estimates of the annual report of the World Bank (WB) Doing Business-2019, Russia is in 31st place among 190 countries in terms of simplified business management. Although over the past five years there has been a steady improvement (112th place in 2013), the situation needs further improvement. Other weak points of the investment climate are international trade and tax payments. The problem of corruption persists. According to Transparency International, at the end of 2017, Russia ranks 135th out of 180 in the Corruption Susceptibility Index (Transparency 2018).

Taking into account the analysis performed, it can be stated that in order to attract FDI to the Russian economy, the importance of political, economic, and regulatory factors should be taken into account. According to many foreign studies, the current political situation testifies to the impossibility of a breakthrough in attracting significant cost volumes of foreign investment from Western countries, primarily the European Union. The main trend in recent years is an increase in Asian investment, including the EAEU. However, their share in the total FDI in the Russian economy is low, although higher growth inspires optimism.

Another major recipient of direct investment from among the countries of the EAEU is **Kazakhstan**, the amount of accumulated FDI in the economy of which at the end of 2017 amounted to \$161.3 billion.

Between 2010 and 2018, FDI in Kazakhstan increased from \$22,246 million to \$24,276 million, or 1.09 times. The dynamics are uneven, with a maximum of \$28,885 million in 2012 and a minimum of \$15,368 million in 2015. The top five investors are the Netherlands (30.3 per cent), the USA (22.0 per cent), Switzerland (10.5 per cent), Russia (6.2 per cent), and China (6.1 per cent) (see Table 3.3).

FDI from EAEU countries grew more dynamically: from \$993.3 million to \$1558.6 million, or 1.57 times, which stimulated the growth of the share of country members in total investments in Kazakhstan from 4.5 per cent to 6.4 per cent between 2010 and 2018. The main investor from the EAEU countries is Russia (96.2 per cent), whose direct investment increased from \$951.6 million to \$1499.2 million respectively, or 1.58 times. Belarus ranks second: FDI increased from \$41.7 million to

Table 3.3 FDI inflow into Kazakhstan ($ million)

Country	*2010*	*2011*	*2012*	*2013*	*2014*	*2015*	*2016*	*2017*	*2018*
Total	22,246	26,467	28,885	24,098	23,809	15,368	21,367	20,960	24,276
The Netherlands	7310.3	8876.0	8692.2	6520.9	6763.3	5744.4	7968.6	5935.2	7349.8
USA	1810.9	1113.4	1975.7	2438.7	4153.4	2770.3	3417.6	3693.2	5344.0
Switzerland	547.3	3199.9	3312.4	1877.4	2366.4	1907.4	2702.2	2964.5	2540.3
Russia	951.6	1000.1	1069.5	1299.2	1583.8	533.6	872.6	1226.6	1499.2
China	1717.6	1693.1	2414.6	2246.0	1807.5	833.9	975.2	1082.5	1489.4
Armenia	–	–	-0.2	0.0	0.4	0.6	0.2	0.0	0.1
Belarus	41.7	85.8	122.5	165.0	202.0	79.5	63.5	81.4	59.3
Kyrgyzstan	-20.3	4.7	-4.1	-59.5	-26.2	-17.6	-3.1	-0.3	4.2
EAEU, total	993.3	1085.9	1192	1464.2	1785.8	613.7	936.3	1308	1558.6
Share of EAEU, per cent	4.5	4.1	4.1	6.1	7.5	4.0	4.4	6.2	6.4

Source: Gross inflow of foreign direct investment in the Republic of Kazakhstan from foreign direct investors by country. National Bank of Kazakhstan. Retrieved from: https://www.nationalbank.kz/?docid=680&switch=rus

$59.3 million between 2010 and 2018, with the maximum volume of $202 million reached in 2014. Two other countries of the Eurasian Union, Armenia ($0.1 million) and Kyrgyzstan ($4.1 million), are the minimum investors in the Kazakh economy.

As far as the sectoral structure is concerned, it is necessary to single out the mining sector (crude oil and natural gas)—55.9 per cent—and the processing industry—14.9 per cent, primarily the metallurgical industry, plastics and rubber products, and chemical industry. In terms of simplified business, Kazakhstan ranks 28th in the evaluation of the World Bank Doing Business-2019 report. The weak points of the investment climate are the obtaining of a permit for electricity (which requires spending 98 days), foreign trade, the execution of contracts, obtaining a loan, paying taxes, protecting the rights of minority investors, and obtaining a building permit. In general, the investment opportunities of the Kazakhstan economy are growing, as the competition for its domestic market between Russia, on the one hand, and China and the EU countries, on the other hand, is intensifying. The main investment attractive sector is undoubtedly the fuel and energy complex.

The third largest recipient from the EAEU countries is **Belarus**. The accumulated FDI is equal to $19.8 billion as of 2017. Investments in the Belarusian economy are contradictory. If their total inflow increased by 1.4 times, mainly due to investments from developed countries, then FDI from the EAEU countries decreased by 1.8 times as a result of a decrease mainly in the growth rate of direct investments from Russia (see Table 3.4).

Table 3.4 FDI inflow into Belarus ($ million)

Country	*2010*	*2013*	*2014*	*2015*	*2016*	*2017*
Total	5569.4	11,083.4	10,168.9	7241.4	6928.6	7634.2
Russia	5055.1	5815.7	5114.8	3264.7	3526.0	2848.9
The United Kingdom	53.6	2804.6	2420.3	2192.5	1389.1	2456.4
Cyprus	59.3	754.0	710.4	648.9	564.1	657.3
Poland	27.0	177.9	134.1	191.3	189.0	316.8
Ukraine	5.5	136.6	117.8	88.9	225.5	251.8
Kazakhstan	0.09	1.6	4.8	1.0	0.8	3.4
Armenia	0.3	9.9	9.0	5.9	6.9	8.0
Kyrgyzstan	0.07	0.01	0	0	0	0
EAEU, total	5055.56	5827.21	5128.6	3271.6	3533.7	2860.3
Share of EAEU, per cent	90.8	52.6	50.4	45.2	51.0	37.5

Source: Belarus and countries of the world—2017 (2018). Pp. 309–310

As a result, the share of the EAEU declined in total FDI from 90.8 per cent to 37.5 per cent between 2010 and 2017. However, the Russian Federation is the main investor in Belarus. From the group of countries of the EAEU, Armenia occupies the second position in terms of investments in Belarus, whose direct investments increased from $0.8 million to $8.0 million, or ten times. Kazakhstan ranks third: its direct investments increased from $0.09 million to $3.4 million, or almost 38 times. Kyrgyzstan is practically not invested.

From the group of the third countries, the main investors are the United Kingdom (32.2 per cent), Cyprus (8.6 per cent), Poland (4.1 per cent), and Ukraine (3.3 per cent). The sector structure of FDI is characterized by the predominance of three industries (the wholesale and retail trade, as well as the repair of vehicles and household appliances, transport and communications).

The investment climate of Belarus is characterized by contradictory characteristics: on the one hand, a favorable geographical position, a developed transport and logistics infrastructure; while, on the other hand, a weakly diversified structure of the national economy, a high role of the state in the economy, strict regulation of investment, and a lack of natural resources (i.e. lack of absolute advantages). At the same time, the country's investment climate is gradually improving. According to Doing Business-2019, Belarus is 37th in the world in terms of simplified business. Areas that require improvement include obtaining credit, paying taxes, and protecting the rights of minority investors.

The volume of accumulated FDI in the **Armenian** economy amounted to $4751 million at the end of 2017. Between 2010 and 2018, the value of attracted FDI increased from $149.99 million to $669.1 million, or 4.46 times (see Fig. 3.1). The trend is mainly upward: there was a decline only in 2013 and then by $58 million.

The geographical structure of FDI is characterized by the predominance of three states—Russia, Jersey, and Germany, the total share of which is 69.1 per cent (see Table 3.5). The leading investor is Russia, which invests a little over half of total FDI in the Armenian economy, as well as almost 100 per cent of FDI from the countries of the Eurasian Economic Union. Thanks to Russian investments, the EAEU is the main investor in the context of groups of states with a share of 54.0 per cent in 2018. The main reason for Russia's dominant role is related to the investments of Russian investors of Armenian origin.

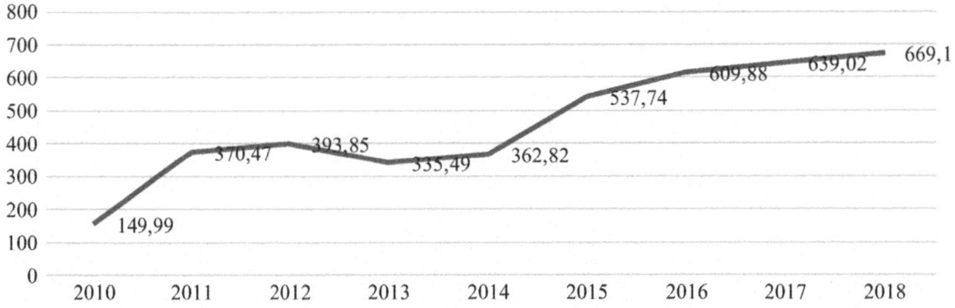

Fig. 3.1 FDI inflow into the economy of Armenia ($ million). (Source: Compiled on the basis of data of the Central Bank of Armenia. Retrieved from: https://www.cba.am/RU/SitePages/Default.aspx)

Table 3.5 Geographical distribution of FDI in the Armenian economy (per cent)

Country	*2014*	*2015*	*2016*	*2017*	*2018*
Russia	36.4	51.8	41.9	13.0	53.8
Jersey	–	–	16.1	11.6	18.4
Germany	16.9	0.9	0.9	15.5	13.9
Lebanon	0.4	7.3	25.2	7.2	4.3
Cyprus	3.4	7.6	55.2	1.6	2.9

Source: Compiled on the basis of data of the Central Bank of Armenia. Retrieved from: https://www.cba.am/RU/SitePages/Default.aspx

The sector profile of FDI is characterized by the predominance of several industries as investment objects: the supply of electricity, gas, steam, and conditioned air (42.8 per cent), the provision of services in the field of mining (17.3 per cent), and real estate (12.1 per cent). The main investor in the supply of electricity, gas, steam, and air-conditioned air is Russia; in the provision of services in the field of mining the main investor is Jersey; in the extraction of other minerals both Russia and Argentina are the main investors; while in real estate the main investor is again Russia.

The inflow of FDI into the Armenian economy is negatively affected by factors such as the lack of internal market capacity, low endowment with natural resources, a small number of large companies, a high level of political risk, and the predominance of the agro-food sector. However, there is

Table 3.6 FDI inflow into the economy of Kyrgyzstan ($ million)

Country	*2013*	*2014*	*2015*	*2016*	*2017*
Total	5487.1	5415.7	5615.4	5335.1	5219.9
China	468.3	221.7	474.4	301.3	303.0
Russia	69.8	60.4	515.5	291.5	98.6
Kazakhstan	52.3	30.6	20.8	23.1	47.0
Germany	6.5	18.2	7.0	0.7	33.6
The United Kingdom	81.7	53.4	189.5	0.7	28.9
The Netherlands	9.5	6.5	13.2	9.4	25.4
Belarus	1.8	0.1	40.7	0.1	0
Armenia	–	–	–	–	–
EAEU, total	123.9	91.1	577	314.7	145.6
Share of EAEU, per cent	2.2	1.7	10.3	5.9	2.8

Source: Kyrgyz Republic 2013–2017 (2018). P.109

also a positive factor—the simplification of running a business, in which Armenia occupies the 41st place in the world according to WB Doing Business-2019. The weakest points of the country's investment climate are obtaining building permits (which requires 98 days), protecting the rights of minority investors, and paying taxes.

In Kyrgyzstan, by the end of 2017, the volume of FDI withdrawn exceeded the amount of accumulated FDI by $107.2 million. A similar situation exists due to the withdrawal of Canadian FDI from the national economy. Between 2013 and 2017, the volume of FDI decreased from $5487.1 million to $5219.9 million, or 1.05 times. The largest inflow was reached in 2015—$5615.7 million (Table 3.6). The main investor is China with a share of 5.8 per cent, although its FDI decreased in the period under review from $468.3 million to $303.0 million. Other large investors are Germany, the United Kingdom, and the Netherlands.

FDI from EAEU countries increased from $123.9 million to $145.6 million between 2013 and 2017, with a maximum of $577 million in 2015. The share of the EAEU in total FDI in Kyrgyzstan increased from 2.2 per cent to 2.8 per cent, respectively. The leading investors are Russia and Kazakhstan, which occupy the second and third positions in the total investment invested. However, the trends are different. If, in the period under review, Russian FDI increased from $69.8 million to $98.6 million, then Kazakh investments, on the contrary, decreased from $52.3 million to $47.0 million. The inflow of Belarusian FDI is extremely uneven, ranging from $40.7 million in 2015 to 0 in 2017. There is no Armenian FDI in the economy of Kyrgyzstan.

As far as sectoral structure is concerned, FDI dominates in manufacturing (37.6 per cent), financial intermediation and insurance (27.3 per cent), and electricity, gas, and steam (13.0 per cent). The share of the mining sector, which Chinese investors prefer to invest FDI (oil refining and gold mining), accounts for 2.6 per cent.

In general, the Kyrgyz economy is characterized by a low level of favorable investment climate, which is associated with a low level of economic development, a precarious domestic market, a low level of labor force skills, and high political risk throughout the 2000s. Kyrgyzstan is much inferior to other EAEU countries in terms of simplified business. According to World Bank (Doing Business-2019), the country is 70th in the world. Such components of the investment climate as obtaining a building permit (it takes 111 days to spend), paying taxes, and executing contracts need to be improved.

3.5 Mutual FDI in the EAEU

Thus, in the EAEU, mutual accumulated FDI is insignificant. The main reasons are associated with weak economic ties between countries and the lack of economic sectors that are attractive for mutual investment. Thus, the sectoral structure of mutual FDI is characterized by the predominance of the oil and gas sector (42.6 per cent), the non-ferrous metallurgy (12.0 per cent), transport (8.8 per cent), communications and IT (8.2 per cent), and the agro-industrial complex (6.5 per cent followed with a long break).

The importance of mutual accumulated FDI for the EAEU individual countries is presented in Table 3.7.

Table 3.7 Matrix of mutual accumulated FDI of the EAEU countries in 2017 ($ million)

Recipient	*Russia*	*Kazakhstan*	*Belarus*	*Armenia*	*Kyrgyzstan*	*EAEU, total*
Russia	X	2948	2054	8	0	5010
Kazakhstan	8212	X	34	0	0	8246
Belarus	8522	57	X	16	2	8597
Armenia	3441	0	0	X	0	3441
Kyrgyzstan	858	605	3	0	X	1466
EAEU, total	21,033	3610	2091	24	2	26,760

Source: Monitoring of Mutual Investments in the CIS countries (2018)

As can be seen from the above matrix, the main investor in the EAEU is Russia (78.6 per cent), which is the only net exporter in mutual FDI. The reasons are related to the capacity of the domestic market, when the share of the Russian Federation in the total GDP of the EAEU in 2017 is 85 per cent, the greater capacity of Russian corporations. It is no coincidence that, at the end of 2016, the share of the outflow of accumulated FDI in EAEU to the country's GDP from Russia was 26.2 per cent against 15.5 per cent to the country's GDP from Kazakhstan, 5.3 per cent from Armenia, 1.4 per cent from Belarus, and 0.03 per cent from Kyrgyzstan. With a large margin, Russia is followed by Kazakhstan (13.5 per cent to the country's GDP) and Belarus (7.8 per cent to the country's GDP), which are also notable direct investment investors in the mutual framework. The extreme unevenness of bilateral investment relations should be noted. For Russia, the main recipients of FDI are Belarus and Kazakhstan (although compared with other member countries, FDIs are very important in the economies of Armenia and Kyrgyzstan); for Kazakhstan, the main recipients are Russia and Kyrgyzstan; and for Belarus, it is Russia.

According to the Eurasian Development Bank, 240 mutual FDI projects are being implemented in EAEU countries, the total accumulated investment in which is estimated to be at least $1 million, as well as more than 300 projects with small investments (Monitoring 2018).

According to the UNCTAD methodology, we can calculate the Investment Intensity Index (III) of mutual FDI:

$$III = \frac{I_{rr} / I_{rw}}{I_{rw} / I_{ww}}$$

where I_{rr}—mutual investments of the region;

I_{rw}—total investment of the region;

I_{ww}—total global investment.

This figure allows us to estimate the amount of FDI invested in the region from the EAEU member-states compared to the expected value based on the region's share in the global FDI.

We will perform calculations based on the data presented in Table 3.8:

III2014 = 0.055/0.001 = 55.

III2017 = 0.032/0.001 = 32.

It can be seen from the calculation that, in addition to the reduction of the total value of FDI, the Investment Intensity Index is also reduced by

Table 3.8 Key indicators for calculating the Investment Intensity Index of mutual accumulated FDI in the EAEU in 2014 and 2017 ($ million)

	2014	*2017*
Mutual FDI in EAEU (I_{rr})	1760	1122
FDI in EAEU (I_{rw})	31,870	34,630
World FDI (I_{ww})	259,178,166	326,235,576

Source: Direct Investment in the Eurasian Economic Union (2018)

1.7 times, that is, EAEU countries are investing more dynamically in non-participating economies than all non-regional countries. Thus, the propensity for mutual FDI is maintained at a low level.

In general, in the investment sphere, EAEU countries do not yet benefit from participation in integration processes in the Eurasian region, which is confirmed by the low share of mutual direct investments and the reduction of the mutual Investment Intensity Index. At the same time, it should be noted that several years have passed since the start of the EAEU's operation and it is too early to sum up. Investment ties are imbalanced and are most developed between Russia-Kazakhstan and Russia-Belarus. Russia remains the main investor and recipient of mutual investments as the largest and most developed economy of the EAEU, considering the economic relations that were formed during the Soviet period.

Negative effects are caused by the low level of economic development of member countries, the differentiation between them according to many macroeconomic indicators (GDP, average per capita incomes, endowment with natural resources, etc.), underdeveloped financial markets, high political risk, weak economic ties between countries, and the lack of economic sectors that are attractive for mutual investment.

3.6 Conclusions

The analysis performed allows us to determine the following main findings.

The multilateral investment regulation among EAEU countries generally corresponds to international standards for the protection of the rights and interests of investors, but at the same time introduces a dissonance in the regulation due to different kinds of interstate agreements. In order to improve the issues under consideration, it is necessary to harmonize the national legislation of EAEU countries and bring it in line with the norms of the EAEU Treaty, as well as develop a single conceptual apparatus. One of the reasons is related to the inconsistency between the national laws and the Treaty on the EAEU of the concept of "investment", which is a cornerstone of the investment legislation of any country.

Between 2014 and 2017, the value of accumulated FDI in EAEU economies increased due to investments from non-member countries. This situation is related both to the factors of the overall economic situation, including the unfavorable situation in the global economy, the fall in fuel prices and low investment demand, as well as the problems of economic development of the EAEU countries, in particular, sluggish GDP growth, high political risk, and an unfavorable investment climate. The share of accumulated FDI in the GDP of the economies of the EAEU is quite substantial and amounts to more than 34 per cent. All EAEU countries are net importers of FDI.

The total amount of FDI invested in EAEU economies between 2010 and 2018 show an upward trend with some exceptions, when it was influenced by objective economic factors, both external and internal nature.

The geographical distribution of FDI in EAEU countries is dominated by investments from non-participating states. The economies of Russia, Kazakhstan, and Belarus have a high share of FDI from offshore countries like Switzerland, Cyprus, the Netherlands, and Luxembourg, which allows us to talk about the return of previously exported capital. These countries are the leading recipients of FDI of a number of EAEU states. An important trend is the diversification of the geographical distribution of investments from third countries at the expense of Asian countries like China and Singapore, especially to Kazakhstan and Russia.

The volume of mutual FDI is low, which is associated with weak economic ties between countries, lack of economic sectors that are attractive for mutual investment, economic problems, and high political risk. The most significant shares of mutual FDI are in Belarus and Armenia, where they constitute more than a third of total investments. Bilateral investment ties are most developed between Russia and Kazakhstan, Russia and Belarus, and Kazakhstan and Kyrgyzstan.

The sectoral structure of accumulated FDI in the EAEU is distinguished by the leading role of the fuel industry due to its high comparative advantages in providing natural resources to individual countries that are major recipients of investments, like Russia and Kazakhstan.

The leading investor and recipient in mutual investments of the EAEU countries is Russia. The main reasons are the large capacity of the domestic market, a higher level of economic development, high comparative advantages in the provision of natural resources, and a favorable geographical position.

Between 2014 and 2017, the mutual Investment Intensity Index decreased, that is, EAEU countries are investing more heavily into the economies of non-participating states. As a result, the volume of mutual FDI remains at a low level.

Overall, the main conclusion from the study made is that in EAEU countries, trade liberalization (the customs union has been in effect since 2010) has stimulated the growth of mutual trade flows yet at the same time negatively affected mutual investments, leading to a decrease in their growth rates, which is also associated with a weak development of regional production chains. Among the factors that also negatively affected the volume of mutual investment, the following should be emphasized: the generally low level of economic development of the member countries (especially in Armenia and Kyrgyzstan); differentiation in the levels of economic development, which has prevailed since the early 1990s; a high proportion of developed countries in the FDI inflow into the economies of Russia, Kazakhstan, and Kyrgyzstan; and a non-high level of international competitiveness of member countries.

As a result, the effect of investment diversion affected the dynamics and volumes of mutual FDI in the EAEU. To obtain the effect of investment creation, it is necessary to intensify investment liberalization of mutual ties and intensify mutual production relations, and therefore, the formation of regional production chains. As the dynamic effect of membership in an integration block is concerned, it manifests itself in the long term, whereas the EAEU has been in effect only since 2015. Consequently, investment creation and growing investment attractiveness due to participation in the EAEU should have an effect, at least in the medium term. In conclusion, in the investment sphere, the EAEU states do not yet benefit from participation in the integration processes.

References

Altomonte, C. (2000). Economic Determinants and Institutional Frameworks: FDI in Economies in Transition. *Transnational Corporations Journal of United Nations, 9*(2), 75–106.

APEC Non-Binding Investment Principles. (1994). Retrieved from https://www.apec.org/Achievements/Group/Committee-on-Trade-and-Investment-2/Investment-Experts-Group.

Belarus and Countries of the World—2017. (2018). *Statistical Reference Book*. Minsk. Retrieved from http://www.belstat.gov.by/ofitsialnaya-statistika/publications/izdania/index_12823/.

Berger, A., Busse, M., Nunnenkamp, P., & Roy, M. (2013). Do trade and Investment Agreements Lead to More FDI? Accounting for Key Provisions Inside the Black Box. *International Economic Policy, 10*, 247–275.

Blomström, M., & Kokko, A. (1997, May). *Regional Integration and Foreign Direct Investment*. Working Paper Series in Economics and Finance No. 172.

CIS Investor Rights Convention. (1997). Retrieved from https://cis-legislation.com/document.fwx?rgn=4732.

Direct investment in the Eurasian Economic Union. (2018). *Statistical Bulletin of 2017* (p. 63). Moscow: Eurasian Commission.

Doing Business. (2019). *Training for Reform*. World Bank Report. Retrieved from https://www.doingbusiness.org/en/reports/global-reports/doing-business-.

Entrepreneur Code of the Republic of Kazakhstan of October 29. (2015). No. 375-V. Retrieved from http://adilet.zan.kz/eng/docs/K1500000375.

EU-Armenia Partnership and cooperation agreement. (1999). Retrieved from https://eeas.europa.eu/sites/eeas/files/eu-armenia_partnership_and_cooperation_agreement_en.

EU-Kazakhstan Enhanced Partnership and Cooperation Agreement. (2017). Retrieved from https://bureau.kz/en/monitoring/international_reports_on_kazakhstan/eu-kazakhstan_enhanced_partnership_and_cooperation_agreement_.

EU-Kyrgyzstan Comprehensive Agreement. (2019). Retrieved from https://www.europarl.europa.eu/doceo/document/TA-8-2019-0004_EN.html.

Federal Law of 09.07.1999 No. 160-FZ "On Foreign Investments in the Russian Federation". (1999). Retrieved from https://en.fas.gov.ru/documents/documentdetails.html?id=13818.

Federal Law of April 29. (2008). No. 57-FZ "On the Procedure for Making Foreign Investments in Business Companies of Strategic Importance to Ensure the Defense of the Country and the Security of the State". Retrieved from https://en.fas.gov.ru/documents/documentdetails.html?id=13918.

Global Competitiveness Report. (2018). Retrieved from http://reports.weforum.org/global-competitiveness-report-2018/competitiveness-rankings/.

Government. (2019). Retrieved from http://government.ru/news/37047/.

Heifetz, B. A. (2016). On the Eurasian Economic Union's Free Investment Zone. *Problems of Economic Transition, 58*(4), 328–347.

Investment Climate in Russia—Foreign Investors Perception. (2015). Ernst&Yang. Retrieved from https://www.ey.com/Publication/vwLUAssets/EY_report_-_Investment_climate_in_Russia_2015/ per cent24FILE/EY-Investment-climate-in-Russia_eng per cent20EY per cent202015.pdf.

Investments in the Kyrgyz Republic 2013–2017. (2018). *Annual Publication*. Bishkek. Retrieved from http://www.stat.kg/media/publicationarchive/ac191131-20a6-4450-bd7e-7af5d106dd69.

Kindleberger, C. P. (1966). European Integration and the International Corporation. *Columbia Journal of World Business, 1*, 65–73.

Kostyunina, G. M. (2019). Mutual Investments in the EAEC Countries. In *Big Eurasia: Development, Security, Cooperation*. Moscow: INION. Retrieved from https://mgimo.ru/upload/iblock/d69/vzaimnye-pryamye-investicii-v-stranah-eaehs-osnovnye-tendencii-i-faktory-vliyaniya.pdf.

Law of March 27. (2003a) No. 66 "On Investments in Kyrgyz Republic". Retrieved from https://investmentpolicy.unctad.org/investment-laws/laws/111/kyrgyzstan-investment-law.

Law of November 4. (2003b) No. 490-II "On State Monitoring of Property in Strategic Economic Sectors". Retrieved from http://adilet.zan.kz/eng/docs/Z030000490_.

Law of July 12. (2013). No. 53–3. On Investments. Retrieved from http://law.by/document/?guid=3871&p0=H11300053.

Law of July 31. (1994) No. ZR-115 "On Foreign Investments in the Republic of Armenia". Retrieved from http://www.parliament.am/legislation.php?sel=show&ID=1552&lang=eng.

Monitoring of Mutual Investments in the CIS countries. (2018). Eurasian Development Bank. *Center for Integration Studies Report, 45*, 75.

OIC Investment Agreement. (1981). Retrieved from https://investmentpolicy.unctad.org/international-investment-agreements/treaties/bit/3092/oic-investment-agreement-1981-.

Pacific Basin Charter on International Investments. (1995). Retrieved from https://investmentpolicy.unctad.org/international-investment-agreements/treaty-files/2883/download.

The Energy Charter Treaty. (1994). Retrieved from https://www.europarl.europa.eu/meetdocs/2014_2019/documents/itre/dv/energy_charter_/energy_charter_en.pdf.

Transparency International. (2018). Corruption Perceptions Index. Retrieved from https://www.transparency.org/news/feature/corruption_perceptions_index_.

Transparency International. 2019. The Corruption Perceptions Index 2019. URL: https://images.transparencycdn.org/images/2019_CPI_Report_EN_200331_141425.pdf

Treaty on the EAEU. (05/29/2014, ed. 04/11/2017). Retrieved from https://cis-legislation.com/document.fwx?rgn=4732.

UNCTAD. (2019). Retrieved from https://investmentpolicy.unctad.org/international-investment-agreement.

UNCTAD. (2020). Retrieved from https://stats.unctad.org/handbook/EconomicTrends/Fdi.html.

US-Central Asia Trade and Investment Facilitation Agreement. (2013). Retrieved from https://ustr.gov/about-us/policy-offices/press-office/press-releases/2013/November/US-Central-Asia-TIFA-Council-Joint-Statement

World Bank data. (2020). Exports of goods and services (per cent of GDP). Retrieved from https://data.worldbank.org/indicator/NE.EXP.GNFS.ZS.

CHAPTER 4

Industrial Cooperation in the EAEU

Yuri A. Savinov and Evgenya V. Taranovskaya

4.1 Introduction

One of the trends in global economic development is an objective movement toward the unification of countries into economic integration groups that are diverse in form and nature. Economic integration allows the full use of each participant's comparative advantages. However, the implementation of economic integration plans is not an easy task, especially if states with different levels of economic development take part. One of the main difficulties at the initial stage is the complexity of developing a formal regulatory framework. This problem is of great importance for many states implementing plans for economic integration on various continents (Libman 2009).

Industrial cooperation evolves with the development of production itself. It was mainly the economic relations between the partners arising from the production and the supply of components and assemblies by one of them to the other in accordance with the technical conditions and needs of one of them on the basis of a contract (subcontract).

Y. A. Savinov (✉) • E. V. Taranovskaya
Russian Foreign Trade Academy of Ministry of Economic Development, Moscow, Russia

N. A. Piskulova (ed.), *The Economic Dimension of Eurasian Integration*, https://doi.org/10.1007/978-3-030-59886-0_4

Legal framework contributes to the full use of the economic potential of the participating countries and allows the intended goals to be achieved. This is also true for countries that are members of the Eurasian Economic Union (EAEU). At the same time, no matter what the political goals of integration, in fact, the main instrument for implementing plans for economic unification is the establishment of comprehensive economic cooperation. Our task is to analyze the development of industrial cooperation within the EAEU.

In the economic literature and in discussions with business representatives, the term "cooperation" also usually refers to the whole range of possible economic relations, including negotiations of a general nature and the execution of specific transactions for the exchange of parts and details in cooperative production. Industrial cooperation, the main element of which is production cooperation, is permanent production relations between relatively independent specialized industrial enterprises, developed in different forms: inter-state joint programs and projects, negotiated contract cooperation, creation of joint ventures, strategic alliances, and inter-state financial-industrial groups.

4.2 Literature Review

Quite a few publications are devoted to the issues of industrial cooperation in various forms. A large part of these issues is considered from a political point of view. Industrial cooperation is the subject of research by many economists.

Finnish economists Ritala and Elonen, in the study of international inter-firm cooperation, focus on the acquisition of comparative advantages by the parties involved in cooperation projects (Ritala and Ellonen 2010). This conclusion is confirmed by a group of Spanish economists who have studied international inter-firm cooperation at the present time (Edwards-Schachter et al. 2013). The British economist Farrell analyzes the impact of institutional factors on the development of international inter-firm cooperation, analyzing the cooperation between enterprises of Emilia-Romagna (Italy) and Baden-Württemberg (Germany; Farrell 2012).

The development of inter-country cooperation in the literature is discussed from different sides and the role of general economic and social factors is largely emphasized.

One of the areas of analysis in economic research is the development of cross-border industrial cooperation. In fact, all EAEU countries, except

Armenia, have common borders and carry out cross-border cooperation. These issues are analyzed in detail in the publication (Klojcnik 2012).

Cooperation in the commercial sphere has expanded, reflecting the processes of direct impact of industrial cooperation on it. Similar relations apply to the field of subcontract, providing the contractor the same opportunity initiative, as the main customer (Recherche et innovation 1993).

4.3 Directions of State Policy for the Development of Industrial Cooperation in the EAEU

In countries with a market economy, the state apparatus produces documents of a general nature, not dealing with private issues of relations between enterprises. Governments reduce the barriers of transaction costs through the creation of formal institutions (e.g., property rights protection or trade liberalization) as well as through the provision of physical infrastructure (e.g., railway network) in the case of its absence.

A specific feature of the achievements set out in the normative documents of the tasks is their recommendatory, not directive, structures (optional for business). State structures develop normative documents, but for their implementation, it is desirable to develop additional tools.

At the same time, since state-owned enterprises are privatized, the state does not accept and implement inter-state investment projects. This requires the interest of private, entrepreneurial structures, but special incentives for this have not yet been developed. As a result, in practice, cooperative projects have the character of bilateral business relations, as a rule, of a supply type (Savinov et al. 2019).

As Savinov et al. (2019) explain it, the main tasks of industrial cooperation and cooperation within the EAEU at the present stage are the following:

- ensuring the creation of conditions for increasing the growth rate and volume of industrial production in the member-states, as well as conditions conducive to the development of mutual trade and fair competition between enterprises of the member-states in the single market of the EAEU;
- ensuring effective cooperation of member-states aimed at increasing the innovative activity of industrial enterprises;

- ensuring the creation of conditions for increasing the share of products of the member-states in the common market of the EAEU and gradually increasing its localization;
- ensuring the creation of conditions for the development of production of new competitive products, export-oriented, and the modernization (technical re-equipment) of existing industries with the creation of new innovative sectors of industry of the member-states;
- ensuring the removal of barriers in the industrial sector;
- ensuring the creation of conditions for attracting investment and increasing the availability of financial resources for industrial enterprises;
- ensuring control over the implementation of the provisions of article 93 and Annex No. 28 to the EAEU Treaty;
- improving the effectiveness of the implementation of the provisions of the Treaty in the field of industrial cooperation and the provision of industrial subsidies (industrial policy in the Eurasian economic Union: three years of integration, 2018).

Industrial cooperation is regulated by section XXIV of the Treaty on the EAEU, which refers to the harmonization of goals, principles, and the main directions of industrial cooperation within the EAEU (approved by the decision of the Intergovernmental commission dated September 8, 2015, № 9), on the basis of which countries conduct an independent industrial policy, based on consultation, policy coordination, monitoring, and analysis of results from the EAEU Economic Commission. The principles of industrial subsidies and protective measures have been agreed upon, mutual information and consultations are under way, joint programs and projects are being developed, and a list of sensitive goods has been approved. Joint research and measures are planned to stimulate cooperation, including the creation of joint technology platforms, industrial clusters, the involvement of small- and medium-sized businesses, and the formation of cooperative chains to produce joint products. For the effective implementation of the decisions taken in the EAEU, the Department of Industrial Policy, cooperating with UNIDO, was established.

To implement the adopted documents on economic integration in the EAEU, Eurasian technological platforms have been developed and adopted, which aim to establish a systematic work on the widespread use of advanced national and global achievements of scientific and technical development, and the mobilization of scientific potential of member-states for solving applied problems in the development of innovative products and technologies, as well as their implementation in industrial production. Fourteen industrial platforms have been developed and more than 100 projects have been approved. In the EAEU, special mechanisms are being formed: technological platforms and clusters "Eurasian supercomputer technology platform," "Light industry," "Eurasian led technology platform," and so on. A special network of industrial cooperation and subcontracting, the functioning of which is facilitated by a single information system for search and organization of orders, subcontracts exchanges. Their implementation will contribute to solving urgent economic problems.

4.4 Inter-Firm Cooperation and Mutual Investments

The development of the process of cooperation in industry is not an end in itself, but should be considered as one of the stages of inter-firm cooperation, which often comes to joint development and joint production of both existing and new products. Therefore, enterprises are setting up new joint ventures in countries with sufficient market capacity. Mutual investments of the parties are a reflection of this process. This factor is extremely important for the cooperation of the economies of EAEU countries, which is one of the goals of the EAEU Treaty. Russia ranks first in terms of investment among EAEU countries. However, it should be recognized that, due to sanctions and fluctuations in energy prices, there has not yet been a significant increase in the growth rate of mutual investments between EAEU member-states, but mutual investments of the EAEU member-states in 2017–2019 began to increase. After a slight decline in 2013–2015, they increased by 15.9 per cent to $26.8 billion (Monitoring of mutual investments in CIS countries—2017). The integration effect is manifested in the growth of mutual investments. As a result, for example, accumulated Russian investments in Kazakhstan amount to almost $13 billion, and Kazakhstan to Russia almost $4 billion.

Russian companies take first place in the export of investments. They account for over 78 per cent of foreign direct investment exports. Second place is taken by Kazakhstan (13.5 per cent) and third by Belarus (7.8 per cent). Of the Russian investor companies in the EAEU, 71 per cent are among the top 25 firms. It is assumed that as the integration processes develop, foreign investments of medium and small firms will begin. Russian companies often occupy significant positions in the EAEU member-states. Thus, in Kyrgyzstan, Russian enterprises operate in almost all important sectors of the economy, which include energy, engineering, agricultural and industrial complement, transport, and the gas industry. Russia is the main foreign investor in Armenia. More than 1300 Russian companies operate in the Republic, and the volume of accumulated investments is $4 billion (40 per cent of all foreign investments). The Republic actively works with the largest Russian companies—Gazprom, Rosatom, Russian Railways, VTB (Former name of VneshTorgBank - Foreign Trade bank), RUSAL (Russian Aluminium Company), and so on. Russia is almost totally owned by the Armenian energy sector. In the gas sector, Gazprom is the monopolist, and in the transmission and distribution of electricity, it is inter RAO UES, which owns JSC "Electric networks of Armenia."

Another new area of industrial investment cooperation is the joint creation of production structures for the development of foreign trade with third countries. Since the end of 2016, an agreement on a free trade zone between the EAEU and Vietnam has been in force. Joint ventures are being prepared to develop exports to third States. For example, Armenia intends to create Assembly plants of Belarusian tractors in the country for their export to Iran. The city of Meghri, located on the border with Iran, on the territory of which a free economic zone is being created, is considered as the location of enterprises for the production of Belarusian tractors and elevators.

As the main bonus, the Armenian side offers Minsk the prospects of penetration into the vast Iranian market, which will be opened thanks to the agreement on a free-trade zone with Iran. The signing of an Interim agreement on the establishment of a free-trade zone between the EAEU and the Islamic Republic of Iran, signed in May 2018 at the Astana economic forum, opens new prospects for the development of industrial cooperation and export development.

The main direction of development and the deepening of economic integration in the EAEU countries is the expansion of cooperation between industrial enterprises. This will make it possible to re-engineer production facilities, increase the competitiveness of products, and expand exports to third countries. Thus, the implementation of major projects in which all the countries of the Eurasian Economic Union would participate is one of the key elements of the Union's development strategy.

Members of the Union do not hide that they would like to enter the global market with Eurasian brands—recognizable, jointly released products and new technologies (Savinov et al. 2019). As an example, large production companies of Belarus, such as "Tractor plant," MAZ, BelAZ, which create about 30–50 per cent of components together with enterprises of the Russian Federation—partners in cooperation. Deputy Prime Minister of the Republic of Belarus I. Petrishenko stressed that it is necessary to promote brands in the EAEU and avoid protectionist measures. "In general, there should be an honest competition policy within the Union, so that our companies in close cooperation interact in the EAEU market and promote our common brand in foreign markets," the Belarusian Deputy Prime Minister said (Co-operation and joint project activity 2018).

4.5 Development of Production Cooperation Projects

Within the framework of the Union, a lot of successful cooperation projects have been implemented: the St. Petersburg tractor plant, with the support of the Ministry of Industry and Trade of Russia and the EEC itself, started production of automated transmissions and plans to produce them up to 6000 per year. It is planned to start production of transmissions for tractors, which are not currently produced in the EAEU countries. As consumers participating in the project, involving the machine-building enterprise of Belarus (Minsk tractor works, Gomselmash) and Kazakhstan ("Agromashholding") is planned. It is such projects that create real cooperative ties that contribute not only to competition, but also to the creation of technological chains between the EAEU countries, which have long been talked about.

An example of the development of such a cooperation is the relationship between the Ural turbine plant (UTZ—holding ROTEK) and the Karaganda turbo-mechanical plant (KTMZ). KTMZ is the leading Kazakhstan power engineering enterprise, specializing in the repair and modernization of steam turbines. It should be noted that the UTZ has been cooperating with the Kazakh enterprise for a long time.

Together they carried out several projects for power plants in Russia and the Republic of Kazakhstan. In 2018, Ural specialists joined forces on the replacement of the high-pressure part of the T-100-130 turbine at Arcelor Mittal Temirtau CHPP (Kazakhstan) on the basis of a contract. This is the first stage of modernization of the unit. As a result of the modernization, the T-100-130 will be fully updated. The UTZ is already implementing the contract: the design and technological study of the order is being completed; the equipment will be manufactured and shipped to the customer in the coming months.

The participation of each country in the processes of international specialization and cooperation contributed to the development of trade between the EAEU member-states. These two activities are closely related.

Due to different levels of economic development, the structure of exports and imports of EAEU member-states differs significantly. Countries with a relatively high level of industrial development—Russia, Belarus, and Kazakhstan—export raw materials and large-scale finished products, that is, processed goods. Based on this, the development of mutual trade is carried out either within the framework of inter-sectoral exchange of goods, or intra-industry. It seems reasonable to determine the specifics of foreign trade relations in the EAEU markets. Based on the trends in the development of cooperative supplies in industrialized countries, it is known that they have a high share of intra-industry cooperation.

For example, trade between Russia and Kyrgyzstan is mainly developing on an inter-sectoral basis. Trade with Armenia is also developing, although the share of finished goods in Armenia's exports is increasing. At the same time, the rapid development of intra-industry specialization and cooperation leads to high rates of export growth in the mutual trade of machinery and equipment between Russia and Belarus. In other words, cooperation is a driving force for the development of mutual trade (Savinov et al. 2019).

The development of inter-firm industrial cooperation is not only symbolic as the achievement of a certain criterion, which is an indicator of the development of cooperation; it also reflects the deep economic processes, the result of which is economic growth on the basis of saving production costs.

After that, the correlation coefficient of the increase in the growth rate of trade turnover from the level of intra-industry cooperation was calculated without taking into account the data in the crisis years (i.e., for 2010–2011 and 2016–2017), and it showed a fairly high figure.

For correct analysis of the presence of correlation on the export structure, it is necessary to maintain some conditional restrictions. As our first step, we withdraw export of defense products from the exports of all countries; the second step was comparing the degree of coincidence of mutual export structures of the two countries and the higher the degree of these coincidences over the years, the more obvious the development of intra-industry cooperation. It can be achieved by the use of the Spearmen coefficient. After that, we propose to determine how great is the impact of the increase in the degree of coincidence of mutual export structures of the two countries on the development of mutual exports (more specifically, on the growth rate of mutual exports between the countries).

On the horizontal axis (abscissa axis), we postpone the dynamics of the degree of conformity of the mutual export structures of the two countries, and on the vertical axis (ordinate axis), we postpone the indicators of export growth rates. Then we build a graph of the mutual correlation of the two indicators (See Fig. 4.1). We get the direct correlation equation, which shows how much the growth rate of export increases (along the ordinate) with an increase in the degree of coincidence of mutual export structures (abscissa indicator), that is, an indicator of increased cooperation and development within industry exports. The coefficient R is called the coefficient of determination.

The coefficient of determination is considered, as a rule, as the main indicator reflecting a measure of the quality of the regression model describing the relationship between the dependent and independent variables of the model. The coefficient of determination shows what proportion of the variation of the explained variable y is taken into account in the model and is caused by the influence of factors included in the model on it (Fig. 4.1).

The same situation is observed in Russia's trade with Kazakhstan. The increase in the coefficient of coincidence of mutual export structures of the two countries (Russia and Kazakhstan) affects the growth rate of mutual exports as shown in Fig. 4.2.

The indicator of the correlation of Spearman's ranks on commodity items in mutual trade from 2010 to 2017 increased from 0.893 to 0.929, which caused the growth of trade turnover of the two countries by 13 per cent.

Mutual trade of the three countries, taken for analysis, includes a greater number of commodity items, primarily due to the development of exchange of engineering products. This can be determined by the increase in the share of these products in mutual trade with the development of

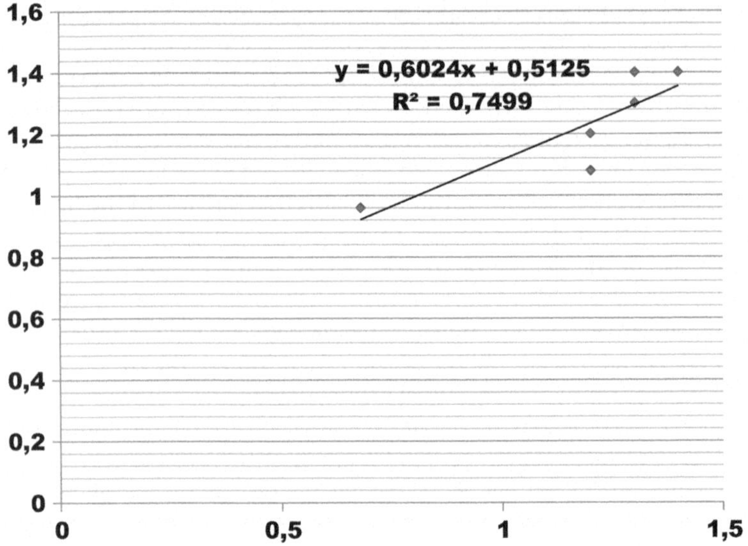

Fig. 4.1 Correlation of the index of increase of trade turnover from the dynamics of the Spearman's coefficient in mutual trade of Russia and the Republic of Belarus. (Note: The dynamics of Spearman's correlation coefficient is marked on the abscissa axis, the movement of the trade turnover index of Russia and the Republic of Belarus on the ordinate axis. Calculated based on: https://www.trademap.org)

economic integration of the countries: in 2018, their share in exports of the Republic of Belarus amounted to 14.8 per cent (in 2017, 17.3 per cent), against 7.8 per cent in 2012. In Russia's exports to Armenia, the share of machinery and equipment increased from 14.5 per cent in 2014 to 23.7 per cent in 2017. In Kazakhstan's exports to Russia, the share of machinery and equipment in 2016–2018 increased from 4.8 to 5.8 per cent. It should be noted that the mutual trade of these two countries was largely affected by the crisis, as a result of which mutual supplies for many types of engineering products were reduced. Some stabilization came at the turn of 2016–2018 and yet trade is unstable: the mutual turnover of engineering products in 2016 amounted to $2.5 billion, in 2017 it fell to $2.1 billion, and in 2018 it already increased to $2.4 billion. During these years, several important agreements on the development of cooperation within the EAEU were signed, which in our opinion plays a significant

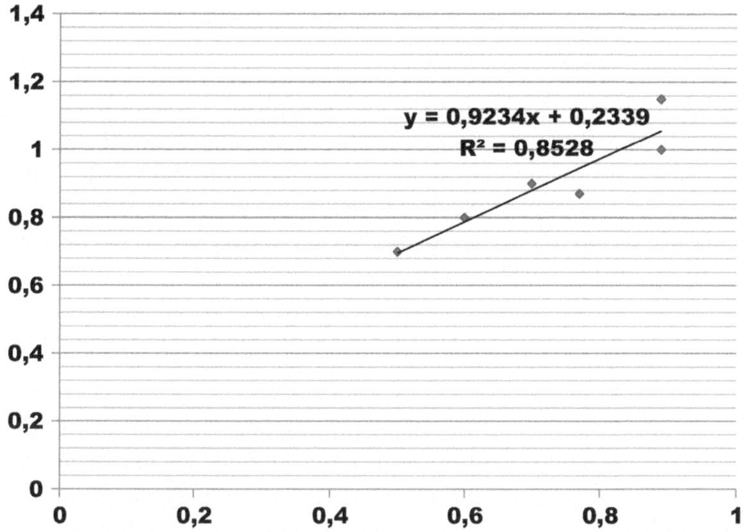

Fig. 4.2 Dependence of the dynamics of the growth rate of mutual trade in machinery and equipment on the indicator of cooperation between Russia and Kazakhstan for 2014–2018. On the ordinate axis—indicators of the Spearman's coefficient; on the abscissa axis—indicators of the growth index of mutual trade in machinery and equipment between Russia and Kazakhstan. The coefficient of determination in the equation is quite high. It shows that with an increase in the degree of coincidence of mutual export structures (i.e., with an increase in the degree of mutual intra-industrial cooperation) by 1, the export growth rate increases by 0.85. This indicates a significant impact of the development of intra-industry cooperation on the growth rate of mutual exports. Calculated based on: https://www.trademap.org

role in the development of mutual trade. The development of intra-industry cooperation relations in 2016–2018 determined the dynamics of mutual trade (Russia and Kazakhstan) (Fig. 4.2).

4.6 Obstacles to the Development of Industrial Cooperation in EAEU Countries

The development of economic integration within the EAEU is facing emerging "growth difficulties," which are explained by different levels of economic development and differences in the choice of methods of cooperation. However, all member countries of the Union are determined to overcome the emerging barriers.

A special emphasis in the development of cooperation within the EAEU should be made on overcoming the key difficulties that limit the development of cooperation in innovation, science, and technology. Among them, the lack of a full legal framework for cooperation, the lack of the required software and financial instruments, as well as the problems associated with the violation of the timing of the preparation of decisions and other documents are particularly highlighted.

There are several completely unused opportunities in the work of the EAEU on industrial cooperation. To date, the practice of cooperation in the field of bilateral and multilateral industrial cooperation has not been fully developed. The policy is not fully synchronized and there is not always an understanding of the opportunities and challenges of Eurasian integration by business and state authorities, despite the numerous documents adopted. As a result, there is fragmentation in cooperation, which needs to be eliminated, to make it more monolithic and complex.

Regarding possible methods of implementing the adopted program documents, usually in state structures, the opinion is expressed that if the normative documents are adopted, then everything is good. In fact, in order to ensure the implementation of the decisions taken, it is necessary to develop measures to implement the agreements and to develop incentives for private companies to participate in the programs adopted. In our opinion:

1. The best incentive for the participation of business entities in the implementation of the announced and approved interstate program is to reduce the tax burden through the issuance of state contracts for the implementation of general programs with general funding. They are possible through fundamental R & D, but there are no joint production programs yet.
2. Joint training of personnel in the production and conduct of business.
3. In order to achieve the goals of the industrial cooperation programs, it is necessary to take steps from goals announcement to the recognition of the need for cooperation on specific types of industrial products; that is, to production cooperation: joint production and contract cooperation.
4. The development of incentives for cooperation seems necessary (the reduction of taxes on cooperated products).

4.7 Conclusions

The development of industrial international inter-firm cooperation serves as a reliable factor in reducing production costs and contributes to an increase in economic growth. This has been proven in the article through the example of export growth in relations between Russia and the Republic of Belarus, as well as in relations between Russia and the Republic of Kazakhstan.

References

Edwards-Schachter, M., Castro-Martínez, E., & Fernández-De-Lucio, I. (2013). *Motives for International Inter-Firm Cooperation on R&D and Innovation.* Literature Overview and Recent Trends. Chapter 11 Quality Innovation by Latif Al-Hakim; Chen Jin. Published by IGI Global, Institute of Innovation and Knowledge Management, Spain & Universitat Politécnica de València. Retrieved from https://www.safaribooksonline.com/library/view/quality-innovation/9781466647695/978-1-4666-4769-5.ch011.xhtml.

Farrell, H. (2012). *The Political Economy of Trust. Institutions, Interests, and Inter-Firm Cooperation in Italy and Germany.* Part of Cambridge Studies in Comparative Politics. p. 256.

Hanahhe, O., et al. (1993). *Recherche et innovation: Le temps des reseaux: Rapport du groupe "Recherche, technologic et competitive"* Commissariat general du plan; P.: Documentation fr., p. 160.

Klojcnik, J. (2012). *Cross-Border Cooperation as a Tool of Development and Cohesion—Experiences in the EU.* ECERS-European Centre for Ethnic, Regional and Sociological Studies, University of Maribor, pp. *113–127. (in English).*

Libman, A. (2009, October). *Models of Market Integration in Central Asia—omparative performance.* Frankfurt School of Finance. MPRA Paper No. 17510. Retrieved from http://mpra.ub.uni-muenchen.de/17510/.

Ritala, P., & Ellonen, H. (2010). Competitive Advantage in Interfirm Cooperation: Old and New Explanations. *(Lappeenranta School of Business, Lappeenranta, Finland) Competitiveness Review, 20*(5), 367–383.

Savinov, Y., Orlova, G., Taranovskaja, E., & Basilashvili, T. (2019). Development of Industrial Cooperstion Within the EAEU. *Russian Foreign Economic Journal, 5*, 54–78. (In Russian).

CHAPTER 5

Perspectives of Common EAEU Oil and Gas Markets

Olga L. Garanina

5.1 Introduction

The Eurasian Economic Union (EAEU) connects major energy producers in Eurasia and plays a crucial role in providing energy supplies and energy security. However, energy-related issues were brought into the post-Soviet integration agenda relatively late, with the establishment of the EAEU in 2015.

The EAEU integration project proposes the creation of common markets for energy resources (oil, oil products, natural gas, and electricity). Although previous integration initiatives in the post-Soviet space introduced some provisions concerning the energy markets, the EAEU stands as the most comprehensive attempt to build integrated energy markets in the post-Soviet space (Zemskova 2018). Notably, the Eurasian Economic Community, launched in 2000 by Russia, Belarus, Kazakhstan, Kyrgyzstan, and Tajikistan, included provisions for joint development of energy

O. L. Garanina (✉)
Graduate School of Management, St. Petersburg University, Saint-Petersburg, Russia
e-mail: o.garanina@gsom.spbu.ru

N. A. Piskulova (ed.), *The Economic Dimension of Eurasian Integration*, https://doi.org/10.1007/978-3-030-59886-0_5

balances and common information support system. It also included a concept for the formation of common energy markets. Later, the Customs Union, founded in 2010 by Russia, Belarus, and Kazakhstan and transformed into a Single Economic Space in 2012, set the common principles and approaches to energy pricing and access to natural monopoly services for markets in electricity, natural gas, oil, and oil products (EEE 2015). In continuation of these initiatives, the EAEU members agreed on the goal to create common markets of energy resources in perspective to 2025 (Concept for the Formation of Common Markets of Oil and Oil Products of Eurasian Economic Union 2016; Concept for the Formation of Common Market of Natural Gas of Eurasian Economic Union 2016).

In theory, energy market integration is expected to raise the level of market competition and to ensure efficient use of resources, which would result in stronger economic growth dynamics through lowering energy costs. Energy market integration also increases the security of supply (Booz & Company 2013). The most prominent example of market integration is the case of the European Union, where energy market reforms were introduced since the end of 1990s. Market integration was accompanied by market liberalization, which included unbundling natural monopolies, promoting competition, and establishing supranational (EU-level) market regulating authorities. Transition to liberalized and integrated markets was perceived as a way to ensure the price benefits and to reach energy security gains.

At a first glance, one can observe that EAEU integration declares a similar goal-setting framework. Energy cooperation intends a step-by-step creation of common markets of energy resources and should also take into account provision for energy security. The objectives of collaboration in the energy domain are defined as (i) efficient use of the energy potential of the member-states and (ii) provision of energy supplies (electricity, gas, oil, and oil products) to member countries (Treaty on the Eurasian Economic Union, art.79). Creating common energy markets is also expected to strengthen the countries' positions in the global energy markets and ensure energy security (Pleshkin 2017; Shenec 2017). However, in the case of the EAEU, market integration reforms are still at their initial stage. The institutional framework is oriented at creating conditions for policy cohesion and promotion of market liberalization, whereas the specific rules, processes, and targets need to be further elaborated.

More precisely, integration of oil, oil products, and natural gas markets intends non-discriminatory access to energy infrastructures within the integration union and promotion of energy trade at market prices.

Common rules will be applied to services of natural monopolies in the energy transportation segment, antitrust regulation, customs and fiscal regulations, and regulation of trading activities and also technical requirements (EDB 2017).

Integration is expected to be implemented in three stages (Program for the Formation of Common Markets of Oil and Oil Products of Eurasian Economic Union 2018; Program for the Formation of Common Market of Natural Gas of Eurasian Economic Union 2018). For oil and oil products, the first stage (2018–2021) intends the development of methodological and organizational basis for market integration and harmonization of legislation; the second stage (2021–2024) will see the development of common rules for access to oil and products transportation infrastructures and approval of the international treaty by the relevant authorities in member-states; and the third stage (prior to January 1, 2025) provides for the entry in force of the international treaty on formation of common markets of oil and oil products. For natural gas, the first stage (until 2020) includes the harmonization of legislative basis for market regulation, information exchange between member-states, elaboration of common rules for access to gas transportation systems, and identification of infrastructural constraints; the second stage (until 2021) will see the functioning of gas trading platforms and ensuring non-discriminatory access of the EAEU market participants to these platforms, provision of access to gas transportation systems for intra-EAEU gas deliveries, and support of consultations for issues related to gas exports to third countries (including for cases where EAEU members may be competitors); at the third stage (by January 1, 2025), the international treaty on the formation of common markets of natural gas should enter into force, and it is expected that by this date, countries will ensure free intra-EAEU gas supplies at market prices and make a decision on transition to equal profitability of gas supplies in EAEU.

However, while assessing the prospects of common energy markets in the EAEU, it should be acknowledged that the EAEU integration project follows several failed attempts to reintegrate the post-Soviet space (Libman 2007; Zhukov and Reznikova 2007). At its origin, the progress of post-Soviet integration was severely challenged by the affirmation of independent politics in the newly sovereign republics. In order to succeed, the EAEU should be supported by a transfer of sovereignty from the national level to supranational institutions, which is not truly achieved at the current stage (Roberts and Moshes 2016). Therefore, the integration results may not reach up to the declared objectives.

The energy industry presents a relevant case for studying the political and economic constraints related to the EAEU integration project, given the strategic importance of oil and gas for members' macroeconomic health and political strategies. This chapter aims to discuss the perspectives and constraints of the EAEU integration with a focus on oil and natural gas industry. We intentionally do not consider the electricity sector, also covered by the EAEU integration framework, due to industry specificity. We show that EAEU energy integration (as concerns oil and gas industry) faces numerous challenges. Differences in terms of resource endowment, relative economic weight of partners, different pricing conditions, and political constraints complicate the harmonization of energy policies between EAEU members.

This chapter is organized as follows. Section 5.2 introduces the role of oil and gas in EAEU economic integration. Section 5.3 discusses energy subsidies. Section 5.4 outlines economic, institutional, and political constraints to the integration process. The last section concludes.

5.2 EAEU Energy Space: Trade and Economic Issues

The EAEU countries play a significant role in global energy markets. If integrated, the EAEU will cover about 8 percent of global oil reserves and 19 percent of natural gas reserves, which corresponds to 14 percent of global oil production and 18 percent of global gas production (Table 5.1).

Although, the bloc is far from being homogeneous with regard to energy and economic issues. The EAEU is characterized by different positions of member countries in the energy trade. It includes Russia, which stands among the world largest oil and gas exporters, and Kazakhstan, which has significant oil and gas endowment, as well as the energy-poor Armenia, Belarus, and Kyrgyzstan. As has been widely studied, energy security interests tend to diverge across energy exporting and energy importing countries: while energy exporters privilege the stability of demand and revenue stream maximization, the net importers seek uninterrupted supplies at affordable prices (Energy Charter Secretariat 2015). Therefore, the EAEU integration model should find ways to reconcile the interests of both energy exporters and energy importers.

Table 5.1 EAEU energy space: an overview

	GDP PPP (billion $, 2017)	*GDP per capita, PPP (thousand $, 2017)*	*Proven reserves, share of world total (percent, 2017)*		*Production, share of world total (percent, 2017)*		*Share of oil, gas and products in total exports (imports) (percent, 2017)*	*Oil rents (percent of GDP, 2017)*
			Oil	*Natural gas*	*Oil*	*Natural gas*		
Armenia	28.3	9.6	–	–	–	–	0.0 (15.7)	0.0
Belarus	179.1	18.8	–	–	–	–	23.4 (27.7)[a]	0.5
Kazakhstan	476.8	26.4	1.8	0.6	2.0	0.7	62.2 (5.0)	10.2
Kyrgyzstan	23.1	3.7	–	–	–	–	2.9 (13.7)	0.1
Russia	3817.2	25.5	6.3	18.1	12.2	17.3	54.8 (0.6)	6.4

Source: BP, UN Comtrade, World Bank

[a]Belarus is a net importer of crude oil and net exporter of refined products

The EAEU includes transition economies with low- to upper-middle incomes. Differently from the EU, where the integration of energy markets occurred at the later stages of the economic integration process and was implemented by high-income economies, in the post-Soviet space, countries have to deal with economic development and energy market integration simultaneously. In this sense, energy cooperation lies at the nexus of macroeconomic stabilization and development policies which exacerbates the level of sensitivity of energy-related issues. Finally, the well-known inequalities in terms of relative economic weight of EAEU members (simply measured through GDP indicators) add to the governability problem of the union.

At the economic level, energy plays a key role in regional development. Oil, gas, and energy products account for about 55 percent of Russian total exports and 60 percent of Kazakh exports in 2017 (the level of dependency may fluctuate over time following the oil price dynamics). Fiscal returns from oil and gas-related activities are major sources of budget revenues, reaching around 40 percent in Russia in 2017 (Tass 2018) and 30 percent in Kazakhstan (EADaily 2019). Due to the high relative weight of Russia in the EAEU, macroeconomic trends in both energy-rich and energy-poor countries follow the oil price cycle, as the latter are dependent on their economic ties to Russia (Becker 2019).

Energy is also a major engine of intra-regional trade in the EAEU. In 2015–2017, natural gas, oil, and oil products accounted for about 35–50 percent of Russian exports to Belarus, 40–55 percent of exports to Kyrgyzstan, 10–20 percent of Russian exports to Armenia, and 10 percent of exports to Kazakhstan (UNCTAD 2019). The high proportion of energy trade explains the rationale for inclusion of energy-related aspects into the integration agenda.

However, energy relations of member countries are to a large extent oriented outside the union. In other terms, intra-regional trade in oil and gas is low in comparison to countries' oil and gas exports outside the EAEU (Tables 5.2 and 5.3).

Measured in terms of market size, the role of the EAEU demand is moderate in comparison to the EU or China. To illustrate, Russian gas exports to the EAEU account for less than 20 percent of Russia's gas exports outside the region. Similarly, the bulk of Kazakh oil exports run outside the EAEU. Hence, integration initiatives cannot be considered with disregard to external context, that is, the relations with the EU and China. The centrifugal forces set a significant obstacle to the integration process.

Finally, one should not forget that the historical legacy of value chains and embedded interdependencies remain important factors of the EAEU integration. The value chain structure was designed in the context of a unified economic space in the Soviet period, and restructuring the energy chains can take a long time. For example, Kazakhstan is used to provide transit for natural gas supplies from Turkmenistan to Russia (except the period of 2016–2019) (RIA Novosti 2019). Until the construction of a pipeline system toward China (launched in 2015), Kazakhstan was dependent on gas from Uzbekistan, which was supplied via Kyrgyzstan, to cover the energy needs of its southern regions (Sharipbaev 2015). Another vivid example is the operation of refining industry and export of oil products by Belarus, which fully relies on crude oil supplies from Russia, leaving space to numerous pricing conflicts for Russian oil and gas supplies.

Table 5.2 Oil industry and trade in the EAEU in 2015 (million tons)

	Armenia	*Belarus*	*Kazakhstan*	*Kyrgyzstan*	*Russia*	*EAEU*
Oil industry indicators						
Production of oil and gas condensate	–	1.6	79.5	0.1	533.2	*614.4*
Refining of oil and gas condensate	–	23.0	16.3	0.1*	281.8	*321.2*
Oil exports (total)	–	1.6	63.5	–	241.3	*306.4*
Oil exports outside EAEU	–	1.6	60.7	–	218.4	*280.7*
Oil products exports	–	16.8	4.8	0.1	171.5	*193.2*
Oil products exports outside EAEU	–	16.7	4.6	0.1	168.7	*190.1*
Oil imports (total)		22.9	0.5	0.01	2.8	*26.2*
Oil imports from outside EAEU	–	–	–	–	–	–
Oil products imports (total)	0.3	1.6	1.8	1.5	1.2	*6.4*
Oil products imports from outside EAEU	0.1	–	1.0	0.6	1.1	*2.8*
Intra-EAEU oil & products trade						
Armenia						
Exports of oil/oil products	–/–	–/–	–/–	–/–	–/–	*–/–*
Imports of oil/oil products	–/–	–/–	–/–	–/–	–/0.2	*–/0.2*
Belarus						
Exports of oil/oil products	–/–	–/–	–/–	–/–	–/0.1	*–/0.1*
Imports of oil/oil products	–/–	–/–	–/–	–/–	22.9/1.6	*22.9/1.6*
Kazakhstan						
Exports of oil/oil products	–/–	–/–	–/–	–/0.2	2.8/–	*2.8/0.2*
Imports of oil/oil products	–/–	–/–	–/–	–/–	0.5/0.8	*0.5/0.8*
Kyrgyzstan						
Exports of oil/oil products	–/–	–/–	–/–	–/–	–/–	*–/–*

(*continued*)

Table 5.2 (continued)

	Armenia	*Belarus*	*Kazakhstan*	*Kyrgyzstan*	*Russia*	*EAEU*
Imports of oil/oil products	–/–	–/–	–/0.2	–/–	0.01/0.7	*0.01/0.9*
Russia						
Exports of oil/oil products	–/0.2	22.9/1.5	0.5/0.8	0.01/0.7	–/–	*23.41/3.2*
Imports of oil/oil products	–/–	–/0.1	2.8/–	–/–	–/–	*2.8/0.1*

Source: Eurasian economic commission. Retrieved June 19, 2019, from http://www.eurasiancommission.org/ru/act/energetikaiinfr/energ/energo_stat/Pages/default.aspx

5.3 Economic Interests Toward EAEU Integration: The Case of Energy Subsidies

Energy pricing mechanisms in the EAEU have their origins in the period of administered economy, when energy was supplied by Russia at low prices. Today, energy prices continue to play a decisive role in the EAEU economic cooperation.

Russia has a long history of price disputes with Belarus, both before and after the establishment of the EAEU. The key issue is the dependency of the latter on Russian de facto energy subsidies (Tarr 2016; Knobel 2017; Libman and Vinokurov 2018). Russia supplies over 90 percent of Belarusian oil consumption, and Belarusian refineries are fully dependent on Russian oil supplies (Kardas and Klysinski 2017). Exports of petroleum products provide over 20 percent of Belarus's total export revenue. Also, Belarus is fully dependent on natural gas supplies from Russia which are delivered at preferential prices. The recent episode of 2016–2017 illustrates a fragile equilibrium in Russia-Belarus energy relations. In 2016, at times when gas prices were falling in Europe, Minsk unilaterally cuts the price for Russian gas from $132 per thousand of cubic meters (tcm) to $73 per tcm. In response, Russia reduced its oil exports to Belarus. The conflict was resolved in 2017 when parties agreed on gas price at the level of $127–130 per tcm for 2017–2019, which is still almost twice lower than gas prices to Europe.[1] Countries also reached an agreement on gas debt regulation, on a return of Russian oil supplies to Belarus, and on a

[1] To compare, average gas prices to Europe in 2017–2018 levelled to $200–245 per tcm. Data from http://www.gazprom.ru/about/marketing/europe/ (accessed 25.06.2019).

Table 5.3 Natural gas industry and trade in the EAEU in 2015 (billion cubic meters)

	Armenia	*Belarus*	*Kazakhstan*	*Kyrgyzstan*	*Russia*	*EAEU*
Natural gas industry indicators						
Natural gas production	–	0.2	45.7	0.03	633.4	679.3
Natural gas export (total)	–	–	12.7	–	192.4	205.1
Natural gas exports outside EAEU	–	–	3.9	–	169.1	173.0
Natural gas imports (total)	2.3	18.8	5.8	0.2	8.7	35.8
Natural gas imports (from outside EAEU)	0.4	–	3.2	–	–	3.6
Intra-EAEU natural gas trade						
Armenia						
Exports to	–	–	–	–	–	–
Imports from	–	–	–	–	1.9	1.9
Belarus						
Exports to	–	–	–	–	–	–
Imports from	–	–	–	–	18.8	18.8
Kazakhstan						
Exports to				0.2	8.7	8.9
Imports from					2.6	2.6
Kyrgyzstan						
Exports to	–	–	–	–	–	–
Imports from	–	–	0.2	–	–	0.2
Russia						
Exports to	1.9	18.8	2.6	0.0		23.3
Imports from	–	–	8.7	–		8.7

Source: Eurasian economic commission. Retrieved June 19, 2019, from http://www.eurasiancommission.org/ru/act/energetikaiinfr/energ/energo_stat/Pages/default.aspx

new preferential loan to Belarus. Moscow and Minsk also confirmed the intention to cooperate in framework of the EAEU integration project (Kardas and Klysinski 2017; Pastukhova and Westphal 2018).

Still, the risk of further occurrences of disputes is not ruled out. Minsk's position is based on the fact that unified gas prices were promised to Belarus with the Union treaty of 1999 between Russia and Belarus. The latter set an ambitious program for economic integration of the two countries, including for energy markets (Starostina et al. 2019). Therefore, Minsk expects gas prices to be close to price to its neighboring Smolensk region in Russia (the prices paid by Belarus are currently about twice higher) (Manenok 2018). A. Lukashenko points to the use of oil and gas by Moscow as a political leverage, where access to cheaper oil and gas is exchanged for a loss of autonomy (Starostina et al. 2019). All in all, it seems that economic integration is indissociable from political alignment. However, it remains under question which degree of political integration can be acceptable.

In the case of Kazakhstan, the major driver of energy dependency on Russia is the access to pipelines to reach the export markets because of the country's landlocked location. Russia's presence in the Kazakh upstream is quite limited. Due to a lack of capital in the 1990s, the development of the Kazakh oil industry largely relied on foreign investments, which account nowadays for 80–90 percent of the capital structure in the newly developed large oil and gas projects in the country (Kuratova 2019). Kazakhstan increased its oil production from 27 million tons in 1991 to 87 million tons in 2017 and gas production from 6 billion cubic meters (bcm) to 27 bcm, respectively (BP 2018). Expansion of oil and gas production required the enlargement of oil export capacities. Major progress was achieved with the construction of the Caspian Pipeline Consortium (CPC) pipeline which absorbs close to 70 percent of Kazakh oil exports (Kazenergy 2017). The route connects oilfields in Western Kazakhstan to the Russian port of Novorossiysk; the deliveries started in 2001. Interestingly, CPC is the only oil export pipeline in Russia which is not operated by Russian state-owned oil pipeline operator Transneft. Another element of Kazakh oil and gas export diversification is the development of infrastructures toward China which allows lessening the degree of dependency on Russia. Thus, coordinating export strategies is the major driver of relationship with Russia rather than subsidies.

A combination of Russian subsidies and security reasons explains the attitudes of Kyrgyzstan. Being dependent on remittances from its migrant workers in Russia, the country is predominantly interested in intra-EAEU labor migration provisions (Tarr 2016). In 2014, Gazprom acquired control over Kyrgyz gas transportation system for a symbolic price of one dollar and engaged itself to invest into the gas infrastructure of the republic, to bring the gasification level in the country from current 22 percent to 60 percent in perspective by 2030 (Topalov 2017). Gazprom ensures gas supplies at an advantageous price of $150 per tcm, to compare to $224–290 per tcm previously paid for the supplies from Kazakhstan and Uzbekistan (Karimov 2019). Gazprom also invests in social objects in the country (i.e. building a school in Bishkek).

For Armenia, alongside security considerations related to the conflict with Azerbaijan in Nagorno-Karabakh region, its entry into the EAEU reduced the gas import price from $271 per tcm to $189 per tcm (Zamakhina 2013). Further discounts were granted in 2015 and 2016, curbing the gas price to $150 per tcm. However, a slight import price increase to $165 occurred in 2019 (Alifirova 2019).

To sum up, Russia's energy relations with the EAEU members seem to be tied with the level of political partnership. Political alignment is compensated by preferential energy supplies granted by Russian state-owned companies. The largest recipient of subsidies is Belarus: the cumulated amount of oil and gas subsidies to Minsk in 2011–2017 is estimated to over $38 billion or 4–14 percent of Belarus' GDP per year during the studied period (Knobel 2017). According to the World Bank (2012), energy subsidies accounted for 14.5 percent of Belarus's GDP in 2001–2008 annually. Although Belarus used to receive the largest transfers, the size of subsidies shows a declining trend (from 10 percent in 2011 and 14 percent in 2012 to 4 percent in 2017). Other countries receive relatively less: for Kazakhstan, the transfers declined from 1.7 percent of GDP to close to zero; and for Armenia, the transfers account for about 1.5 percent of GDP (Knobel 2017).

This situation has its natural limitations, given the macroeconomic difficulties and revenue maximization motives in Russia. In relation to this, a major current issue is the reduction of fiscal benefits granted to the EAEU members by Russia. Until recently, Russia used two major fiscal instruments in domestic oil and gas industry, notably the export duties and mineral tax. Export duties ensured support to domestic consumers, meaning that domestic prices differed from export prices by the amount of export duty. Mineral tax was applied at the wellhead production level. It is a traditional national instrument of revenue sharing between energy companies and the state. The EAEU agreements lowered the price of Russia's energy supplies by the amount of export duty, as duties are not applicable in intra-EAEU trade. However, for the next years, Russia is planning to implement a tax maneuvre which means reducing export duty to a zero level, and on the contrary increasing the mineral tax. This will negatively affect the EAEU countries. In particular, Belarus assesses its losses from this Russian tax maneuver to $11 billion in the period till 2024 (Starostina et al. 2019).

Energy pricing and related disputes illustrate the dominance of "redistributive motive" in the EAEU integration (Knobel 2017, 2018). In other words, the EAEU integration is primarily based on a distribution of subsidies rather than on an increase of economic activity driven by a more efficient use of resources.

In turn, energy market integration will require a harmonization of pricing methods across the EAEU members. It will also require alignment of regulatory framework which may become controversial. The next section outlines key political economic constraints to this process.

5.4 Constraints to the Integration Process

The occurrence of energy-related disputes in the EAEU shows the vulnerability of the integration project at its current stage. As argued by Wilson (2019), non-cooperative behavior and a high level of conflict in energy relations (energy perceived as a "weapon" in inter-state politics) can be explained by several reasons, which are the following: (i) the energy sector is of particular importance for domestic economy, (ii) maintenance of domestic political regime depends on energy rents, and (iii) energy is used as a foreign policy tool. In the EAEU, the energy sector makes a significant contribution to the national budget of energy exporters, while energy subsidies are significant integration drivers for energy-dependent EAEU members, putting energy at the core of domestic and foreign policy interests. The importance of economic and political stakes related to the energy market integration project increases the level of conflict and therefore makes the project more fragile. In turn, a gradual shift away from the historical legacy of subsidization along the energy value chain, as well as the progress of economic development indicators in the region, could provide ground for developing win-win partnership models in a competitive market and institution-building.

Market integration progress will also depend on the progress of domestic market reforms implemented in the EAEU member countries, as well as on other external factors.

5.4.1 Domestic Market Reforms

The EAEU energy market integration is constrained by the progress of liberalization reforms at the domestic level. Harmonizing pricing mechanisms is a pre-condition for market integration. A major element of a liberal market model is the fair pricing of energy resources, which in turn requires the development of oil and gas trading platforms. These platforms should have high market liquidity indicators to establish prices as efficient market signals. Market integration also requires cross-border connectivity of networks, harmonization of transportation tariffs, and ensuring equal access to transportation facilities.

These conditions are not yet united in the case of the EAEU. Ad hoc measures introduced recently in Russia to freeze gasoline prices (agreement between the government and the ten largest companies adopted in 2018) provide an example of restrictions to market-based regulatory framework at the domestic level. The Russian natural gas industry undergoes a gradual deregulation process. Therefore, the declared goal of establishing common markets in the EAEU, in its absolute sense, does not appear realistic under closer analysis due to a current transitory phase of market reforms at the domestic level. This also opens the question of the search for an adequate model for market integration of EAEU members, given the current stage of market development in each member country. In accordance with the programs for the formation of common markets of oil, oil products, and natural gas, regulatory harmonization should start by a comparative study of legislation among the EAEU members, to be implemented in 2019. Thus, the design of the EAEU energy markets remains to be negotiated in subsequent years. As for natural gas, the decision on implementation of the principle of equal profitability of gas prices in the EAEU is expected only in 2023.

Another systemic aspect where harmonization seems difficult stems from different roles assigned to state-owned and private companies: while in Russian oil model, the state-owned companies (Rosneft, Gazprom) have a dominant market position and benefit from privileged access to upstream segment, major oil and gas projects in Kazakhstan are led by international privately owned companies. The compatibility of Russian and Kazakh petroleum models, and possible implications for specific forms of market integration, is not fully clear (Inozemtsev 2019).

The two aforementioned factors translate to (i) a relatively long time period assigned to the process of energy market integration in the EAEU and (ii) regulatory flexibility of the integration process. In fact, the Treaty on the EAEU and corresponding program documents adopted by 2019 (Program for the Formation of Common Markets of Oil and Oil Products of Eurasian Economic Union 2018; Program for the Formation of Common Market of Natural Gas of Eurasian Economic Union 2018) rather set the framework for further negotiations to propel the market integration, than introduce binding regulations.

5.4.2 *External Factors*

Integration initiatives in the EAEU can also be seen as Russia's attempt to reaffirm its economic presence in the region and to increase the bargaining power in negotiations with the EU and China through creating a regional bloc. However, recent macroeconomic difficulties make the integration project fragile and vulnerable to external shocks of both economic (i.e. oil price fluctuations) and political (i.e. sanctions against Russia) natures. The deterioration of the economic climate in Russia downgrades the attractiveness of joining an integration project led by Russia. More generally, integration dynamics in the EAEU area is subject to ups and downs of the oil price cycle.

Finally, the creation of common markets for energy resources is a part of the integration agenda in the EAEU space. Faster or slower progress in other issue areas will affect the development of energy market integration project.

5.5 Conclusions

Creating common markets for energy resources is an important element of the EAEU integration agenda. Energy market integration is expected to ensure efficient use of the energy potential of EAEU members, secure internal energy supplies, and to increase the role of the EAEU in international energy markets. The integration project intends to foster energy trade at market prices and ensure non-discriminatory access to energy infrastructures within the integration union.

However, the EAEU energy market integration project faces numerous challenges. First, it has to reconcile the energy security interests of major energy exporters (Russia, Kazakhstan) with those of net importers (Belarus, Armenia, Kyrgyzstan). Second, it has to find a delicate balance between the market integration and gradual transition toward competitive market on one hand and historical legacy of energy subsidies granted by Russia to post-Soviet republics on the other hand. Third, it has to harmonize the different regulatory norms applicable at each national context.

Given these challenges, the integration project sets a framework for further negotiation and specification of its common regulatory base. Integrating markets for energy resources can only be a gradual process.

References

Alifirova, Y. (2019, January 3). Gazprom Armenia kompensiruet. Tsena na rossiiskiy gaz dlia Armenii vyrosla, no vnutrennie tarify sokhraniatsia na prezhnem urovne. *Neftegaz.ru*. Retrieved June 25, 2019, from https://neftegaz.ru/news/Trading/195780-gazprom-armeniya-kompensiruet-tsena-na-rossiyskiy-gaz-dlya-armenii-vyrosla-no-vnutrennie-tarify-sokh/.

Becker, T. (2019). Russia's Economy and Regional Spillovers. *Stockholm Institute of Transition Economics*. Working Paper No. 48, June.

Booz & Company. (2013). *Benefits of an Integrated European Energy Market*. Final Report for European Commission Directorate-General Energy, July 20. Retrieved June 26, 2019, from http://ec.europa.eu/energy/infrastructure/studies/doc/20130902_energy_integration_benefits.pdf.

BP. (2018, June). Statistical Review of World Energy.

Concept for the Formation of Common Market of Natural Gas of Eurasian Economic Union (2016). Adopted May 31, 2016, Decision 7 of the Supreme Eurasian Economic Council. (in Russian).

Concept for the Formation of Common Markets of Oil and Oil Products of Eurasian Economic Union (2016). Adopted May 31, 2016, Decision 8 of the Supreme Eurasian Economic Council. (in Russian).

EADaily. (2019, February 8). Zavisimost' gosbudzheta Kazakhstana ot neftianykh dokhodov vyrosla—Expert. *EADaily*. Retrieved June 25, 2019, from https://eadaily.com/ru/news/2019/02/08/zavisimost-gosbyudzheta-kazahstana-ot-neftyanyh-dohodov-vyrosla-ekspert.

EDB. (2017). Eurasian economic Union. St Petersburg, EDB Centre for Integration Studies, [Russian version, retrieved June 25, 2019, from https://eabr.org/upload/iblock/aeb/EDB_Centre_2017_Monograph_EAEU_RUS_1.pdf].

EEE. (2015). *Energy*. Moscow: Eurasian Economic Commission.

Energy Charter Secretariat. (2015, March). International Energy Security: Common Concept for Energy Producing, Consuming and Transit Countries. Energy Charter Secretariat.

Inozemtsev, V. (2019, February 12). Chto ne tak s evraziyskoi integratsiei. *RBC*. Retrieved from April 5, 2019, https://www.rbc.ru/newspaper/2019/02/13/5c6277b79a7947ca4c388822.

Kardas, S., & Klysinski, K. (2017). The Story that Never Ends. A New Stage in the Energy Dispute between Russia and Belarus. *OSW Commentary* 242. Retrieved from April 15, 2019, from https://www.osw.waw.pl/sites/default/files/commentary_242.pdf.

Karimov, D. (2019, February 7). Prodiktovano traditsiey. *Rossiyskaya Gazeta*. Retrieved August 15, 2019, from https://rg.ru/2019/02/07/dlia-kirgizii-sotrudnichestvo-s-rossiej-imeet-osobuiu-vazhnost.html.

Kazenergy. (2017). National Energy Report 2017. Retrieved June 26, 2019, from http://www.kazenergy.com/upload/document/energy-report/National_Energy_Report-ENGLISH_03.09.pdf.

Knobel, A. (2017). The Eurasian Economic Union. Development Prospects and Possible Obstacles. *Problems of Economic Transition, 59*(5), 335–360.

Knobel, A. (2018, December 18). Kak nalogovyi manevr rassoril Moskvu i Minsk. *RBC*. Retrieved from https://www.rbc.ru/newspaper/2018/12/18/5c1785399a79473cde10ccbe.

Kuratova, A. (2019). Analiz istochnikov finansirovaniya neftegazovykh proektov na primere gruppy stran. Natsionalniy Bank Kazakhstana. Departament platezhnogo balansa i valutnogo regulirovaniya. Analiticheskaya zapiska. May 2019. Retrieved June 26, 2019, from https://nationalbank.kz/cont/Анализрercent20источниковpercent20финансированияpercent20нефтегазовыхpercent20проектовpercent20наpercent20примереpercent20группыpercent20стран4.pdf.

Libman, A. (2007). Regionalisation and Regionalism in the Post-Soviet Space: Current Status and Implications for Institutional Development. *Europe-Asia Studies, 59*(3), 401–430. https://doi.org/10.1080/09668130701239849.

Libman, A., & Vinokurov, E. (2018). Autocracies and Regional Integration: The Eurasian Case. *Post-Communist Economies, 30*(3), 334–364. https://doi.org/10.1080/14631377.2018.1442057.

Manenok, T. (2018, July 19). Po kakoi tsene Belarus' budet pokupat' rossiiskiy gaz s 2020 goda? *Belrynok*. Retrieved June 26, 2019, from https://www.belrynok.by/2018/07/19/po-kakoj-tsene-belarus-budet-pokupat-rossijskij-gaz-s-2020-goda/.

Pastukhova M., & Westphal, K. (2018, January 5). Eurasian Economic Union Integrates Energy Markets—EU Stands Aside. *SWP Comments*.

Pleshkin, M. (2017). Sozdanie obshchikh rynkov enegeticheskikh resursov. Presentation at a conference "Eurasian Economic Integration: New Challenges and Opportunities", Eurasian Economic Commission, American Chamber of Commerce in Russia, U.S.-Russia Business Council, Moscow, December 7. Retrieved April 15, 2019, from http://usrbc.org/uploaded/web/Events/2017/20171207percent20EECpercent20Pleshkin.pdf.

Program for the Formation of Common Market of Natural Gas of Eurasian Economic Union (2018). Adopted 6 December 2018, Decision 18 of the Supreme Eurasian Economic Council. (in Russian).

Program for the Formation of Common Markets of Oil and Oil Products of Eurasian Economic Union (2018). Adopted 6 December 2018, Decision 23 of the Supreme Eurasian Economic Council. (in Russian).

RIA Novosti. (2019, May 3). Kazakhstan spustia tri goda vozobillionovil transit turkmenskogo gaza v Rossiu. *RIA Novosti*. Retrieved June 25, 2019, from https://ria.ru/20190503/1553238806.html.

Roberts, S., & Moshes, A. (2016). The Eurasian Economic Union: A Case of Reproductive Integration? *Post-Soviet Affairs, 32*(6), 542–565. https://doi.org/10.1080/1060586X.2015.1115198.

Sharipbaev, K. (2015). Kazakhstan bolche ne zavisit ot importnogo gaza—Kaztransgaz. Retrieved June 24, 2016, from http://www.kaztransgas.kz/index.php/ru/press-tsentr/novosti-kompanii/802-kazakhstan-bolshe-ne-zavisit-ot-importnogo-gaza-kaztransgaz.

Shenec, L. (2017, August 29). Sroki dlia sozdania obshchikh energorynkov—szhatye. Neobkhodimo uskorenie. Eurasian Economic Commission. *News*. Retrieved June 15, 2019, from http://www.eurasiancommission.org/ru/nae/news/Pages/29-08-2017-2.aspx.

Starostina Yu., Tkachev, I., Khimiachvili, P., & Feinberg, A. (2019, April 17). Rossiya peredala Belorussii plan dal'neishei integratsii. *RBC*. Retrieved June 15, 2019, from https://www.rbc.ru/economics/17/04/2019/5cb751019a7947caf9263ea3?from=center.

Tarr, D. G. (2016). The Eurasian Economic Union of Russia, Belarus, Kazakhstan, Armenia, and the Kyrgyz Republic: Can It Succeed Where Its Predecessor Failed? *Eastern European Economics, 54*(1), 1–22. https://doi.org/10.1080/00128775.2015.1105672.

Tass. (2018, February 8). Experty: zavisimost' ekonomiki RF i budzheta ot nefti snova nachala vozrastat'. *Tass*. Retrieved June 25, 2019, from https://tass.ru/ekonomika/4941082.

Topalov, A. (2017, February 28). Moskva poddast kirgizam gaza. *Gazeta.ru*. Retrieved June 25, 2019, from https://www.gazeta.ru/business/2017/02/28/10549985.shtml?updated.

Treaty on the Eurasian Economic Union. Astana, May 29, 2014 (redaction 15 March 2018).

UNCTAD. (2019, August 15). UNCTADStat Data Center. Retrieved from https://unctadstat.unctad.org/EN/.

Wilson, J. D. (2019). A Securitisation Approach to International Energy Politics. *Energy Research & Social Science, 49*, 114–125.

World Bank. (2012). *Belarus Country Economic Memorandum*. Washington, DC: World Bank.

Zamakhina, T. (2013, December 3). L'goty dlia souznika. *Rossiiskaya Gazeta*. Retrieved April 15, 2019, from https://rg.ru/2013/12/02/putin-armenia-site.html.

Zemskova, K. (2018). The Common Energy Market of the Eurasian Economic Union. Implications for the European Union and the Role of the Energy Charter Treaty (ECT). Occasional Paper. Energy Charter Secretariat.

Zhukov, S., & Reznikova, O. (2007). Economic Integration in the Post-Soviet Space. *Problems of Economic Transition, 50*(7), 24–36. https://doi.org/10.2753/PET1061-1991500702.

CHAPTER 6

Transport and Logistics in the EAEU

Egor V. Pak

6.1 Introduction

Transport and logistics might be one of the most promising dimensions of the EAEU. Large distances, scattered industrial facilities and a high deterioration rate of transport infrastructure turn out to be the key prerequisites for fostering transport and logistics cooperation in the EAEU. Moreover, transport and logistics may be one of the non-energy drivers laying down the bases for exploiting transit potential of the EAEU in international transport corridors East-West and North-South. EAEU transit potential can be utilized both in regional (within the EAEU) and in transcontinental (in the framework of Greater Eurasia) formats.

Thus, the research hypothesis stands for the fact that, by creating an efficient transport and logistics complex, the EAEU states may contribute to greater connectivity within the EAEU and via its territory both deepening the Eurasian economic integration.

E. V. Pak (✉)
MGIMO University, Moscow, Russia
e-mail: egor_pak@mail.ru

N. A. Piskulova (ed.), *The Economic Dimension of Eurasian Integration*, https://doi.org/10.1007/978-3-030-59886-0_6

6.2 Literature Review

Transport and logistics, as one of the areas of economic integration in the EAEU, have not been fully and objectively studied. Fundamentally this might be a logical result of a top-down approach (dominance of politics over economics) in the integration process in the EAEU. For this reason, some research (mainly that of the foreign scholars) on transport and logistics in the EAEU and Eurasian integration at large is heavily politicized (Laruelle 2015; Sergi 2018). For instance, as of today, transport and logistics are viewed as one of the instruments of geopolitical dominance (Sidaway and Woon 2017; Summers 2017). Taking this into consideration, the paper aims to undertake a holistic and mainly economic, *albeit* critical, view on current trends, problems and prospects of transport and logistics cooperation in the EAEU.

The existing research on the topic could be broken down into two blocks: (1) study of transport and logistics cooperation in the EAEU coupled with the analysis of the existing transport and logistics complex of the EAEU and (2) discussion on challenges and prospects of transit flows via the EAEU in international transport corridors East-West and North-South.

Prospects and failing points of transport and logistics cooperation in the EAEU have been investigated by Vinokurov (2018), Larin (2017), Pak (2018a), Domnina and Zaboev (2017), Lane and Samokhvalov (2015), Dutkiewicz and Sakwa (2014), and Dragneva and Wolczuk (2017). More specifically the role of Belarus in transport and logistics complex of the EAEU has been highlighted by Shurubovich (2018) and Ivut et al. (2015). Related interests of Kazakhstan have been studied by Turaeva (2018), Syroezhkin (2018), Contessi (2018) and Kassenova (2017).

As of today, the EAEU possesses a relatively untapped transit potential. Strategic measures that could utilize the Union's potential in the international transport corridors East-West and North-South have been scrutinized by a group of scholars from the Market Economy Institute of the Russian Academy of Sciences (Zoidov et al. 2016; Tsvetkov et al. 2018, 2019) and Centre for Eurasian Studies of the Eurasian Development Bank (EDB) (2018a, b). Organizational and technical measures that could boost transit flows via the EAEU in transport corridors in question have been outlined by Vardomsky and Turaeva (2018) and Shcherbanin (2018).

Another promising route that might develop the EAEU's transit potential is the Northern Sea Route. Route's specifics, challenges and prospects in the framework of the development of transport and logistics cooperation in the EAEU have been analyzed in the report by the Russian International Affairs Council (RIAC) (2015), Kheyfets (2018) and Solvang et al. (2018).

The paper assumes that China's Belt and Road Initiative (BRI) might also contribute to the deployment of the EAEU transport and logistics agenda. Economic, technological and organizational peculiarities of the EAEU-BRI conjunction have been investigated by Luzjanin (2017), Scriba (2016), Yakovlev (2018), Pak (2018b), Sternberg et al. (2017), Ostrovskii (2017), Laruelle (2018) and Pomfret (2019). More specifically Russia's interests in the conjunction process have been identified by Makarov and Sokolova (2016), Bennett (2016) and Kaneshko (2017).

An interesting perspective on utilizing the EAEU transit potential could be captured from the concept of Greater Eurasia involving the EAEU states, other CIS members, China, India, Iran and all other countries concerned. Related roles and interests of the EAEU member-states in terms of transport and logistics, as well as possible projects' influence on the EAEU transit agenda, have been investigated by Dynkin et al. (2018), Lavrikova et al. (2018), Diesen (2019), van der Togt (2017) and Tsvyk (2018).

Thus, this paper stresses that the deployment of transport and logistics agenda meets economic interests of all the EAEU member-states, as the announced economic and technological modernization (including transit issues) within the EAEU can hardly be effected without an efficient transport and logistics complex.

6.3 Key Performance Indicators

The paper assumes that in 2010–2018 Eurasian integrative mechanisms have positively influenced the dynamics of key transport and logistics performance indicators: freight turnover and the volume of goods transported. From the quantitative side, the EAEU member-states and the entity as a whole have witnessed an increase in freight turnover and the volume of goods transported. From the qualitative perspective the EAEU has seen railway and auto segments strengthening their positions, which

Table 6.1 Freight turnover of the EAEU states in 2010–2018 (billion tkm)

	2010	*2011*	*2012*	*2013*	*2014*	*2015*	*2016*	*2017*	*2018*
Armenia	3.1	3.6	4.3	4.2	4.2	3.8	3.9	4.2	4.4
Belarus	128.1	134.3	131.7	130.8	131.4	126.0	125.2	133.2	139.0
Kazakhstan	381.0	444.4	475.3	493.3	553.9	512.1	518.0	564.4	601.8
Kyrgyzstan	2.2	2.4	2.6	2.7	2.5	2.5	2.5	2.6	2.8
Russia	4752.0	4915.0	5056.0	5084.0	5080.0	5091.0	5213.1	5486.5	5643.0
EAEU	5271.7	5499.7	5669.9	5715.0	5772.0	5735.4	5862.7	6190.9	6391.0

Source: Compiled by the author based on the data from National Statistics Agencies of Armenia, Belarus, Kazakhstan, Kyrgyzstan and Russia. Retrieved from https://www.armstat.am/ru/, http://www.belstat.gov.by/, http://stat.gov.kz/, http://www.stat.kg/ru/, www.gks.ru

might be a cautious sign of a non-energy shift in the EAEU economy, including development of transit flows.

Thus, freight turnover of the EAEU in 2018 has leveled at roughly 6.4 trillion ton per kilometer (tkm) (+3.2 per cent compared to 2017) overall showing an upward trend starting from 2010 (Table 6.1).

Given its distances and transit flows passing through their territory, Russia and Kazakhstan logically account for 97.7 per cent of the overall EAEU freight turnover. In average annual terms in 2010–2018 EAEU freight turnover has increased by 2.4 per cent. Out of the troika[1] states Kazakhstan has secured the largest increment (+5.8 per cent), far ahead of Russia (+2.2 per cent) and Belarus (+1.0 per cent). In their turns, freight turnover of Armenia and Kyrgyzstan in average annual terms in 2015–2018 (for the sake of methodological accuracy, related calculations start from 2015 when the states joined the EAEU) has increased by 5.0 per cent and 3.8 per cent, respectively. Thus, other things being equal, positive increments in the freight turnover of all of the EAEU states might be sustained by the integration mechanisms.

In 2010–2018 the structure of freight turnover by modes of transport has undergone a change with railway and auto segments, having gained greater shares at the expense of the pipeline one. Pipeline and railway modes have historically played vital role in the EAEU economy. Large distances and the domination of energy resources in the overall merchandise exports have presupposed substantial shares of both modes in the structure of the EAEU freight turnover (Table 6.2).

[1] Hereinafter founding members of the Eurasian integration that led to the creation of EAEU—Belarus, Kazakhstan and Russia—are referred to as troika states.

Table 6.2 Freight turnover of the EAEU by modes of transport in 2010–2018 (per cent)

	2010	*2011*	*2012*	*2013*	*2014*	*2015*	*2016*	*2017*	*2018*
Air	0.1	0.1	0.1	0.1	0.1	0.1	0.1	0.1	0.1
Auto	5.6	6.2	7.1	7.0	7.1	7.2	7.3	7.2	7.4
Inland waterway	1.0	1.1	1.4	1.1	1.2	1.2	1.3	1.1	1.0
Railway	43.1	44.0	44.2	45.0	45.3	44.6	45.0	45.4	45.9
Maritime	2.0	1.0	0.8	0.8	0.8	0.9	0.6	0.8	0.7
Pipeline	48.2	48.0	46.3	46.5	47.0	46.2	45.7	45.3	44.8
Total	100	100	100	100	100	100	100	100	100

Source: Compiled by the author based on the data from National Statistics Agencies of Armenia, Belarus, Kazakhstan, Kyrgyzstan and Russia. Retrieved from https://www.armstat.am/ru/, http://www.belstat.gov.by/, http://stat.gov.kz/, http://www.stat.kg/ru/, www.gks.ru

In 2018, the share of railway mode (that can carry wider range of cargo, i.e. containers), in the structure of freight turnover, leveled at 45.9 per cent compared to 43.1 per cent in 2010, whereas the related share of pipeline mode, on the contrary, diminished from 48.2 per cent in 2010 to 44.8 per cent in 2018. Such a shift might be a direct consequence of the EAEU transit deployment agenda in international transport corridors East-West and North-South (with their multimodal status, yet, predominant role of railway mode). According to the EDB (2018b) figures, transit flows via the EAEU in the East-West corridor reached 262,000 TEU[2] in 2017, which is 1.8 times higher than that in 2016. Besides, a decline in the related pipeline share might also be a consequence of the overall downturn in the share of energy segment (mainly transported via pipelines) in the EAEU mutual trade in 2010–2018.

The rise of auto share (from 5.6 per cent in 2010 to 7.4 per cent in 2018) might be a result of the development of cross-border shipments (between the EAEU members) being remarkably vibrant between Belarus and Russia, Armenia and Russia, and Kyrgyzstan and Kazakhstan.

EAEU volume of goods transported has been overall on the rise in 2010–2018, having reached its maximum of 12.76 billion tons in 2018 (Table 6.3).

[2] A twenty-foot equivalent (TEU) is an internationally accepted metric to measure containerized trade on the basis of a twenty-foot container with the following dimensions: length = 6.10 m, width = 2.44 m, height = 2.59 m. One TEU roughly equals to 21.6 tons.

Table 6.3 Volume of goods transported in the EAEU states in 2010–2018 (billion tons)

	2010	*2011*	*2012*	*2013*	*2014*	*2015*	*2016*	*2017*	*2018*
Armenia	0.01	0.01	0.01	0.01	0.01	0.01	0.01	0.03	0.03
Belarus	0.45	0.49	0.48	0.44	0.46	0.45	0.42	0.44	0.46
Kazakhstan	2.43	2.96	3.22	3.49	3.75	3.73	3.73	3.95	4.10
Kyrgyzstan	0.04	0.04	0.04	0.04	0.03	0.03	0.03	0.03	0.03
Russia	7.75	8.34	8.52	8.26	8.01	7.57	7.95	8.07	8.14
EAEU	10.68	11.84	12.27	12.24	12.26	11.79	12.14	12.52	12.76

Source: Compiled by the author based on the data from National Statistics Agencies of Armenia, Belarus, Kazakhstan, Kyrgyzstan and Russia. Retrieved from https://www.armstat.am/ru/, http://www.belstat.gov.by/, http://stat.gov.kz/, http://www.stat.kg/ru/, www.gks.ru

Again, Russia and Kazakhstan secure almost 96 per cent of the overall volume of goods transported in the EAEU. In average annual terms in 2010–2018 the volume of goods transported in the EAEU increased by 2.2 per cent. Out of the troika states Kazakhstan has seen the largest increment (+6.9). In its turn, the volume of goods transported of Armenia and Kyrgyzstan in average annual terms in 2015–2018 (for the sake of methodological accuracy, related calculations start from 2015 when the states joined the EAEU) has increased by 44.2 per cent and 3.6 per cent, respectively. Thus, other things being equal, positive increments in the volumes of goods transported in all of the EAEU states might be sustained by the integration mechanisms.

Auto mode has historically accounted for the largest share in the EAEU structure of volume of goods transported. In 2010–2018, the auto segment strengthened its positions having increased its share from 69.4 per cent in 2010 to 72.2 per cent in 2018 (Table 6.4).

This revealed rise of auto mode share in the overall structure of the EAEU volume of goods transported has been mostly captured in 2015–2018. To some extent, it could be a direct consequence of Armenia and Kyrgyzstan's membership in the EAEU. Auto mode has historically mostly been used to execute exports of Armenian and Kyrgyz agricultural products to Russia and Kazakhstan, respectively. As of today, it accounts for almost 70 per cent of the overall structure of volume of goods transported of Armenia and around 95 per cent in the overall structure of volume of goods transported of Kyrgyzstan.

Thus, the research has captured upward dynamics of key performance indicators of the EAEU transport and logistics industry, as well as strengthening role of the railway and auto segments in related structures. More

Table 6.4 Volume of goods transported of the EAEU by modes of transport in 2010–2018 (per cent)

	2010	*2011*	*2012*	*2013*	*2014*	*2015*	*2016*	*2017*	*2018*
Air	0.0	0.0	0.0	0.0	0.0	0.0	0.0	0.0	0.0
Auto	69.4	70.3	71.6	71.5	71.4	71.8	72.1	71.6	72.2
Inland waterway	1.0	1.0	1.2	1.5	1.7	1.9	1.0	1.0	0.9
Railway	16.1	15.9	15.2	14.0	14.3	14.3	14.7	15.3	14.4
Maritime	0.4	0.4	0.2	0.3	0.4	0.4	0.2	0.2	0.2
Pipeline	13.0	12.5	11.8	11.5	11.6	12.0	12.0	11.9	12.3
Total	100	100	100	100	100	100	100	100	100

Source: Compiled by the author based on the data from National Statistics Agencies of Armenia, Belarus, Kazakhstan, Kyrgyzstan and Russia. Retrieved from https://www.armstat.am/ru/, http://www.belstat.gov.by/, http://stat.gov.kz/, http://www.stat.kg/ru/, www.gks.ru

specifically, Kazakhstan has turned out to be the main beneficiary of this tendency, having showed the greatest average annual growth rates in 2010–2018 in both freight turnover and volume of goods transported.

Summing this up, the positive dynamics revealed generally correlate with the overall dynamics of mutual trade between Armenia, Belarus, Kazakhstan, Kyrgyzstan and Russia in 2010–2018. EAEU mutual trade showed a solid increase in 2010–2012, then decline in 2013–2016 and then rise again in 2017–2018. In its turn, EAEU freight turnover and volume of goods transported were on the rise in 2010–2014, then dropped in 2015 before rebounding in 2016–2018. As such, the relative inconsistency means that physical volumes of the EAEU mutual trade (that are in fact transported) in 2014–2016 were more stable or even on the rise in some segments than the related value (which suffered from the devaluation of national currencies and overall adverse external economic conditions).

6.4 Market Analysis

The transport and logistics industry of the EAEU is characterized by low integrity of the transport and logistics services rendered; a lack of truly supranational policy; and a high moral and technical deterioration rate of infrastructure.

It has been stressed that modern economic growth sustained by global value chains is highly dependent on the availability of integrated transport and logistics services not limited to transportation, but including warehousing, handling, tracking, planning, managing customer-supplier relationships and so on (Christopher 2016; Ballou 2007). More specifically, this integrity comes from third- and fourth-party logistics providers[3] (3 and 4PL) maintaining the door-to-door delivery from the supplier side to the end-customer within the whole chain. Hertz and Alfredsson (2003) state that it is the integrated transport and logistics services that currently form value in Supply Chain Management and, thus, make the economy buoyant.

As of today, the EAEU market of transport and logistics services implies a low level of integrity in rendering transport and logistics services and, as a result, the dominance of first- and second-party logistics providers (1 and 2 PL). In its turn, 3 and 4PL together account for less than 10 per cent (in 2015 less than 5 per cent) of the overall EAEU market of transport and logistics services that is roughly four times less than that in the world (Table 6.5).

Little integrity in transport and logistics services available in the EAEU has presupposed a low level of development of transport and logistics

Table 6.5 Structure of the EAEU market of transport and logistics services in 2018 (per cent)

Types of transport and logistics services	*EAEU*	*World*
1PL and 2PL	92	58
3PL	6	25
4PL	2	17
Total market of transport and logistics services	100	100

Source: RBC Group. Marketing research of express-delivery market of Russia in 2014–2018, forecast till 2023. Retrieved from https://s.rbk.ru/v4_marketing_media/demo/8/96/115529961204968.pdf

[3] Logistics service providers differ from each other by the range of transport and logistics services rendered and, thus, value added. First-party logistics provider (1PL) operates locally and renders limited range of services, that is, transportation by his own vehicles. Second-party logistics provider (2PL) operates globally and renders greater range of services, that is, transportation (usually done by his own vehicles), warehousing and handling. Third-party logistics provider (3PL) usually referred to as operator renders full range of services, including transportation, warehousing, handling, route-building, tracking, insurance, customs clearance and so on, under the door-to-door delivery concept. Fourth-party logistics provider (4PL) usually referred to as integrator offers a more integrated range of services than that of 3PL which includes planning and managing customer-supplier relationships throughout the whole supply chain.

outsourcing and high share of transport and logistics costs in the economy. Transport and logistics outsourcing in the EAEU accounts for roughly 35 per cent out of all transport and logistics services rendered which is substantially lower than that of the world (55 per cent) and the EU (65 per cent) (RIAC 2017). In its turn, the share of transport of logistics in the overall cost of goods sold in the EAEU ranges from 20 to 25 per cent, which is almost two times higher than in the world and in the EU (RIAC 2017).

The insufficient share of integrated transport and logistics services has also led to the lower capitalization of the EAEU transport and logistics market. The capitalization of the EAEU market of transport and logistics services is estimated at around $350 billion, far behind NAFTA/USMCA ($1.5 trillion) and EU ($1.3 trillion) (RIAC 2017).

Another reason for the low integrity in transport and logistics services achieved comes from the existing features of transport and logistics infrastructure (both stationary and rolling stock) of the EAEU. As of today, it is heavily outdated, with infrastructure building mainly funded by the state. According to the RIAC (2017) and EDB (2018b) estimates, average technical and moral deterioration rate of the EAEU transport and logistics infrastructure is around 70 per cent with major problems concentrated predominantly in the railway segment. At the same time the state is the leading investor into EAEU infrastructure, accounting for more than 70 per cent of the overall funding infrastructure (Pak 2018a). As Zoidov et al. (2017) put it, the share of private funds in the private-public partnership (PPP) projects compared to the GDP in the EAEU is less than 1 per cent, which is lagging behind other emerging economies such as Brazil (20 per cent) and India (10 per cent).

Finally, this low level of integrity in transport and logistics industry is, *inter alia*, a consequence of lack of truly supranational transport and logistics policy in the EAEU. As of today, the EAEU executes a coordinated (agreed) transport policy at the platform of the Eurasian Economic Commission (EEC), whereas some of the regulations (in some cases of crucial importance for member-states) are still to be done at the national level of the EAEU members. For instance, designing, planning and implementation instruments of coordinated (agreed) transport policy are predominantly held at the inter-governmental level of the EAEU members. At the same time, the format of the EAEU transport policy as it is does not cover all modes of transport. Thus, substantial progress under the framework of coordinated (agreed) transport policy of the EAEU has been made only in railway and auto segments, pointing at their leading role in the EAEU economy. As for auto mode, the integrating states have fully liberalized all auto shipments within the EAEU and launched the Programme on Liberalization of Cabotage[4] Auto Shipments in the EAEU for 2016–2025. As for railway mode, major integration-induced achievements include the application of unified railway tariffs within the EAEU (including transit directions); the introduction of the corridor of their fluctuations; setting common principles of access to the services of neighboring parts of railway infrastructure; and the creation of the Unified Transport and Logistics Company—Eurasian Rail Alliance to facilitate containerized transit flows via the EAEU in the East-West transport corridor.

Nonetheless, the EAEU states have alleged to move toward a common regulative mechanism in the transport and logistics area. It has been agreed that by 2025 the EAEU states will eliminate all the barriers (including non-tariff ones) on all modes of transport, will form a single transport space and introduce a common market of transport and logistics services. Overall, even in such an abridged format, the policy offers cargo delivery via EAEU territory in East-West transport corridor (e.g. in China-EU trade direction) on average 3–3.5 times faster than that via the Southern Sea Route that takes roughly 45–60 days (Pak 2018b).

To sum this up, the EAEU's existing transport and logistics industry can hardly sustain the economic and technological modernization announced and needs substantial renovation. In this case, Eurasian integrative mechanisms might be a good impetus for this motion should the member-states accumulate the necessary technological, financial and organizational resources at the platform of the EEC to pour them into the initiatives, including infrastructural, that might carry regional synergetic effect.

6.5 International Focus

Given the low integrity of transport and logistics services rendered, the EAEU states are insubstantially involved into world exports of transport and logistics services. As of today, developed economies are the main exporters of transport and logistics services and account for around 60

[4] Autocabotage stands for the situation when a transport and logistics company registered in one EAEU state is allowed to execute shipments between the points in another EAEU state.

per cent of the related exports. To be more specific, according to the ITC figures, top-five in exports of transport and logistics services in 2018 include the US ($92.3 billion), Germany ($68.7 billion), Singapore ($51.5 billion), France ($47.5 billion) and China ($42.3 billion).

In their turn, Russia is ranked 14th ($22.1 billion), Kazakhstan is ranked 45th ($3.98 billion), Belarus is ranked 45th ($3.85 billion), Armenia is ranked 102nd ($253.7 million) and Kyrgyzstan is ranked 106th ($251.3 million). In 2010–2018 all EAEU member-states increased their role in world exports of transport and logistics services. In its turn, within this period, Kazakhstan saw the largest average annual growth in exports of transport and logistics services (+8.3 per cent) well ahead of Russia (+5.2 per cent) and the EAEU at large (+5.8 per cent) (Table 6.6).

When considered as a trading block, the EAEU is not heavily involved in international trade in transport and logistics services lagging behind the EU, NAFTA/USMCA and ASEAN (Table 6.7).

Table 6.6 Exports of transport and logistics services from the EAEU states in 2010–2018 ($ billion)

	2010	*2011*	*2012*	*2013*	*2014*	*2015*	*2016*	*2017*	*2018*
Armenia	0.15	0.17	0.17	0.17	0.18	0.16	0.19	0.23	0.25
Belarus	2.96	3.49	3.57	3.79	3.73	2.92	2.93	3.45	3.85
Kazakhstan	2.28	2.21	2.59	2.90	3.93	3.61	3.28	3.46	3.98
Kyrgyzstan	0.15	0.17	0.18	0.18	0.16	0.19	0.17	0.21	0.22
Russia	14.87	17.35	19.20	20.75	20.54	16.64	17.13	19.81	22.08
EAEU	20.42	23.40	25.67	27.75	28.54	23.44	23.70	27.16	30.38

Source: Compiled by the author based on the data from International Trade Centre (ITC). Retrieved from www.trademap.org

Table 6.7 Share of regional economic entities in world trade in transport and logistics services in 2010–2018 (per cent)

	2010	*2011*	*2012*	*2013*	*2014*	*2015*	*2016*	*2017*	*2018*
ASEAN	7.3	7.3	7.2	7.4	7.2	7.4	7.1	7.4	7.5
EAEU	2.6	2.8	2.9	3.1	2.9	2.6	2.8	2.9	3.0
EU (28)	39.9	40.2	39.7	40.3	42.4	41.7	42.4	43.2	44.3
NAFTA/USMCA	11.1	11.3	11.3	11.4	10.7	11.3	11.5	11.1	10.9
MERCOSUR	1.1	1.1	1.1	1.1	1.0	1.0	1.0	0.9	0.9

Source: Compiled by the author based on the data from International Trade Centre (ITC). Retrieved from www.trademap.org

However, if compared to other integrative blocks, in average annual terms in 2010–2018 the EAEU increased its share in world exports of transport and logistics services by 1.8 per cent, being ahead of the EU (+1.3 per cent) and ASEAN (+0.3 per cent). On the contrary, NAFTA/ USMCA and MERCOSUR saw a negative tendency: -0.2 per cent and -2.5 per cent, respectively. The paper assumes that Eurasian integrative mechanisms might have contributed to this process given national, *albeit* coordinated (under the framework of coordinated (agreed) transport policy), policies of the EAEU states on securing transit flows in international transport corridors East-West and North-South.

In the course of integration, the EAEU states have also slightly strengthened their positions in Logistics Performance Index (LPI), a distinguished international metric to measure the quality and competitiveness of transport and logistics complex of a particular state. However, the EAEU members are still well behind the LPI leaders (mostly developed economies) such as Germany (ranked 1st in 2018, 2016, 2014), Sweden (ranked 2nd in 2018 and ranked 3rd in 2016) and Belgium (ranked 3rd in 2018 and ranked 6th in 2016).

Out of the EAEU states, in Global LPI 2018 Kazakhstan was ranked 71st being ahead of Russia (ranked 75th), Armenia (ranked 92nd), Belarus (103rd) and Kyrgyzstan (108th). Moreover, in all Global LPI ratings Kazakhstan has been ranked higher than other EAEU members (Table 6.8).

Thus, the paper stresses that, by participating in the Eurasian economic integration, the EAEU members have overall increased their role in international trade in transport and logistics services, as well as raised the competitiveness of their transport and logistics complexes.

Table 6.8 Global LPI scores of the EAEU states in 2012, 2014, 2016 and 2018

	2012	*2014*	*2016*	*2018*
Armenia	2.56	2.67	2.21	2.61
Belarus	2.61	2.64	2.40	2.57
Kazakhstan	2.69	2.70	2.75	2.81
Kyrgyzstan	2.35	2.21	2.16	2.55
Russia	2.58	2.69	2.57	2.76

Source: International Logistics Performance Indexes 2010, 2012, 2014, 2016 and 2018. Retrieved from: https://lpi.worldbank.org/international/global

6.6 Green Transport and Logistics in the EAEU

One of the promising areas of transport and logistics cooperation in the EAEU might be introduction of green technologies into the industry. The research suggests that green transport might contribute to deepening integration in the EAEU by raising the energy-efficiency of the rolling stock as well as by creating a green segment of transport machine building.

Green technologies might be one of the decisive instruments when modernizing the EAEU rolling stock, that is, trucks. According to the EEC (2018) figures, auto segment accounts for around 70 per cent of overall CO_2 emissions done by transport. From this perspective it has been revealed that Belarus exploits the most up-to-date and eco-friendly fleet of trucks (Table 6.9).

Despite the obvious necessity of auto fleet overhaul there is no serial manufacturing of electric vehicles (both trucks and cars) in the EAEU. Out of the EAEU states, Kazakhstan and Russia have pioneered trial output of electric cars.

As the EEC (2018) estimates it, as of 2018, there are 1800 electric cars registered in Russia, which is two times more than in 2017. Alongside with electric cars of foreign design Russia's major car manufacturer AutoVAZ has introduced its own product—Lada Ellada.

In its turn, there have been 119 units of electric cars registered in 2014–2017 in Kazakhstan, out of which 79 units were of Tesla origin and 17 units of Nissan origin. The first electric car trial of KIA origin assembled in Kazakhstan was in 2014 at the facilities of Asia Auto (city of Ust-Kamenogorsk). In 2016 the first trial lot of 27 units of electric cars of JAC origin was manufactured at the facilities of SaryarkaAutoProm (city of

Table 6.9 Ecological characteristics of Belarus, Kazakhstan and Russia auto fleet in 2018 (per cent)

	Share of trucks of Euro-4 and Euro-5 standards in the overall structure of auto fleet	*Share of trucks not older than 5 ages in the overall structure of auto fleet*
Belarus	50	37
Kazakhstan	25	15
Russia	15	7
Total	100	100

Source: Compiled by the author based on the data from National Statistics Agencies of Belarus, Kazakhstan and Russia. Retrieved from http://www.belstat.gov.by/, http://stat.gov.kz/, www.gks.ru

Kostanay). Finally, the first Russian electric car Lada Vesta EV assembled in Kazakhstan was introduced in the course of EXPO-2017 (EEC 2018).

From the regulatory side, the EAEU's existing coordinated (agreed) transport policy, due to its non-supranational status, is not empowered to introduce binding ecological norms and regulations on transport, despite the fact that diminishing negative impact on environment and people have been stated as major priorities of the policy.

However, some progress in motion toward green transport has been achieved. Starting from January 1, 2018, all types of auto vehicles (both trucks and cars) manufactured in the EAEU or imported into the EAEU are to be equipped with engines solely of Euro-5 standard. According to EEC (2018) estimates, such a measure will allow the reduction of the content of harmful substances in the emissions of the EAEU auto fleet by 1.5 times. By 2020 the EEC (2018) is expected to ban the manufacturing and distribution of marine low viscosity fuel (used by inland waterway segment) with sulfur containment of more than 0.5 per cent.

Thus, development of green transport and logistics in the EAEU is on the way. The introduction of green technologies into the auto segment might contribute to the overhaul of the EAEU rolling stock and turning it into the eco-friendly area of economy. However, green transport and logistics in the EAEU face objective regulatory vacuum.

6.7 Conclusions

The paper argues that transport and logistics is one of the most promising dimensions of integration in the EAEU despite the fact that the economic achievements of the EAEU are still modest due to the external shocks as well as the specifics of integration building. Nonetheless, the analysis carried out has revealed that in 2010–2018 the transport and logistics industry has overall positively reacted to the development of Eurasian integrative mechanisms.

The EAEU has seen an increase in two basic industry performance indicators—freight turnover and the volume of goods transported. Russia and Kazakhstan account for the overwhelming share both EAEU freight turnover and the volume of goods transported. From the qualitative side, the railway and auto segments have raised their shares in the structure of EAEU freight turnover and the volume of goods transported. Thus, the progress achieved has been a direct consequence of the development of railway transit via the EAEU in international transport corridor East-West and North-South, as well as intensification of cross-border shipments by auto mode (mainly secured by Armenia and Kyrgyzstan).

Eurasian economic integration has led to qualitative changes in the EAEU transport and logistics market by raising the share of integrated transport and logistics services available. Thus, the share of 3 and 4PL in the related market structure increased in 2015–2018. However, the EAEU is still far behind the world, EU and NAFTA/USMCA indicators of the development of integrated transport and logistics services, the share of transport and logistics outsourcing and capitalization of transport and logistics market.

Integrative mechanisms, because of the transit deployment agenda, have also raised EAEU global competitiveness in the transport and logistics area. First, the EAEU has overall increased its involvement into international trade in transport and logistics services. Yet, the EAEU is still far behind the EU, NAFTA/USMCA and ASEAN figures. Second, the EAEU states have strengthened their positions in the Global LPI rankings.

Finally, green transport might be another potential area of transport and logistics cooperation in the EAEU. By introducing green technologies into the industry, the EAEU states might contribute to modernization of the industry and economy at large.

However, the paper stresses that the lack of a supranational transport policy in the EAEU hampers any widening and deepening of integration in the EAEU (including in terms of transit flows), as well as the EAEU's involvement into regional transport and logistics initiatives. For instance, when implementing EAEU-BRI conjunction, the EEC (under the framework of coordinated [agreed] transport policy) is not authorized to negotiate the details of the project leaving the floor for exclusively member-states' national dialogue with China.

References

Ballou, R. (2007). The Evolution and Future of Logistics and Supply Chain Management. *European Business Review*. Retrieved from https://www.researchgate.net/publication/235318339_The_Evolution_and_Future_of_Logistics_and_Supply_Chain_Management.

Bennett, M. (2016). The Silk Road Goes North: Russia's Role Within China's Belt and Road Initiative. *Area Development and Policy, 1*(3), 341–351.

Christopher, M. (2016). *Logistics and Supply Chain Management* (5th ed.). New York: Financial Times/Pearson Education.

Contessi, N. (2018). Foreign Policy Diversification and Intercontinental Transport Corridors: The Case of Kazakhstan's Railways Diplomacy. *Europe-Asia Studies, 70*, 759–790.

Diesen, G. (2019). *Russia's Geoeconomic Strategy for a Greater Eurasia*. London: Routledge.

Domnina, S., & Zaboev, A. (2017). Eurasian Integration: On the Way to New Logistics. *Logistics and Supply Chain Management, 2*, 49–64. (In Russian).

Dragneva, R., & Wolczuk, K. (2017). The Eurasian Economic Union. Deals, Rules and the Exercise of Power. *Clatham House Research Paper*. Retrieved from: https://www.chathamhouse.org/sites/default/files/publications/research/2017-05-02-eurasian-economic-union-dragneva-wolczuk.pdf.

Dutkiewicz, P., & Sakwa, R. (2014). *Eurasian Integration—The View from Within*. London: Routledge.

Dynkin, A., Telegina, E., & Khalova, G. (2018). The Role of the Eurasian Economic Union in the Formation of Great Eurasia. *World Economy and International Relations, 62*, 5–24.

Eurasian Development Bank. (2018a). *Belt and Road Transport Corridors: Barriers and Investments*. Saint-Petersburg: EDB Centre for Integration Studies.

Eurasian Development Bank. (2018b). *Silk Road Transport Corridors: Assessment of Trans-EAEU Traffic Growth Potential*. Saint-Petersburg: EDB Centre for Integration Studies.

Eurasian Economic Commission. (2018). Transport and Infrastructure Department. Retrieved from www.eurasiancommission.org/en/act/energetikaiinfr/transport/Pages/default.aspx.

Hertz, S., & Alfredsson, M. (2003). Strategic Development of Third Party Logictics Providers. *Industrial Marketing Management, 2*, 139–149.

International Trade Centre. Trade Map. Retrieved from https://www.trademap.org/Index.aspx.

Ivut, R., Zubritsky, A., & Zinevich, A. (2015). Transit Capacity Development in the Republic of Belarus in the Context of Its Transport-Logistical System Formsation. *News of Science and Technologies, 1*, 19–33. (In Russian).

Kaneshko, S. (2017). Russia and China in the Age of Grand Eurasian Projects: Prospects for Integration between the Silk Road Economic Belt and the Eurasian Economic Union. *Cambridge Journal of Eurasian Studies, 1*, 1–15.

Kassenova, N. (2017). China's Silk Road and Kazakhstan's Bright Path: Linking Dreams of Prosperity. *Asian Policy, 24*, 110–116.

Kheyfets, B. (2018). Northern Sea Route as a New Transit Route of One Belt—One Road Initiative. The International Affairs. Retrieved from https://interaffairs.ru/jauthor/material/2047.

Lane, D., & Samokhvalov, V. (2015). *The Eurasian Project and Europe: Regional Discontinuities and Geopolitics*. London: Palgrave Macmillan.

Larin, O. (2017). Prospects for the Eurasian Economic Union's Transportation Systems Integration. *National Strategy Issues, 4*, 152–170. (In Russian).

Laruelle, M. (2015). Kazakhstan's Posture in the Eurasian Union: In Search of Serene Sovereignty. *Russian Analytical, 165*, 7–10.

Laruelle, M. (Ed.). (2018). *China's Belt and Road Initiative and Its Impact in Central Asia*. Washington, DC: The George Washington University, Central Asia Program. Retrieved from https://voicesoncentralasia.org/chinas-belt-and-road-initiative-and-its-impact-in-central-asia/.

Lavrikova, Y., Andreeva, E., Ratner, A., & Sobolev, A. (2018). Ural Vector of Arctic Opening up in Context of Big Eurasian Space Becoming. *Russian Foreign Economic Journal, 7*, 21–34. (In Russian).

Luzjanin, S. (2017). One Belt—One Road Initiative: Russian Vision and Problems of Conjunction. *China in World and Regional Politics. History and Modernity, 22*, 27–36.

Makarov, I., & Sokolova, A. (2016). Coordination of the Eurasian Economic Union and the Silk Road Economic Belt: Opportunities for Russia. *International Organizations Research Journal, 11*, 29–42.

Ostrovskii, A. (2017). Prospects to Interface the Silk Road Economic Belt and the Eurasian Economic Union Projects. *Herald of Russian Academy of Sciences, 87*(6), 480–490.

Pak, E. (2018a). Public-Private Partnership in the EAEU Transit Economy: Russia and Central Asian States. *MGIMO Review of International Relations, 5*(62), 174–183. (In Russian).

Pak, E. (2018b). Turkey and the EAEU in Regional Transport Systems: Rivals or Partners? *Perceptions, 23*(2), 135–153.

Pomfret, R. (2019). The Eurasian Landbridge and China's Belt and Road Initiative: Demand, Supply of Services and Public Policy. *World Economy, 1*, 1–12.

Russian International Affairs Council. (2015). *Northern Sea Route*. Retrieved from https://russiancouncil.ru/en/northernsearoute#transit.

Russian International Affairs Council. (2017). *EAEU Development Prospects up to 2025*. Moscow: Russian International Affairs Council.

Scriba, A. (2016). The Eurasian Economic Union and the Silk Road Economic Belt: Players, Interests and Implementation Challenges. *International Organizations Research Journal, 3*, 67–79. (In Russian).

Sergi, B. (2018). Putin's and Russian-led Economic Union: A Hybrid Half-Economics and Half-Political 'Janus Bifrons'. *Journal of Eurasian Studies, 9*, 52–60.

Shcherbanin, Y. (2018). International Transport Corridor 'North-South': What Worked Out. *Transport of the Russian Federation, 6*, 3–6. (In Russian).

Shurubovich, A. (2018). International Transit in the Economic Model of Belarus. *World of Changes, 2*, 174–189. (In Russian).

Sidaway, J., & Woon, C. (2017). Chinese Narratives on 'One Belt, One Road' in Geopolitical and Imperial Contexts. *The Professional Geographer, 59*(4), 1–13.

Solvang, H., Karameridis, S., Valantasis-Kanellos, N., & Song, D.-W. (2018). An Explanatory Study on the Northern Route as an Alternative Shipping Passage. *Maritime Policy and Management, 45*, 495–513.

Sternberg, T., Ahearn, A., McConnell, F. (2017). Central Asian 'Characteristics' on China's New Silk Road: The Role of Landscape and the Politics of Infrastructure. *Land, 6*(3), 1–16.

Summers, T. (2017). China's 'New Silk Roads': Sub-National Regions and Networks of Global Political Economy. *Third World Quart, 37*, 1628–1643.

Syroezhkin, K. (2018). Problem of pairing EBSR and 'Nurly Zhol'. In A. Krylov, A. Kuznetsov, & G. Chufrin (Eds.), *Post-Soviet Area: The Role of External Factors. Collection of Articles.* Moscow: Institute of World Economy and International Relations of the Russian Academy of Sciences. (In Russian).

Tsvetkov, V., Ziyadullaev, N., Zoidov, K., & Medkov, A. (2019). *Transit Economy: Theory, Methodology, Practice.* Moscow: Economic Education Publishing House. (In Russian).

Tsvetkov, V., Zoidov, K., Medkov, A., & Chernyshov, M. (2018). *The Formation of a Global Eurasia: The Problems of Interfacing Transit Systems.* Moscow: Market Economy Institute of the Russian Academy of Sciences. (In Russian).

Tsvyk, A. (2018). Greater Europe or Greater Eurasia? In Search of New Ideas for the Eurasian Integration. *RUDN Journal of Sociology, 2*, 262–270.

Turaeva, M. (2018). New Realities of Eurasian Transport Space: Kazakhstan Transit. *The Bulletin of the Institute of the Russian Academy of Sciences, 3*, 25–39. (In Russian).

Van der Togt, T. (2017). Bridging the Diving Lines in Greater Eurasia. *Russia in Global Affairs.* Retrieved from https://eng.globalaffairs.ru/number/Bridging-the-Dividing-Lines-in-Greater-Eurasia-18764.

Vardomsky, L., & Turaeva, M. (2018). *Development of the Post-Soviet Transport Corridors in Terms of Contemporary Geopolitical and Economic Challenges.* Moscow: Institute of Economics of the Russian Academy of Sciences. (In Russian).

Vinokurov, E. (2018). *Introduction to the Eurasian Economic Union.* Cham: Palgrave Macmillan.

Yakovlev, A. (2018). Eurasian Economic Union and the Chinese Initiative 'One Belt—One Road'. Opportunities for Cooperation. *Bulletin of the Institute of the Russian Academy of Sciences, 1*, 204–211. (In Russian).

Zoidov, K., Medkov, A., & Zoidov, Z. (2016). *Transit Economy's Development—A Basis for Stability, Security and Modernization of Russia and Central Asian Countries.* Moscow: Central Economic Mathematical Institute of the Russian Academy of Sciences. (In Russian).

Zoidov, K., Medkov, A., & Zoidov, Z. (2017). *Public-Private Partnership—The Basis of Innovative Development and Security in the Transit Economy.* Moscow: Economic Education Publishing. (In Russian).

CHAPTER 7

Scientific, Technical, and Educational Cooperation in the EAEU

Petr I. Kasatkin, Ludmila S. Salnikova, and Veronika M. Fatykhova

7.1 Introduction

Integration processes in the Eurasian economic union may be characterized as «pragmatic Eurasianism» (Kofner 2019), aimed at achieving concrete, mutually beneficial goals without an ideological component. In the modern world—marked by a rapid growth of knowledge-driven economy—addressing this task is only possible with an impetus on developing science and higher education. Scientific and technical interactions not only facilitate pragmatic economic interactions, but also strengthen interpersonal ties, giving rise to humanitarian integration.

The EAEU appears to be experiencing difficulties forming a common scientific, technical, and educational space, due in part to member-states' fears of losing national sovereignty, as well as a lack of any exact mechanisms for studying concrete arrangements or methods for accounting for

P. I. Kasatkin (✉) • L. S. Salnikova
MGIMO University, Moscow, Russia

V. M. Fatykhova
Ministry of Foreign Affairs of the Russian Federation, Moscow, Russia

N. A. Piskulova (ed.), *The Economic Dimension of Eurasian Integration*, https://doi.org/10.1007/978-3-030-59886-0_7

the interests of other members, leading to delayed integration (Obukhov and Golovko 2018). In order to overcome these challenges, the EAEU is working slowly yet consistently towards creating specialized funds to finance scientific and educational projects, developing relevant regulations, and eliminating bureaucratic barriers to innovation.

EAEU integration has a unique competitive advantage: using their Soviet experience, and building on the cooperation mechanisms developed within the former USSR (Torkunov 2019a). Russia is the engine of Eurasian scientific-educational integration due to its considerable economic and human resources, laying the foundation for a number of major multilateral projects with great potential for strengthening integration. Noteworthy among these projects are the Eurasian technological platforms, prioritizing the development areas of mutual interest. In the educational sphere, considerable effort is also made to strengthen cooperation between leading universities, develop joint programs, open branches in member-states, and promote academic mobility.

The chapter is organized as follows. After the introduction, the second part deals with key aspects of scientific-educational cooperation in the EAEU. It explains the "pragmatic Eurasianism" approach to integration processes within the Union which also pertains to scientific and educational cooperation. It also analyzes the economic preconditions for further integration in this sphere. Part 3 analyzes the existing multilateral projects in scientific research. Parts 4 and 5, respectively, deal with prospective areas of cooperation and challenges in the scientific-technological and educational spheres. Part 6 concludes the chapter with an assessment of the EAEU's prospects for further scientific and educational integration.

7.2 Scientific-Educational Cooperation in the EAEU: Key Aspects

The year 2019 marks the fifth anniversary of signing the EAEU Treaty and the 25th anniversary of the idea of modern Eurasian integration. It is possible to claim that, for the past few years, the Eurasian Economic Union has actualized itself as a dynamically developing, open integration association which has become an integral part of the major economic processes in Eurasia. According to Y. Kofner, the manager of the Eurasian sector of the Centre for Comprehensive European and International Studies of the National Research University Higher School of Economics (CCEIS NRU

HSE), enough time has passed to make it possible to call the theory of the modern Eurasian integration "pragmatic Eurasianism", as it follows a purely pragmatic approach to the activity of the EAEU. It is the pragmatic setting of economic targets, but not the ideological contents, that takes the central place in the wording of the EAEU Treaty and in the logic of building institutions of Eurasian integration (Kofner 2019).

The assessment of cooperation in the scientific, technical, and educational spheres of the EAEU from the standpoint of "pragmatic Eurasianism" seems to be the most exact. In this context, social and humanitarian cooperation amongst the member countries of the Eurasian Union gains a new insight. As Professor and Diplomat A. Smbatyan notes, "without education, without science, without dealing with cultural, ethnic questions, it is extremely difficult to build relations between the peoples and the states. For people to understand each other, for the achievement of the atmosphere of absolute mutual trust, we especially need contacts created only by humanitarian cooperation—through culture, art, education. It is impossible to imagine the formation of the Eurasian Union without cooperation in these spheres... Sooner or later we will surely come to it. And why not get ahead of events and, in the closest time, start building these bridges which, for certain, will facilitate the development of the economic relations?" (Jun 2017)

In the context of the fourth industrial revolution, the strengthening of humanitarian cooperation on inter-state scientific, technical, and educational programs of EAEU countries is an important factor of the harmonization and integration of many scientific disciplines and technologies, and national and universal values that lead to breakthroughs; these are innovative discoveries which form the backbone for the creation of a new economy—"the economy of knowledge", free from ideological and political clichés.

At the same time, it should be noted that forming this common scientific, technical, and educational space is not easy. On the one hand, all the participants of the Union that are represented by higher education institutions, research establishments, or industrial and administrative structures understand the need of interaction in this sphere. On the other hand, representatives of the political establishment of member countries have some vigilance concerning the forced rapprochement with Russia that is caused by fears of losing national sovereignty. As it appears, realizing the mutual benefits of scientific, technical, and educational cooperation in the integration association is to be based on the principles of the inviolability of the national sovereignty of each state of the Union. The methods and instruments of European integration cannot be mechanically carried over to the EAEU.

The EAEU has a unique advantage—the opportunity to make use of the experience Russia accumulated during the Soviet period, so as to create new formats of communication based on models and networks already approved. Researchers of the Russian Foundation of Fundamental Research and the Institute of World Economy and International Relations of the Russian Academy of Sciences believe that the intensification of the multilateral scientific, technical, and educational cooperation in the EAEU lays the foundation for the modernization of national economies as well as promoting the accumulation of the economic and political potential of the whole association, as the elimination of customs, legislative and further barriers in the field of high technologies creates favorable conditions for the restoration of the connections lost after the collapse of the USSR and the creation of new research and production chains. It is also promoted by the fact that, historically, the scientific schools were localized in Russia (Moscow, St. Petersburg, Siberia and the Volga region), and the objects of the hi-tech industry (in particular, microelectronics, thin chemistry and pharmaceutics, biotechnologies) developed in the republics that creates the EAEU's competitive advantages (Federation Council of the Federal Assembly of the Russian Federation 2015).

According to the Eurasian Economic Commission (EEC), in 2017 the EAEU included 4926 organizations, which were carrying out research and advanced development, from which 3944 were in Russia (80 percent).

Research and development costs in the EAEU are growing, but still remain low compared to Western nations. The internal costs of research and development in 2017 were distributed as follows: Armenia—$24.6 million, Belarus—$319.5 million, Kazakhstan—$211.3 million, Kyrgyzstan—$8.2 million, Russia—$17.4 billion (nearly 97 percent of the total internal costs of the EAEU for research and advanced development) (Eurasian Economic Commission 2018d). Over a ten-year period—from 2007 to 2017—the internal costs of research and advanced development in the Union have seen a sizeable increase, by 20 percent on average. That said, research and development costs as a share of GDP remain comparatively low. According to the World Bank, in 2017 R&D expenses reached 0.23 percent of the GDP in Armenia, 0.59 percent in Belarus, 0.13 percent in Kazakhstan, 0.11 percent Kyrgyzstan, and 1.11 percent Russia (by contrast, Israel spent 4.58 percent of its GDP on research, and the USA 2.8 percent) (The World Bank 2017).

Russia plays a key role in the scientific and technical cooperation of the EAEU, bearing the main share of R&D expenses and possessing the greatest human resources. At the same time, Russia promotes the idea of the Eurasian transfer of technologies in order to share and exchange its experience with scientists of the neighboring states on a mutually advantageous basis within bilateral and multilateral projects.

7.3 Current and Completed Projects

Given the emerging nature of the association and the deterrents mentioned above, it should be noted that the number of complete multilateral projects in R&D scientific research and advanced development at the end of 2018 was not substantial: pipeline transport development; nuclear research on the basis of the Joint Institute for Nuclear Research in Dubna; joint implementation of space projects by Russia, Belarus and Kazakhstan; and the interstate EurAsEC target program of "Innovative biotechnologies" (26 projects of the Russian, Belarusian, Kazakh and Tajik scientists in the field of microbic and DNA technologies for food, biological and environmental safety), as well as the interstate target program of the implementation of the projects of the recultivation of the territory of Kyrgyzstan and Tajikistan to mitigate the impact of uranium mining. The issue of the creation of joint ventures for the production of hi-tech hoisting-and-transport equipment is also being worked out (Scientific and technical cooperation as a factor of Eurasian economic integration—Annual Report 2015).

The cornerstone of the listed projects is the agreed decision, adopted in 2016, to form the priority Eurasian Technological Platforms (ETP) as tools of the international scientific-technological and innovative-production cooperation of the scientific organizations, governmental institutions, business and industrial enterprises in the format of the implementation of specific projects. In fact, the ETP is a system mechanism and an innovative platform for discussion, maintaining advanced research and development and their introduction in the economic practice. At the moment, the formation of 13 priority technological platforms is supported: "Space and Geoinformation Technologies", "Biomedicine", "Supercomputers", "Photonics", "Light-emitting diodes", "Technologies of extraction of solid minerals", "Technologies of ecological development", "EurasiaBio", "Technology of food and processing industry of agrarian and industrial complex", "Agriculture", "Consumer goods manufacturing", "Technologies of metallurgy and new materials", "Industrial technologies of providing construction industry" (Eurasian Studies 2018).

The list of technological platforms, including 417 scientific and industrial institutions of the EAEU, is not final and can be corrected and enlarged further. Such mobility indicates that EAEU member-states are studying international scientific and technological experience and trying to coordinate corresponding national interests in order to deepen the research and production cooperation in these hi-tech areas.

One of the successful projects is the ETP "Space and Geoinformation Technologies—Products of Global Competitiveness", which started the formation of the EAEU's Integrated system on providing space and geoinformation services on the basis of the national data sources of the remote sensing of the Earth. The founders of the platform are "The Kazakhstan Garysh Sapary Oil Company Limited" (Astana, Kazakhstan); the non-commercial joint-stock company "Almaty University Of Power snd Communication" (Almaty, Kazakhstan); the private limited company "International Space Technologies" (Moscow, Russia); LLC "SOVZOND Company" (Moscow, Russia); Lomonosov Moscow State University (Moscow, Russia); the scientific and engineering republican unitary enterprise "Geographic Information Systems" of Belarus NAS (Minsk, Belarus); and BSU of V.I. Lenin (Minsk, Belarus) (Eurasian Commission 2016). This project is indicative of the modern integration realities of the Eurasian space. Firstly, by means of the space ETP, the parties express their intention to cooperate within a strategic realm of space exploration, which has been provoking serious international discussions for many years. This signals to international partners that the association views itself as durable and its plans as long-term (Kasatkin et al. 2019). Secondly, the participants of the project are located in the capitals and the largest cities of the member countries where their main scientific potential is concentrated. The leading research organizations are to become the leaders of the scientific thought who will be followed by the regional institutions by means of interaction and exchange of experience.

7.4 Areas of Further Scientific and Technological Development

In December 2018 at the meeting of the Supreme Eurasian Economic Council, the President of Russia, V. Putin, designated the further direction of this research and industrial cooperation: "cooperation of the states of the EAEU in the sphere of providing space services, including the creation of the general group of orbital devices and advance of geoinformation services for the markets of the third countries, appears to have prospects. It is possible to think over the adoption of a joint program of the scientific and technological development" (Sputnik 2018).

For implementing the plans drawn up by the ECE, a set of proposals were made:

- to create a special fund for financing scientific research, including special funds for financing venture projects;
- to carry out the unification and harmonization of legal regulation in the field of scientific, technical, and innovative cooperation, including the additional fine-tuning of the funding mechanisms for the projects in the scientific and technological sphere and the formation of a common digital industrial space;
- to include a provision on the scientific, technical, and educational cooperation in the EAEU Treaty (Eurasian Economic Commission 2018d).

According to Chokan Laumulin, researcher of the Center of Development Studies of the University of Cambridge (Great Britain), the EAEU has the potential to alter the industrial picture of the world: the EAEU's own landscape could change completely owing to the joint development of three directions—non-silicon electronics, superconductivity, and cryogenics. The world's electronic industry approaches the limit of silicon's conductivity of 1 electron/volt, single-crystal silicon being its basic element. The most outstanding physicists, including Professor G. Lonzarich (former head of the group of quantum matter of the Cavendish Laboratory of the University of Cambridge), developed the theories that if the experiments with polymers and rare-earth metals continue in Eurasia, it is possible to substantially increase the efficiency of semiconductors, which will increase the conductivity and lead to a revolution in the electronic industry. As for superconductivity, research under the conditions of low temperatures can help to discover new properties of these materials and to change mankind's energy perception by means of reducing energy losses during transportation (30–40 percent of losses) from remote centers of generation. Russia and Kazakhstan possess large reserves of various rare-earth metals, experiments with which will increase the efficiency of solar battery chips that, in the long term, will give cheap energy to many Asian countries where sunny days are numerous. This scientist believes that the EAEU preserves a potential environment, scientifically and educationally, for reproducing human capital. An example of that are science cities which are penetrated by the ideas, experience and space for scientific experiments; their atmosphere invites communication between scientists, and the development of theories and training. The only thing that is needed is a balanced state policy which will attract prospective young people, as well as raising the social status of the scientists and the prestige of the science. However, besides the direct financing of the researchers' activity and material and technical resources, it is necessary to reduce the extent of the bureaucratization of the science in the EAEU. According to C. Laumulin, scientific and technological research in the EAEU represents nothing but the global demand of the time, which will result in changing the political, social, and economic realities (Heritage 2016).

The share of the EAEU in the international market of knowledge-intensive products is only 2.5 percent, compared with the 80 percent share of the market of high technologies held by the states of the Group of Seven. (Gavrilyuk 2015). In many respects, such a low share is due to the consequences of the disintegration of the scientific and industrial associations and the loss of the connections acquired during the Soviet period in the 1990s, and also the fact that, in the USSR, a powerful scientific and technical complex coexisted, paradoxically, with the lack of practical application of the results of R&D research and development in the civil sphere.

Despite this, the EAEU has serious chances of effectively developing and strengthening its global positions. The keys to the sustainable development of the EAEU economies which have a positive impact on the development of science and education are: bolstering the sectors of the economy and the enterprises which make highly processed products and deepen the amount of scientific and technological cooperation; and corporate integration. It is necessary to develop the institutions of both national and interstate stimulation of the technological and scientific cooperation and innovative activities within the development of the sixth wave of innovation, as the scientific and technological competitiveness serves one of the main indicators of the dynamism of the development of the Eurasian integration (Gavrilyuk 2015).

For this purpose, it is important not so much to increase the public financing of science as to take measures for the productive transfer of technologies among the five Eurasian countries (Glazyev 2012), including the transfer of know-how, technological information, innovative developments, patents for inventions, engineering, and joint development projects carried out by the enterprises (Terebova 2010). The Eurasian transfer of technologies will allow the member countries to effectively commercialize the results of scientific developments and to generate new investments and technologies. To make the realization of such an approach successful, it is necessary to create a new institution—an international network of centers for transferring technologies in the EAEU. This will facilitate the spread of technological information and the search for collaborators for new projects, and promote the increasing, innovative commercialization of the results of this scientific research, as well as also promoting the transfer of technologies to areas remote from their centers of production (Gavrilyuk 2015).

Another prospective direction of Eurasian cooperation, which is closely connected with science and education, is the creation of a digital space in the EAEU and the implementation of the EAEU's digital agenda before the year 2025. The introduction of digital technologies in cross-border interaction within the association plays an important role in increasing its regional and global connectivity as well as competitiveness (Pak 2020). Digitalization is likely to have a synergetic effect on all EAEU economies. It is expected that more widespread broadband internet access will increase the GDP of the association by 1.7 percent, the rising international throughput will bring another 0.66 percent, and electronic trading will yield a 0.88 percent GDP increase. Digitalization will also create 2–4 million jobs. The elimination of standard and legal barriers will further add $46.5 billion to the GDP of the Union (Eurasian Economic Commission 2018).

7.5 Educational Cooperation—Challenges and Prospects

The formation of the common market of the EAEU, including the implementation of its digital agenda, assumes the free movement of human resources that requires special attention to the development of human capacity and poses a question about the development of a coordinated educational policy. In 2017–2018 in Russia, there were 766 higher educational institutions of state and non-state-owned legal entity forms (taking into account branches, about 1000); in Armenia there were 61 higher educational institutions; in Belarus 52; in Kazakhstan 122; and in Kyrgyzstan there were 51 such institutions. The number of higher education students in the EAEU exceeded 5 million people: in Russia 4.28 million students; in Armenia 94.7 thousand; in Belarus about 300 thousand; in Kazakhstan more than half a million people are getting higher education; and in Kyrgyzstan more than 162 thousand people are (Eurasian Economic Commission 2018). Simple arithmetic shows that in all the countries of the EAEU the number of students fluctuates at the level of 2–3 percent of the total number of the population, which demonstrates a rather comparable higher education coverage of the citizens, and, therefore, is a favorable factor for the creation of the general educational space in the long term.

In this context, the indicators of the academic mobility of students within the integration association are also important. 86,788 students from EAEU member countries studied in Russia in the academic year of 2017/18: 3049 from Armenia; 10,792 from Belarus; 65,700 from Kazakhstan; 7247 from Kyrgyzstan. In the same year 1156 citizens from the EAEU studied in Armenia; 1857 people in Belarus; 2229 in Kazakhstan; 4817 in Kyrgyzstan (Eurasian Economic Commission 2018). These statistics show that Russia remains the most attractive destination for Eurasian students; first of all, this shows Russia's competitive advantage in the export of educational services, and, secondly, this allows member-states to exchange experience and to build in educational strategies adequate to labor market demands.

Examples of the Eurasian Educational Cooperation are the national Slavic universities, the EAEU Network University, branches of Russian higher educational institutions in countries of the Union, and the Eurasian Association of Universities (EAU). The EAU carries out its activity by means of organizing conferences, forums, and the development of interuniversity connections and contacts. Since its foundation (1989) the EAU has held 13 congresses, including in Moscow, Astana and Minsk, at which the problems of national education, forming a uniform educational space, and cooperation between universities in the educational and scientific spheres were discussed (Eurasian Association of the Universities 2019).

Lomonosov Moscow State University has five branches in post-Soviet cities—Astana, Baku, Dushanbe, Yerevan, and Tashkent—where about 2500 students study and joint academic scientific research is conducted in Russian. About 500 professors of MSU visit these branches every year. One recent achievement of leading Russian higher education institutions is the creation of an open remote education national platform which can be spread over to EAEU countries as well. It should be noted that, according to forecasts by scientists, by the year 2030 there will be about 180 new professions and specialties in the Eurasian labor market, including Russia, and about 50 professions will become low demand. Therefore, the states of the Union need to realize general measures for preventing the problems of qualified personnel deficiency, or economic backwardness which will lead to a migration imbalance. It is possible to carry this out by means of modernization and the improvement of the higher education system, and by interaction amongst employers and higher educational institutions which will increase the compliance of educational services to the changing demands of the labor market (Eurasian Economic Commission 2018). The new systems of practical cooperation—being built today within the EAEU—demand thousands of qualified employees for their upkeep and should understand what the EAEU is and how it works. Therefore, for the preparation of such staff in the Eurasian space, a uniform educational standard and general educational policy are necessary (Torkunov 2019b).

On April 12, 2016, at the meeting of the Council of the Eurasian Association of Universities, the memorandum of the creation of the Network EAEU University—representing an association of higher education institutions of EAEU member countries, led by Tomsk State University, Lomonosov Moscow State University and St. Petersburg State Economic University—was signed (Eurasian Economic Commission 2018). The pilot project is the one-year master program "Eurasian Research". The Gumilev Eurasian National University (Kazakhstan), Al-Farabi Kazakh National University, the Belarus State University, the Armenian-Slavic National University, and some other higher education institutions also participate in the project (The Rhythm of Eurasia 2016). On September 1, 2016, Tomsk State University started the joint network master's program for training specialists in the field of Eurasian integration with the universities of Kyrgyzstan and Kazakhstan. On September 1, 2017, St. Petersburg State University started the network master's program "The Personnel for Eurasian Economic Integration" (Rusinov 2016). The project of the Eurasian Network University is actively promoted by the Russian part, but it has not received intergovernmental status so far, owing to lack of support from all the members of the EAEU, thus remaining a framework initiative for universities.

For the purpose of cooperation in the spheres of education, science, and finance, for the personnel, and for scientifically ensuring the effective interface of the national financial systems in the EAEU, Network Financial Institution functions include the Russian-Armenian (Slavic) university, the Belarus State Economic University, the Yeltsin Kyrgyz-Russian Slavic University, "The Financial Academy" (Kazakhstan), the Financial University under the Government of the Russian Federation, and St. Petersburg State Economic University. Within the NRU HSE, since 2017, the Eurasian sector has been working on a multipurpose division created within the Center of Complex European and International Research of the Faculty of the World Economy and World Politics of the NRU HSE, implementing educational programs and research. Also, there is the exchange of information, as well as scientific and practical events in the field of Eurasian Economic Integration. In the RANEPA there is the master's program "International Relations and Integration Processes in Eurasia", within which specialists are trained in the field of international relations, specializing in the Eurasian perspective, and leaders of digital transformation of the international social, political and economic processes are conducted (Eurasian Economic Commission 2018).

The Eurasian Information and Analytical Consortium (EIAC) is the association of expert and educational organizations of the member-states, and was created on April 17, 2018, on the basis of the association of assistance to the development of the analytical potential of the personality, society and state "Analytics", Financial University under the Government of the Russian Federation and the Institute of Scientific Information on Social Sciences in the RAS. The purpose of the EIAC is to promote the efficiency of the integration processes of EAEU countries on the basis of their information and analytical provisions (Eurasian Economic Commission 2018).

The Russian-Armenian (Slavic) University mentioned above was created by agreement between the Government of the Russian Federation and the Government of Armenia in 1997. For the EAEU, the functioning of this university is an indicative model of the interaction of the two member countries of the Union, as it is a higher educational institution under joint jurisdiction of the Russian Federation and the Republic of Armenia and uses the status of a state university of Russia and Armenia. Training at the University is conducted in Russian, Armenian and other foreign languages, according to more than 60 specialties within eight institutes. Active research activities are carried out; it is home to centers of cooperation with employers, and international cooperation directed to the integration of the Russian Academy of Public Administration into world educational and scientific space is developing, in particular having signed cooperation agreements with more than 200 foreign higher education institutions from 40 countries (Russian-Armenian (Slavic) University 2019).

On April 13, 2016, at the initiative of the Ministry of Education and Science of the Russian Federation in Moscow, the first meeting of Ministers of Education and Science of the countries of the Union occurred. During this, all the parties (except for Kazakhstan) signed the Memorandum of Cooperation on educational, scientific, and technological cooperation within the Eurasian space; this provides the formation of the advisory boards in the field of science and higher education. However, this initiative has not gone any further than the declarations on intent in many respects, because of the position of Kazakhstan and, partly, Belarus, which shows their discontent in connection with the outflow of students to Russian higher education institutions which can have negative consequences for the labor market of the donor countries (June 2017). In connection with this, Nur-Sultan and Minsk counteract the inclusion of the regulations on scientific, technical, and educational cooperation in the EAEU Treaty.

In the academic and educational environment, there are discussions concerning the transition of the Eurasian states to the Bologna system: today four countries of the EAEU are participants of the Bologna Process, and Kyrgyzstan adopted the two-level higher education system in 2011 but has not yet become an official participant of the Bologna Process. That the system of values—the social, political and economic relations in the EAEU and the European Union where the Bologna Process has proved its efficiency—is significantly different and cannot but affect the scientific and educational complex, which also reflects these features. This issue is studied by Belarusian researcher L. Titarenko, who believes that the EAEU states need to approach the implementation of the Bologna principles with care and to develop their own educational integration projects which would promote regional and national interests and not just "the interests of global development, in many respects only deepening the processes of social inequality both in economy, education and in science" (Titarenko 2018). This is connected with the fact that "the idea of the internationalization of the market of education advanced by western countries is an expression of the market needs of these countries in their advance to the non-western space (including the Post-Soviet countries)" (Titarenko 2018). This remark gains a special importance today as the EAEU countries share the principles of the Soviet education system, which has indisputable advantages. Furthermore, today one of the major tasks in this direction is the preservation of and adaptation to modern conditions of the best practices of both the organization of educational process and of interuniversity cooperation. Moreover, certain national specifics in the sphere of higher education, which should not be rejected as they are caused by deep welfare reasons, are characteristic of all the states of the economic space; with the proper adaptive approach it is not an obstacle for the harmonization of the EzaAEAEU's educational systems. According to M. Lebedeva, it is important for the European and Eurasian educational spaces to intersect with each other "not to create tension between various educational models, but, on the contrary, to contribute to the mutual enrichment and development" (Lebedeva 2017).

7.6 Conclusion

The analysis of the modalities of scientific and educational cooperation in the EAEU shows that it is restrained by fears held by the political establishment "to dissolve" the sovereignty in integration. Objective social and economic problems are masked under propagandistic slogans about "the exploitation of the republics by Moscow" and the consequences of "the Soviet oppression". There is a need to develop the ideology of Eurasian integration which will be able to explain the advantages of the common economic space. At this point a special role is played by the joint work of the partners of the program of scientific research into the social and humanitarian profile, which promotes a favorable perception of the ideas of new Eurasianism by the population. The ideological justification of the community and the reciprocity of member countries' interests, when increasing cooperation between the universities, will allow the restoration of the humanitarian dimension of integration for the formation of the common educational space and the harmonization of labor law (Tkachuk and Mityaev 2018).

Speaking about the difficulties of the current state of scientific and educational cooperation in the EAEU, it is possible to locate the meta-problem which is characteristic of the majority of spheres of integration cooperation. It is the lack of any exact mechanisms for studying concrete arrangements or ways of accounting for the interests of other member-states—this leads to delayed integration. Besides, it creates the serious threat of negative intervention by extraregional players who seek to achieve their own economic and political goals (Obukhov and Golovko 2018). Measures for strengthening support for integration projects by the population act as a guarantee of successful implementation of joint innovative projects, and have to be directly promoted by the scientific and technical cooperation which carries a real increase in the level and quality of the life of the population, as well as favorably influences the formation of a system of Eurasian values (Andronova et al. 2018).

The Eurasian Economic Union has enormous potential for strengthening the national economies of its member countries, accumulating volumes of the internal cooperation, and taking the lead at the regional and, later, global level. Today it is extremely important to provide an advanced integration processes and association competitiveness by means of increasing the knowledge intensity of the economies of EAEU member-states; this can be reached by effective scientific, technical, and educational cooperation, the adjusted transfer of technologies, the implementation of joint educational and scientific projects, and through carrying out research by mixed groups of scientists.

References

Andronova, I., Belova, N., Ganeeva, M., & Moseykin, Y. (2018). Scientific and Technical Cooperation Within the EAEU as the most Important Factor of the Loyalty of the Population of the Member Countries to the Integration Association and Its Attractiveness for New Members. *The RUDN Bulletin. Series: Sociology, 1*(18), 117–130.

Eurasian Association of the Universities. (2019). *About the Association*. Retrieved from http://www.eau-msu.ru/about.

Eurasian Economic Commission. (2018a). *Education*. Retrieved from http://www.eurasiancommission.org/ru/act/integr_i_makroec/dep_stat/econstat/Pages/education.aspx.

Eurasian Economic Commission. (2018b). *In the Union the Eurasian Personnel Potential is Developed*. Retrieved from http://www.eurasiancommission.org/ru/nae/news/Pages/10-05-2018-1.aspx.

Eurasian Economic Commission. (2018c). *Report on the Realization of the Main Directions of Integration within the Eurasian Economic Union*. Retrieved from https://clck.ru/GDAvz.

Eurasian Economic Commission. (2018d). *Science and Innovations*. Retrieved from http://www.eurasiancommission.org/ru/act/integr_i_makroec/dep_stat/econstat/Pages/science.aspx.

Eurasian Economic Commission. (2018e). *The Digital Agenda of the EEU to the Year 2025: Prospects and Recommendations. Review of the World Bank Group*. Retrieved from eurasiancommission.org/ru/act/dmi/SiteAssets/ОбзорWB.pdf.

Eurasian Studies. (2018). *Eurasian Technology Platforms: Description, Directions, Financing Methods*. Retrieved from http://eurasian-studies.org/archives/8263.

Federation Council of the Federal Assembly of the Russian Federation. (2015). *Scientific and Technical Cooperation as a Factor of the Eurasian Economic Integration*. Retrieved from http://www.council.gov.ru/media/files/rAMxT-Gk0OVCzWQHTXaq4AwGba6Iplopl.pdf.

Gavrilyuk, A. V. (2015). A Transfer of Technologies in the Conditions of the International Economic Integration of the Countries of the EEU. *Public Administration. Electronic Bulletin, 52*, 101–119. Retrieved from http://cyberleninka.ru/article/n/transfer-tehnologiy-v-usloviyah-mezhdunarodnoy-ekonomicheskoy-integratsii-stran-eaes.

Glazyev, S. Y. (2012). To a Steady Growth Through a Fair World Economic Order. *The Russian Economic Magazine, 2*, 59–61.

Heritage. (2016). *New Discoveries Will Change the Industrial Reality in the EAEU*. Retrieved from http://nasledie.ru/?q=node/6583.

Jun, S. M. (2017). Education as the Sphere of Cooperation within the Eurasian Economic Union: Problems and Prospects. *Bulletin of Tomsk State University. History, 50*, 89–92.

Kasatkin, P. I., Kovalchuk, J. A., & Stepnov, I. M. (2019). The Modern Role in the Formation of the Digital Wave of Kondratiev's Long Cycles. *Voprosy Ekonomiki, 12*, 123–140.

Kofner, Y. (2019). Pragmatic Eurasianism: Four Approaches for Better Understanding the Eurasian Economic Union. Russian International Affairs Council. Retrieved from: https://russiancouncil.ru/en/blogs/GreaterEurasiaEnglish/pragmatic-eurasianism-four-approaches-for-better-understanding-the-eur/

Lebedeva, M. M. (2017). International Political Processes of Integration of Education. *Education Integration, 3*(88), 385–394.

Obukhov, A., & Golovko, N. (2018). Reconstruction of the World-System Approach in the Context of the Integration Processes in Modern Eurasia. *The Bulletin of the Novosibirsk State Pedagogical University, 2*(8), 173–185.

Pak, E. (2020). Transit Potentials of Russia and Kazakhstan. World Economy and International Relations, 64(11), 132–138

Rusinov, A. (2016). Cooperation on Education Within the Eurasian Economic Union (EAEU). In *The Ministry of Education and Science of the Russian Federation*. Retrieved from http://nic.gov.ru/Media/Default/Images/anons/inter-2016/PDF/25_A.C.Rusinov.pdf.

Russian-Armenian (Slavic) University. (2019). Retrieved from http://www.rau.am/rus/.

Sputnik. (2018). The EAEU Can Adopt a General Program of Scientific and Technological Cooperation. Retrieved from https://ru.sputniknews.kz/politics/20181206/8379480/putin-otkrytie-veehs-prezidenty.html.

Terebova, S. V. (2010). A Transfer of Technologies as an Element of the Innovative Development of the Economy. *Problems of the Development of the Territory, 4*, 33–35.

The Eurasian Economic Union Treaty. (2014). Retrieved from http://www.consultant.ru/document/cons_doc_LAW_163855/.

The Rhythm of Eurasia. (2016). *'The Eurasian Network University' Will Train the First Experts in the Sphere of the EAEU Integration in 2017*. Retrieved from http://www.ritmeurasia.org/news%2D%2D2016-04-19%2D%2Devrazijskij-setevoj-universitet-v-2017-godu-podgotovit-pervyh-specialistov-v-sfere-integracii-eaes-23067.

The World Bank. (2017). *Research and Development Expenditure*. Retrieved from http://data.worldbank.org/indicator/GB.XPD.RSDV.GD.ZS.

Titarenko, L. G. (2018). The Place and Role of the Integration of the Higher Education Systems in the International Cooperation of the EAEU Countries. *Big Eurasia: Development, Safety, Cooperation, 1-2*, 319–321.

Tkachuk, S., & Mityaev, D. (2018). 'Soft Power' of Science and Education in the Development of the Eurasian Economic Integration. *Integration: Eurasian Ark. Economic Strategies, 2*, 182–188. Retrieved from http://www.inesnet.ru/wp-content/mag_archive/2018_02/es2018-02-182-188_Tkachuk_Mityaev.pdf.

Torkunov, A. V. (2019a). Diplomacy of the Academic Community: The Past and the Present. *World Economy and International Relations, 9*(63), 22–28.

Torkunov, A. V. (2019b). University as a Part of National Economy. *Voprosy Ekonomiki, 12*, 111–122.

CHAPTER 8

Digital Economy Developments Within the EAEU

Anna V. Abramova and Elina Thorne

8.1 Introduction

Digital technologies are transforming the global economy, introducing new challenges for every country. Digital economy has become the next step in the evolution of electronic commerce and electronic business, being a key pillar for infrastructure information–communication technologies (ICTs). The ICT sector has hardware, software and computer and telecommunication services as its main subsectors. Significant advances during the past decade in all the ICT industry subsectors made it possible to make the shift for broader use of information and telecommunication technologies for data analysis, automation and robotization. That has become the basis for the digital economy.

Key technological trends in ICT market—artificial intelligence, blockchain, big data and 3D printing—have brought new opportunities in

A. V. Abramova (✉)
MGIMO University, Moscow, Russia

E. Thorne
Collectly, Los-Angeles, CA, USA

N. A. Piskulova (ed.), *The Economic Dimension of Eurasian Integration*, https://doi.org/10.1007/978-3-030-59886-0_8

production and all the types of commercial activities. Besides, digital economy is contributing to the further development of existing global value chains (GVCs) supporting trade, technology transfer and FDI. For some sectors the advances in ICT technologies make it possible to change the structure of the value chain making it shorter or influencing the geographical distribution of production, while at the same time making it possible to create new types of value chains based on data. According to the UNCTAD Digital economy report, this new type could be named Data value chains (UNCTADa 2019). Regional segments of GVCs provide the basis for economic integration supporting interconnectivity (OECD 2013). ICTs plays important role in eliminating technical barriers in foreign trade that can contribute significantly for EAEU development. Information, though still scarce, on the level of use of e-commerce in the EAEU is provided, but the latest data from UNCTAD give the example of Belarus enjoying around 45 per cent of all orders for SMEs received by Internet (UNCTAD 2019).

Digital economy development is recognized as one of the key pillars for further EAEU regional integration development. It should be underlined that digital transformation is challenging for EAEU member-states because of the high level of technological development of some EAEU members. On the one hand, the regional market is influenced by the growing Chinese ICT power, and competition from the EU and the USA. On the other hand, the Asian economies in the EAEU are benefiting greatly from their collaboration with Russia under the umbrella of digital economy development initiative in the EAEU.

Still, however, the digital economy developments in the EAEU were not widely discussed in the literature, being one of the new trends in regional cooperation in the region.

Research of the ICT infrastructure development in EAEU member states, including country rankings, was produced by the experts from the World Bank Group and Asian Development Bank. Data bases, reports, and working papers outlining the ICT infrastructure developments, e-government and e-commerce progress are published by UN agencies, including ITU data sets for ICTs and UNCTAD (UNCTAD 2017, 2019).

EAEU Digital trade developments, being an integral part of the digital economy, are discussed in the report of the Eurasian Economic Commission (EAEU 2019).

Digital economy is able to contribute to different aspects of social life including education (Kasatkin et al. 2019) and may bring significant challenges for the EAEU's social and economic development. Digital economy is predicted to become one the most important components to create the basis for long-term development in the EAEU and support the region upgrading in GVCs providing the access to more value-added operations. Up to now, there has been scarce research covering these issues (Mcglinchey and Johnson 2007; Uffelmann 2011; Sheryazdanova Butterfield 2017; Wilson 2009).

The chapter is organized as follows. The first part introduces EAEU member-states' current positions in the global ICT market, these countries' readiness for digital economy, and current digital divide between the EAEU. The next part discusses the main pillars for further regional development including the discussion of EAEU Digital Agenda and official development assistance (ODA) contribution in narrowing the existing digital divide.

8.2 EAEU Current Positions in the Global Digital Economy

The level of digital economy development in the region can be estimated with the application of indexes produced by international institutions, access to ICT infrastructure, ICT trade and e-commerce developments.

EAEU digital economy development is far from homogeneity. The digital divide between the member-states still exists, in spite of the contribution from midterm initiatives for the single digital space creation initiated in 2016 by the Eurasian Economic Council.

The level of ICT development and readiness for the digital transformation of the economy of member-states could be assessed using the aggregated data from International Telecommunication Union (ITU) ICT Development Index, ITU Global Cybersecurity Index, UN E-Government Survey, and UNCTAD B2C E-commerce. These indexes reflect the level of ICT infrastructure, e-commerce, and e-public services development, making it possible to estimate the digital divide in the global economy. These indexes provide the basis for the digital divide assessment within EAEU (see Table 8.1).

The ITU ICT Development Index reflects the level of ICT infrastructure development and ICT usage and skills, combining 14 indicators for

Table 8.1 International indexes covering ICT and digital facilities development in EAEU (the latest available data)

Index/ EAEU country	*Republic of Armenia*	*Republic of Belarus*	*Republic of Kazakhstan*	*Kyrgyz Republic*	*Russian Federation*
ITU ICT Development Index (2017)	75	32	52	109	45
ITU Global Cybersecurity Index (2018)	79	69	40	111	26
UN E-Government Survey	87	38	39	91	32
UNCTAD B2C E-commerce (2017)	78	44	51	117	43

Source: ICT development index 2017. ITU 2017. https://www.itu.int/net4/ITU-D/idi/2017/index.html; ITU Global Cybersecurity Index 2018. ITU (2018). Retrieved from: https://www.itu.int/dms_pub/itu-d/opb/str/D-STR-GCI.01-2018-PDF-E.pdf; UN E-Government Survey 2018. Retrieved from https://publicadministration.un.org/egovkb/Portals/egovkb/Documents/un/2018-Survey/E-Governmentpercent20Surveypercent202018_FINALpercent20forpercent20web.pdf, https://unctad.org/en/PublicationsLibrary/tn_unctad_ict4d09_en.pdf, UNCTAD B2C E-commerce index. UNCTAD Technical Notes on ICT for Development N°9, 2017. Retrieved from https://unctad.org/en/PublicationsLibrary/tn_unctad_ict4d09_en.pdf

the 176 states. The ITU Global Cybersecurity Index reflects the ability of the states to address cybersecurity risks. The index is based on the analysis of the legal environment, technical infrastructure, organizational measures, and capacity building and cooperation measures for 175 states. The UN E-Government Survey provides understanding of the e-government services development, ranking 193 UN member-states. The last index to be considered—UNCTAD B2C E-commerce—is one of the newest for UN, covering 152 states to provide the understanding of the countries' progress in e-commerce development in the B2C sector. The latter was chosen as one e-commerce segment from which the majority, by and large, of UN member-states collect data.

The indexes reflect significant disproportions in ICT infrastructure development within the EAEU. The member-states could be arranged into two groups with Russia, Belarus and Kazakhstan occupying leading roles. Russia, being one of the recognized global ICT technological leaders, is enjoying the highest rankings for ICTs and e-commerce development. It is followed by Belarus and Kazakhstan, which are now implementing

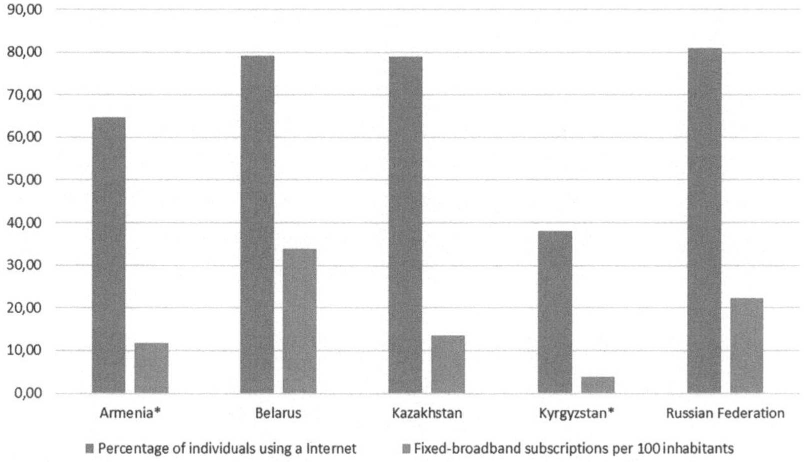

Fig. 8.1 ICT connectivity in EAEU member-states, 2018. (Source: Compiled by the author based on ITU ICT database. Retrieved from: https://www.itu.int/net4/ITU-D/icteye/#/countries. *The latest data for Armenia and Kyrgyzstan for percentage of individuals using Internet is available for 2017)

national strategies in order to support their local ICT markets and promote the export activities. The second group could be composed of Armenia and Kyrgyzstan, which are facing an insufficient level of ICT connectivity, being highly dependent on ICT technologies imports with a lack of inclusion in e-commerce. However, transport infrastructure projects in the region are also contributing to the increase in digital connectivity in EAEU member-states from Central Asian (OECD 2018).

According to ITU ICT data, Armenia and Kyrgyzstan face a lack of fixed broadband connectivity and Internet usage, which are both essential for e-commerce and digital services implications (see Fig. 8.1)

The digital divide in Internet connectivity is highly dependent not only on equipment availability but also on price policies of telecommunication companies. For developing countries, the share of expenditure on mobile and Internet connections is high in terms of their share in total household expenditures. The latest improvements of international indexes for ICT and digital services development for EAEU member-states were supported by a price reduction for the fixed-broadband basket (see Fig. 8.2). Nonetheless, the pricing for fixed-broadband Internet connection still

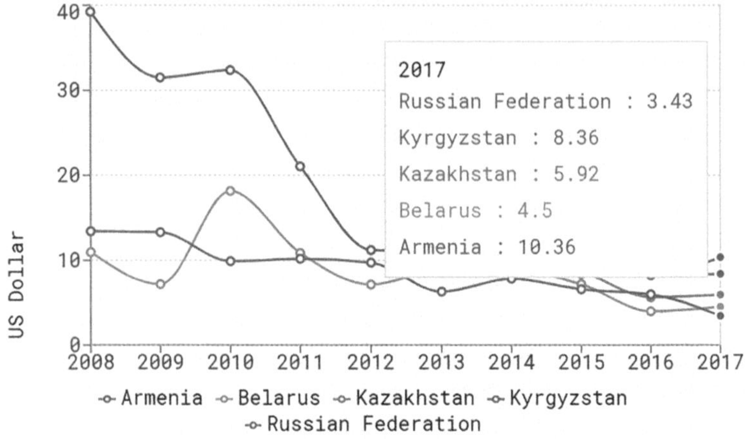

Fig. 8.2 Fixed broadband basket for EAEU member-states, 2008–2017, in $. (Source: Compiled by the author based on ICT Price Baskets (IPB). Retrieved from: https://www.itu.int/net4/ITU-D/ipb/)

varies within the EAEU, with the lowest in Russia $3.43 to the highest $10.36 in Armenia.

This low level of fixed-broadband connections is partly compensated by the high level of mobile connectivity in the EAEU. In 2018, all the member-states saw the indicator for mobile-cellular telephone subscriptions per 100 inhabitants overcoming the level of 122. That makes comparisons with developed economies possible.

One of the key drivers for the expansion of mobile Internet in the region was low pricing. According to experts from Cable.co.uk, in 2019 Kyrgyzstan was the EAEU leader for the average cost of 1 GB of mobile Internet with $0.027, and the most expensive one between the member-states was recorded in Belarus of $2.65 as it was ranked the 50th of 230 countries.[1] However, even a low price is not very conducive for mobile Internet penetration in Armenia and Kyrgyzstan, where the mobile connection share in 80 per cent of households represents 10 per cent of their expenditures (World Bank 2017).

[1] Worldwide mobile data pricing: The cost of 1 GB of mobile data in 230 countries. Cable.co.uk 2019. https://www.cable.co.uk/mobiles/worldwide-data-pricing/.

ICT infrastructure development is dependent on ICT goods imports of which EAEU member-states are net-importers (EDB 2019). ICT production is concentrated in South-East Asia with engineering designing carried out in the USA and Europe. During the past decades, the production of certain types of ICT equipment was allocated in Russia and Belarus, but it was not able to cover the local market demand for mobile phones, PCs, and other types of information technology and telecommunication equipment. Being mostly focused on assembling of ICT goods, Russia had a successful example of creating the regional value chain for mobile phone production, called Yotaphone, with its design in Russia and further production of components and assembling in China (Abramova and Garanina 2016).

The EAEU is more competitive in software and computer services, having Russia and Belarus as leaders in these fields. Nonetheless, it's worth mentioning that in outsourcing operations Russian and Belarusian companies are often competing, especially in price competition. Still, for all EAEU member-states software and computer services are considered important patterns for midterm development. The EAEU digital agenda is expected to support EAEU ICT exports for 50–74 per cent by 2025 (World Bank 2018a).

Nowadays, according to World Bank Database, the EAEU share in global exports of ICT services in 2017 was 1.2 per cent, having Russia and Belarus as the largest exporters between the member-states. The World Bank is considering all the shipments and deliveries of services abroad. Russia was responsible for around 71 per cent, seeing a steady increase in ICT service exports during the past decade despite the economic instability and sanctions that doubled from the level recorded for 2007 reaching $4.6 billion in 2017. The joint share of Armenia, Kyrgyzstan and Kazakhstan in ICT service exports is slowly increasing and reached around 6 per cent in 2017. Unfortunately, at the moment no assessment is provided for intra-regional trade in software and computer services between EAEU member-states.

Nevertheless, dependency of the member-states on ICT service exports is different between the countries, with the highest in Belarus (EDB 2019). For national ICT markets, this trend is positive and negative at the same time. On the one hand, it reflects the certain level of competitiveness achieved by local companies. On the other hand, when the country faces a low level of national consumption of software and computer services, this restrains the digital economy development within the country and makes it dependent on the economic situation in export destination as it was with India.

The other pillar for digital economy development is e-commerce. According to the classification introduced by Asian Development Bank Institute, European and Central Asian states could be split in three groups depending on the level of digital economy development—emerging, transition and transforming digital countries. EAEU member-states are considered emerging ones, lacking logistics infrastructure and online payments (Tan Shawn 2017). According to the Eurasian economic commission, the share of the EAEU in global digital trade is less than 1 per cent (EAEU 2019). The e-commerce market is influenced mainly by developments in Russia and China being the largest player in the field in Eurasia. It must be noted that Chinese business is enlarging its presence through different channels having the main One Belt, One Road program as its main umbrella project which is also promoting Chinese e-commerce companies in the EAEU. in OBOR E-commerce is considered essential for supporting the cross-border trade between the countries involved.[2] Besides, digital giants Huawei and Alibaba are investing in digital economy in Central Asia, supporting digital transformation in Kazakhstan and Kyrgyzstan. Russian digital companies, providing ICT services and software, are contributing the digital market development in EAEU. The leaders are Yandex, 1C, Kaspersky and so on.

8.3 Main Pillars for the Further Development of Digital Economy in the EAEU

The main drivers for digital economy development in the region are the adoption of the EAEU digital agenda, and step-by-step progress in the roadmap implementation for member-states supported by private and public companies' investments and Official Development Assistance (ODA) which supports solving the digital divide problem.

However, several tracks, including EAEU digital agenda implementation, midterm programs from multilateral organizations, and traditional and emerging donors, are progressing to pave the digital economy development in the EAEU.

[2]Vision and Actions on Jointly Building Silk Road Economic Belt and 21st-Century Maritime Silk Road. 2015/03/28 http://en.ndrc.gov.cn/newsrelease/201503/t20150330_669367.html.

The package of documents adopted by EAEU member-states provides the legal and regulation framework for regional digital projects. It is expected that regional level initiatives enhance the synergy from the implementation of the national digital economy programs adopted in 2015–2017 in EAEU member-states—“Digital Agenda of Armenia 2030” Strategy (2017), the Informatization Development Strategy for 2016–2022 (2015) and Decree “On the Digital Economy Development” (2017) in Belarus, “Digital Kazakhstan” State Program for 2018–2022 (2017), National Sustainable Development Strategy for 2018–2040 including State Informatization Project (2017) in Kyrgyzstan, “Digital Economy” National Program until 2024 (2017) in Russia.

Digital economy issues have been in the EAEU agenda since 2016 with the adoption of the Supreme Eurasian Economic Council the decision 135 on digital economy (EAEU 2016) and signing the Declaration on the EAEU Digital agenda. It was stated that digital economy is required for further economic development in the member-states, as it contributes to economic integration in the region, the improvement of public services, creating a better environment for innovations and increasing employment in high-tech industries and supporting competitiveness.

The next milestone in providing a legal basis to support digital transformation was the adoption of the EAEU Digital agenda until 2025 and creation of the high-level working group for its implementation in 2017.

The EAEU Digital agenda until 2025 is aimed to support the member-states transition to the next level of technological basis and economic growth, the creation of new markets and industries, improved competitiveness, and stimulation of the economic integration. Digital initiatives of the member states are at in the heart of Digital agenda implementation. Four main pillars are considered: digital transformation of the industrial sectors and cross-sectoral projects; transformation of services markets, the financial sector and labor through digital trade improvements; fin-tech innovations, venture capital investments in the field and increase in productivity and labor migration; and digital transformation management and infrastructure and information security. Relying on the matrix of these four pillars, the Eurasian Economic Commission (ECC) is arranging Digital Agenda Initiatives in eight groups covering digital trade, data flows, digital traceability, regulatory sandboxes, technology transfer and industrial cooperation, digital transport corridors to support logistics and supply chain effectiveness.

Joint efforts from the introduction of the Digital Agenda are considered more effective in comparison with the only national-level approach. The EAEU Digital Agenda until 2025 is expected to contribute heavily in economic developments in the region. According to the World Bank study the creation of a common digital space could contribute $42.3 billion to EAEU GDP. Digitalization is expected to support manufacturing, retail and services (World Bank 2018a). Digital services could be the main beneficiaries with the growth of the share in total exports from its current level of 28.3 up to the target 34–36 per cent in 2025 as indicated in EAEU Digital Agenda.

The Digital Development Agenda is now passing the first stages of implementation that are hard to assess. Nevertheless, the commitment to the digital transformation between member-states is high and promises positive midterm results.

The other pillar for digital economy development in EAEU member-states are development projects of international organizations with the leading role of development banks. The largest investors are the World Bank Group (WBG) and European bank for Reconstruction and Development (EBRD), according to the Eurasian Development Bank (EDB) (EDB 2019).

The EBRD mainly supported telecommunications infrastructure in EAEU member-states. At the moment the EBRD have a portfolio of the ICT projects at different stages in Russia, Kazakhstan, Kyrgyzstan and Belarus. In Armenia, there is no direct support to ICTs apart from indirectly through some finance provided in energy and power sector. In general, the share of ICT projects in the EAEU in the Bank's portfolio in the region for the period 1997–2018 is relatively low, varying from state to state. On the one hand, EAEU member-states from Central Asia are becoming more attractive for the donors' community who see the growing amount of support provided for digital development. On the other hand, the EBRD in Russia is not putting new projects in the pipeline since the Ukrainian crisis in 2014.

One of the ambitious plans in the EAEU has been introduced by WBG in Kyrgyzstan—Digital CASA Kyrgyz Republic Project (World Bank 2018b). The Digital CASA regional program for Central and Southern Asia aims to support digital economy development in the landlocked Asian economies. The finance provided by WBG for digital economy development in Kyrgyzstan totals $50 million—$39 billion of this financial support is planned to be invested in connectivity improvements and data centers, digital platforms and smart solutions, while the rest is for enabling the environment for the digital economy and management. In other member-states, WBG is supporting ICT connectivity through midterm initiatives. The only exclusion is Russia, having had no new projects in the pipeline since 2014.

The EDB, supporting through investment activities the ICT development in EAEU member-states, is another large multilateral donor institution in the EAEU. The EDB includes information technologies in the list of sectoral priorities to support development in partner countries. This is stated in the EDB Strategy for development for the period 2018–2022. At the moment six projects in ICT infrastructure development in the EAEU are in the pipeline.

UN agencies, having the mandate to support ICT and digital economy development, are less implemented in the EAEU. UN institutions are mainly providing support through technical assistance. UNCTAD is contributing digital economy development through support in ICT data collection. One of the most successful UNCTAD projects in supporting connectivity and trade in the EAEU is Customs Automation—ASYCUDA. UNCTAD is promoting the project in the EAEU with Kazakhstan as the pioneer system's user in the EAEU. In Kazakhstan the customs clearance duration recorded a fourfold reduction to 16 minutes instead of 1 hour after the implementation of the Secure e-Borders system component based on ASYCUDA (UNCTADb 2019).

Aid for Trade (AfT) initiative is contributing digital economy development having transport and storage, communications and energy generation and supply as a main infrastructure element for ODA commitments.

AfT is also boosting e-trade developments along with the EAEU Digital Agenda until 2030. AfT provided to EAEU member-states, excluding Russia (having donor status), totaled at $360.2 million in 2017, less than 1 per cent of the world AfT finance. Kazakhstan announced the donor status providing emergency finance but stays in the reciepients' group for AfT. The largest recipient was Armenia, enjoying more than a half of the total AfT to EAEU member-states (Table 8.2).

According to the OECD, recipient AfT Questionnaire assistance in boosting trade is considered an important part of further trade-related infrastructure improvements in Kazakhstan and Kyrgyzstan (OECD 2019). For communication sector development, these two countries

Table 8.2 Aid for Trade disbursements 2006–2017 in selected EAEU member-states ($ million)

	2006–2008 avg.	*2009–2011 avg.*	*2012–2014 avg.*	*2015*	*2016*	*2017*
Armenia	101.9	163.9	104.6	204.0	168.2	201.0
Belarus	4.0	14.7	12.2	14.1	15.7	22.3
Kazakhstan	100.3	58.5	33.8	15.9	34.2	7.8
Kyrgyzstan	54.5	82.6	129.6	156.2	114.8	129.2
Total Aid for Trade in EAEU	260.5	319.7	280.3	390.2	332.9	360.2

Source: Aid for Trade at a Glance 2019. Economic Diversification and Empowerment. OECD–WTO (2019)

received around $1 million in 2017. According to the WTO–OECD AfT report, commitments to ICT development are now mainly provided in the form of technical assistance to support improvements in sector regulations that later make the local market more attractive for FDI in hardware (OECD–WTO 2019). AfT is supported both at multilateral and bilateral levels in the EAEU. Japan, the United States, ADB, and International Development Association are in the list of the largest donors of AfT for EAEU member-states.

8.4 Conclusion

Digital economy development in the EAEU has great potential for enhancing economic growth in the region through growing connectivity, increase in e-commerce flows, the reduction of transactions costs and the implementation of digital government facilities.

The digital divide in ICT adoption and digital development is one of the obstacles to be eliminated through regional programs. Digital economy is considered to be the main contributor for long-term development in the EAEU. The ambitious regional initiative EAEU Digital Agenda until 2025 is considered to support digital economy growth, with a focus on improvements in industrial and services sectors, growth of internal and external trade relying on e-commerce, and logistic improvements through better and wide use of ICT facilities.

The leading role within the EAEU in digital agenda implementation belongs to Russia, Belarus and Kazakhstan. The leaders enjoy a high level of connectivity, growing exports in ICT services, and automation of public services. E-government digital services implementation is the highest in Russia, having Moscow as the most digitized city.

Kazakhstan and Kyrgyzstan are seeing progress in connectivity, being supported also by the Chinese One Belt, One road initiative. This project is running alongside the assistance provided through different mechanisms of development aid. Development banks, in collaboration with traditional donors, are contributing to digital economy development in the EAEU.

Further digital economy developments are dependent on the consequence implementation of the EAEU digital agenda, which provides the basis and pushes the digital transformation in member-states. ODA commitment in the ICT sector and AfT projects are expected to support the narrowing of digital divide between more advanced economies enjoying high-level of ICT connectivity and usage (Russia, Belarus and Kazakhstan) and those who lack these infrastructure and ICT skills (Armenia, Kyrgyzstan).

References

Abramova, A., & Garanina, O. (2016). The Role of Sanctions in the Internationalization of Russian Multinationals Toward China: The Case of Energy and ICT Sectors. In *The Challenge of Bric Multinationals*. Published online: November 29; 451–479.

EAEU. (2016). Supreme Eurasian Economic Council the Decision 135 on Digital Economy. Retrieved from https://docs.eaeunion.org/docs/en-us/01414600/cncd_13012017_135.

EAEU. (2019). Digital Trade Report.

EDB. (2019). Digital Potential of the Eurasian Development Bank Member-States. Retrieved from https://eabr.org/upload/iblock/0d5/EABR_Digital_Potential_06_2019.pdf.

ITU. (2018). ITU Global Cybersecurity Index 2018. Retrieved from https://www.itu.int/dms_pub/itu-d/opb/str/D-STR-GCI.01-2018-PDF-E.pdf.

ITU ICT Development Index. (2017). https://www.itu.int/net4/ITU-D/idi/2017/index.html.

Kasatkin, P. I., Kovalchuk, J. A., & Stepnov, I. M. (2019). The Modern Universities Role in the Formation of the Digital Wave of Kondratiev's Long Cycles. *Voprosy Ekonomiki, 12,* 123–140 (In Russian). https://doi.org/10.32609/0042-8736-2019-12-123-140.

Mcglinchey, E., & Johnson, E. (2007). Aiding the Internet in Central Asia. *Democratization*, 14(2), 273–288, 83–94.

OECD. (2013). *Interconnected Economies: Benefiting from Global Value Chains.* Paris: OECD.

OECD. (2018). *Enhancing Competitiveness in Central Asia, Competitiveness and Private Sector Development*. Paris: OECD Publishing.

OECD. (2019). Aid for Trade Self-assessments from Partner Countries. Retrieved from https://www.oecd.org/aidfortrade/aidfortradeself-assessments frompartnercountries.htm.

OECD–WTO. (2019). Aid for Trade at a Glance 2019. Economic Diversification and Empowerment. OECD-WTO.

Sheryazdanova, G., & Butterfield, J. (2017). E-government as an Anti-corruption Strategy in Kazakhstan. *Journal of Information Technology & Politics., 14*(1), 83–94.

Tan Shawn, W. (2017). *Digital Trade in Europe and Central Asia*. ADBI Working Paper Series No. 751, June. Retrieved from https://www.adb.org/sites/default/files/publication/324996/adbi-wp751.pdf.

Uffelmann, D. (2011). Post-Russian Eurasia and the Proto-Eurasian Usage of the Runet in Kazakhstan: A Plea for a Cyberlinguistics Turn Area Studies. *Journal of Eurasian Studies, 2*(2011), 172–183.

UN. (2018). UN E-Government Survey 2018. Retrieved from https://publicadministration.un.org/egovkb/Portals/egovkb/Documents/un/2018-Survey/E-Government per cent20Survey per cent202018_FINAL per cent20for per cent20web.pdf.

UNCTAD. (2017). UNCTAD Information Economy Report 2017. Digitalization, Trade and Development. Retrieved from https://unctad.org/en/PublicationsLibrary/ier2017_en.pdf.

UNCTAD B2C E-commerce Index. (2017). UNCTAD Technical Notes on ICT for Development N°9. Retrieved from https://unctad.org/en/Publications Library/tn_unctad_ict4d09_en.pdf.

UNCTAD. (2019). UNCTAD Digital economy report 2019. https://unctad.org/system/files/official-document/der2019_en.pdf.

UNCTADa. (2019). UNCTAD Digital Economy Report 2019. Retrieved from https://unctad.org/en/PublicationsLibrary/der2019_en.pdf.

UNCTADb. (2019). ASYCUDA Newsletter. Retrieved from https://unctad.org/en/PublicationsLibrary/dtlasycuda_misc2019d1_en.pdf.

Wilson, A. (2009). Computer Gap. *Problems of Post-communism, 56*(4), 41–51.

World Bank. (2017). Reaping Digital Dividends: Leveraging the Internet for Development in Europe and Central Asia. Retrieved from https://www.worldbank.org/en/region/eca/publication/digital-dividends-in-eca.

World Bank. (2018a). The EAEU 2025 Digital Agenda: Prospects and Recommendations—Overview Report. Retrieved from http://documents.worldbank.org/curated/en/850581522435806724/pdf/EAEU-Overview-Full-ENG-Final.pdf.

World Bank. (2018b). World Bank Financed Project to Support Digital-Transformation in Kyrgyz Republic. Retrieved from https://www.worldbank.org/en/news/press-release/2018/03/20/new-world-bank-financed-project-to-support-digital-transformation-in-kyrgyz-republic.

CHAPTER 9

Labour Mobility in the Eurasian Economic Union: New Opportunities and Challenges

Anna N. Tsibulina

9.1 Introduction

The Eurasian Economic Union (EAEU) is a rather new integration entity. In a very short time, it has reached a stage of a Common Market with free movement of goods, services, capital and labour. It should be noted, therefore, that all the members states of the EAEU are former Soviet republics. There have been various integration initiatives prior to the establishment of the EAEU but none of them have gone that far regarding the liberalization of free movement of workers. Just after the collapse of the USSR some experts believed that it would be easy to preserve and develop existing economic and social ties. The reality turned out to be different.

As long as the economic situation in some of the CIS countries started to worsen in the 1990s, the labour force started to move to more attractive destinations in terms of availability of jobs, higher salaries and better living conditions. Russia became the main centre of attraction for migrants

A. N. Tsibulina (✉)
MGIMO University, Moscow, Russia
e-mail: a.tsibulina@inno.mgimo.ru

N. A. Piskulova (ed.), *The Economic Dimension of Eurasian Integration*, https://doi.org/10.1007/978-3-030-59886-0_9

because the older population of the CIS countries had good knowledge of the Russian language and degrees obtained in accordance with the single education standards. Due to high numbers of illegal migration and increasing threats of criminal activities, the CIS countries including Russia tightened their labour migration regulation. Within the EAEU, the paradigm regarding the labour migration has changed to now being predominantly perceived as an instrument for smoothing social and economic disparities between the member-states and a source of economic development.

In general, the literature on the EAEU Labour Market is rather limited. The works usually cover certain aspects of its functioning such as legislative regulation (Aliev 2016; Iontseva 2016) or situations in the labour markets of its member-states (Sagynbekova 2017; Luzina et al. 2019). A very substantial overview of the EAEU Labour Market is given by E. Vinokurov (2018) in Introduction to the Eurasian Economic Union.

This chapter explores the preconditions for the efficient functioning of the EAEU Common Labour Market and its strong and weak sides. The first part of the chapter details the main characteristics of the national labour markets and migration policies, demographic and employment developments. Then, we describe the current regulatory system of the EAEU labour market with a focus on workers' rights and regulatory gaps which still exist. The final part of the chapter analyses the importance of the free movement of labour for the economies of the EAEU member-states, citizens' attitudes to labour migrants and possible initiatives which could improve the functioning of the common labour marker. The chapter ends with conclusions.

9.2 National Labour Markets in the Eurasian Economic Union

The member states of the Eurasian Economic Union differ significantly from each other in terms of the size of their territories, their level of economic development, and the size of their population. Those have an impact on the situation in their labour markets as well. For example, the Russian labour market exceeds in aggregate the labour markets of the Republic of Kazakhstan and the Republic of Belarus by about five times. As we can see in Table 9.1 the population of Armenia is almost nine times smaller than that of Russia and its natural increase has been slowing down. The population has been declining in all EAEU countries in the recent

Table 9.1 Dynamics of the main labour market indicators in the EAEU member states

Country	*Year*	*The number of the resident population on January 1*	*Occupational ratio (per cent)*	*Unemployment rate (per cent)*
Armenia	2015	3,010,598	48.1	18.5
	2016	2,998,577	45.6	18.0
	2017	2,986,151	46.2	17.8
Belarus	2015	9,480,868	68.2	5.2
	2016	9,498,364	73.2	5.8
	2017	9,504,704	74.4	5.6
Kazakhstan	2015	17,415,715	72.2	5.1
	2016	17,669,896	72.9	5.0
	2017	17,918,214	72.9	4.9
Kyrgyzstan	2015	5,985,062	60.9	7.6
	2016	6,019,480	60.3	7.2
	2017	6,140,200	59.1	6.9
Russia	2015	146,069,531	70.3	5.6
	2016	146,544,710	70.9	5.5
	2017	146,544,372	61.8	5.2
EAEU	2017	184,006,230	63.1	5.4

Source: Eurasian Economic Commission (2019a)

years. The biggest natural population decrease in 2017 took place in Russia and amounted for 135,818 people, and in Belarus 16,775 people. The ratio of the employed population to average resident population aged 15–64 is highest in Kazakhstan and Belarus at about 73 per cent. Armenia and Kyrgyzstan have the highest unemployment rates at around 17 and 7 per cent, respectively (Eurasian Economic Commission 2019a).

Wage rates differ substantially across the member-states, implying that workers might have a stimulus to leave their native countries in search of better salaries. The lowest average monthly nominal wages in 2018 were in Kyrgyzstan ($238.6) and Armenia ($357.6), while the highest one was in Russia ($699.1). Since 2015—the year of establishment of the EAEU—that indicator has increased in Russia (by $138), Belarus (by $63) and Kyrgyzstan (by $29), considerably decreased in Kazakhstan (by $96), and stayed basically unchanged in Armenia (by $1.5). The minimum guaranteed wages have increased in all the member-states except Armenia where it remained practically the same for the period 2015–2018. The minimum wage has almost doubled in Russia (from $85.6 in 2015 to $165.9 in

2018) and in Kyrgyzstan (from $12.8 in 2015 to $23.8 in 2018) (Eurasian Economic Commission 2019a).

The intensity of labour flows within the EAEU is also dependant on the national migration policies of the member-states. Besides that, migration can help to address negative demographic trends such as ageing and population decline. In 2011, the President of the Russian Federation Vladimir Putin stated that the migration inflow was needed at around 300 thousand people per year (Putin 2012). The State Migration Policy Concept for the period 2019–2025 was signed by President Putin in October 2018; the previous concept, approved in 2012, was therefore terminated. The new policy concept aims to create such a migration situation that will help to improve social and economic conditions, demographic development and guarantee state security. It is also stipulated in the Concept that Russia's international cooperation in the field of migration should ensure the mutual interests of EAEU member-states. The total number of workers Russia needed to attract was 144,583 in 2019. The highest demand for workers was observed in the sectors of construction (52,075), skilled workers in large and small enterprises (20,545) as well as metal and machine building workers (16,090) were also in need (Talukdar 2019).

The migration and demographic policy of Belarus is quite similar to the Russian policy in this field. It also considers migration as an instrument for economic development. Kazakhstan also actively accepts migrants, including those who come based on ethnic affinity (the program for the return of ethnic Kazakhs—oralmans) to maintain the ethnocultural balance, as well as labour migrants compensate for the shortage of labour resources. Armenia and Kyrgyzstan are more oriented towards stimulating emigration, developing ties with their diasporas abroad and attracting their funds to the development of the national economy (Ryazantsev 2017).

The Russian Federation remains the leading EAEU country in accepting labour migrants from the other member-states. In 2018, around 352 thousand citizens of Kazakhstan, 21 thousand citizens of Armenia, 13 thousand citizens of Belarus and 111 thousand citizens of Kazakhstan entered Russia as labour migrants. The second country of destination for labour force from the EAEU is Kazakhstan. It is interesting to note that the share of labour migrants from Russia who arrive there annually is the biggest, comprising 24,816 people in 2018. In comparison, the number of labour migrants who came from Kyrgyzstan, a neighbouring country to Kazakhstan, was just 5493 people in 2018 (Eurasian Economic Commission 2019b). The number of Russian workers who go to Belarus has been increasing since 2016. In 2018, it reached its record number of 4126 people, though in previous years that number had been slightly more than 2000 people per year. The least attractive countries within the EAEU for labour migrants are Kyrgyzstan and Armenia. The total number of citizens from the member-states who entered Armenia in 2018 was 54, and no workers at all entered Kyrgyzstan since 2016.

The highest shares of self-employed people are in Armenia (41 per cent in 2018) and Kyrgyzstan (35 per cent in 2018) according to the data of the World Bank (World Bank 2019). Self-employed workers include four sub-categories of employers, own-account workers (without hired employees), members of producers' cooperatives, and contributing family workers (generally unpaid). The levels of workers with higher and secondary vocational education in Armenia (29 and 20 per cent in 2015, respectively) and in Kyrgyzstan (21 and 10 per cent in 2015, respectively) are also lower than in other member-states. The abovementioned characteristics of the labour markets could allow the countries to gain certain benefits due to the EAEU's need to increase the level of business activity among their populations (Vinokurov 2018).

9.3 Free Movement of Labour: Regulatory Framework

Free movement of labour is laid down in the Treaty on the Eurasian Economic Union that entered into force in 2015. Chapter XXVI of the Treaty covers issues related to the free movement of workers within the Union. Article 97 stipulates the abolition of any restrictions for the protection of labour markets of member-states. Restrictions can only be applied on the basis of ensuring national security (e.g. protection of economic sectors of strategic importance) and public order. Even though the Treaty prohibits imposing any restrictions, there are still cases when employers violate the law and refuse to hire citizens of certain nationalities (Osadchaya 2017; Vinokurov 2018).

Workers of the member states are not required to have their education documents (certificates, diplomas) recognized, unless they are going to work in educational, legal, medical or pharmaceutical spheres. If a person wants to work in those spheres, he or she will have to undergo a procedure of recognizing the education documents in accordance with the national legislation of the member state where he/she intends to work. Workers from EAEU countries do not have to obtain employment permits (so called "patents" which are normally one-year long) as happens in the case of workers coming from other CIS countries. At the same time there are some difficulties regarding the recognition of education documents. Those difficulties usually arise from certain differences in national education systems (Kasatkin et al. 2019). For instance, Master of Business Administration (MBA) and Doctor of Business Administration programs are regarded as additional postgraduate education in Russia. The situation is the opposite in Kazakhstan where the same programs have the status of professional postgraduate training programs and graduates obtain degrees of MBA or DBA. That is formally those diplomas cannot be recognized in both countries (Aliev 2016). Recognition of doctorate degrees and academic statuses is necessary in accordance with the bilateral agreements in EAEU member-states. Russia and Belarus have much better integrated education systems and thus doctorate degrees and academic statuses are automatically recognized in both countries.

The Treaty gives workers from the Union the right to bring their family members to live in a country of employment. Besides that, family members enjoy rights to receive free medical assistance (including urgent and non-urgent care), education (including pre-school education) for their children, and some other types of social protection on the same conditions as the nationals of the member state. However, healthcare systems in member-states differ considerably, resulting in additional complications for migrant workers when they need to get medical assistance. Workers can stay in a host country as long as they have a valid employment contract, or a civil law contract and they can also join trade unions. The period of employment in one of the EAEU countries will become a part of a worker's total record of employment, thus allowing them to get all the social benefits foreseen by national law. The level of income tax is now the same as for nationals of a host state. The size of income tax is 13 per cent in Russia and workers from the EAEU countries have to pay exactly the same amount, while workers from other countries have to pay 30 per cent income tax.

Upon arrival in a member state, a potential worker should fill out a migration card and indicate "work" as a purpose of visit. If he/she wants to stay in the country for more than 30 days in order to find a job, then he/she should register with the competent authority. The total duration of stay without a labour contract is 90 days (30 days without a need for registration plus an additional 60 days). Rights and obligations of workers are also stipulated in the Treaty.

Despite the considerable advantages provided by the Treaty there are still some practices which needed to be overcome. Low-skilled workers have traditionally preferred to work without labour contracts for a number of reasons: lack of information on required documents, long and complicated bureaucratic procedures, higher taxes for workers. Employers who hire low-skilled workers are also often reluctant to sign labour contracts with migrant workers due to the need to pay labour taxes. Thus, labour migrants might become a part of the shadow economy in the EAEU.

Another issue that complicates the regulation is the existence of various bilateral agreements on labour migration which might jeopardize the liberal provisions of the EAEU Treaty. The member-states should harmonize their national legislation in accordance with the provisions of the Treaty in order to avoid development of alternative controls on free movement of labour.

In the report on barriers, exemptions and restrictions in the EAEU (so called "White Paper") prepared by the Eurasian Economic Commission (EEC) in 2017, only one restriction was identified (Eurasian Economic Commission 2017). This is the non-availability of equal conditions of provision of pension guarantees to nationals of member-states in the territory of the member-states. The Board of the Commission in 2016 approved a draft of an international agreement to address the issue of pension provision in the EAEU. The draft agreement aims to create and protect equal rights for workers in the field of pension provision and developing cooperation on pension issues between the member-states (Aliev 2016; Eurasian Economic Commission 2018). It is important to specify in the agreement that each state will pay a worker a pension calculated based on his/her duration of employment in that state. It is envisaged in the draft agreement that the size of pensions cannot be reduced, and their payment cannot be suspended or terminated on the basis of the residence of the worker in the territory of another member state (Aliev 2016; Eurasian Economic Commission 2018). At its meeting on 2 February 2018 the Eurasian Intergovernmental Council called the Eurasian Economic Commission and the member-states to continue work on aligning positions on pension regulations and the agreement provisions. Finally, the Agreement on the Provision of Pensions for Workers in the EAEU was signed in 2019 at a meeting of the Supreme Eurasian Economic Council and ratified by all the member-states in 2020. It is expected to enter into force in 2021. According to the Agreement, a member-state will pay a retired worker a monthly pension based on the length of his/her service when in that state.

Another obstacle identified by the EEC is the lack of unified approaches available in the Union regarding implementation of administrative procedures in internal borders between member-states (White Paper). The department on Labour Migration in the EEC is the main body responsible for this kind of work and also for guidance and implementation of the common migration policy, harmonization and (or) unification of the legislation, the removal of barriers to the free movement of labour, and promotion of cooperation among member-states.

The Treaty grants many benefits and rights to potential labour migrants, but the question of which institution must be responsible for protection of the labour migrants' rights has so far not been solved. The Eurasian Economic Commission cannot bring a member state or an employer to the Court of the Eurasian Economic Union if they do not comply with the Union's legislation. This implies that disputes are to be solved at the political level. In order to improve the situation with implementation and compliance with the legislation an online resource called "Information Portal of the Eurasian Economic Union" has recently been launched. Any individual can refer a case to the Eurasian Economic Commission via this portal and its officials will give clarifications or at least register the problem for further analysis.

9.4 The Common Labour Market: First Results

The free movement of labour allows the important factor of production as labour to be efficiently allocated among the member-states of an integration entity. This implies that labour moves to where it can receive the highest return within an economic union, then total output for the union as a whole will be maximized (Larry 2007). In an economic union where standards of living, unemployment rates and wages differ substantially across member-states, the free movement of labour can also smooth social disparities and tensions.

That is the case of the EAEU, in a manner. The unemployment rate in Armenia was close to 18 per cent in 2017, while in the other EAEU countries this indicator was between 5 and 6 per cent. The lowest minimum guaranteed wage is $23.8 in Kyrgyzstan and the highest one is Russia at $165.9 (Eurasian Economic Commission 2019a). The free movement of workers leads not only to lower levels of unemployment in countries where migrants come from, but also means inflow of money into a country through money transfers (remittances) of citizens who work abroad.

In 2017, remittances from migrant workers represented 32 per cent of Kyrgyzstan's GDP and that was the largest share among the EAEU countries (see Fig. 9.1).

In 2017, the share of remittances in the GDP of Armenia was 13 per cent—the second-largest share among the EAEU. The importance of remittances for a country's GDP is minimal for Russia and Kazakhstan as they account for 1 per cent of GDP. In Belarus, this indicator is around 2 per cent of GDP. Russia is the main country where remittances come from; its share in the EAEU intra-regional inflow of remittances is 60 per cent and around 27 per cent in the total EAEU inflow of remittances.

Remittances from Russia account for more than 90 per cent of all the remittances coming from the rest of the EAEU to member-states. Remittances from Russia amounted to 25 per cent of GDP of Kyrgyzstan and to 8 per cent of Armenian GDP in 2017. Kazakhstan is the main source of remittances for Russia among the EAEU and its share is 74 per cent in total remittances sent within the EAEU (The Global Knowledge Partnership on Migration and Development (KNOMAD 2019). That

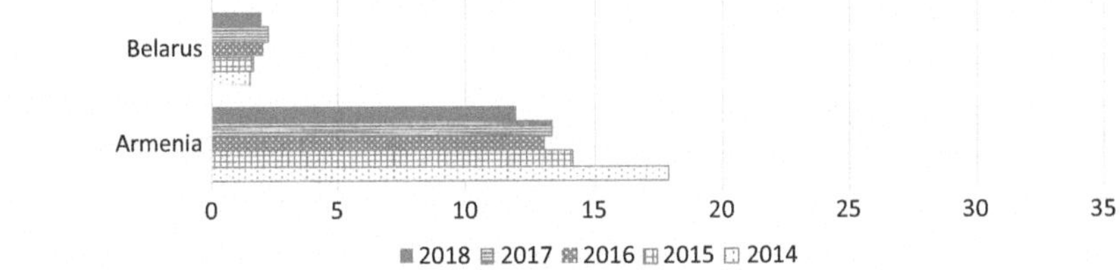

Fig. 9.1 Personal remittances, received (per cent of GDP). (Source: Compiled by the author based on data from the World Bank. Retrieved from https://data.worldbank.org/indicator/BX.TRF.PWKR.DT.GD.ZS?end=2019&start=1993&view=chart)

implies that the majority of EAEU countries depend on the demand in the Russia's labour market and economic situation in the country.

Most of the countries have been experiencing migration outflow (see Fig. 9.2) except for Russia and Belarus.

Besides economic gains that migration might bring to the citizens and the integration entity as a whole, it might be a source of both social gains and risks. The positive outcome of increased labour migration would be a better social and cultural integration between member-states. At the same time, a large inflow of foreign workers might lead to social tensions between migrant and native employees. Citizens' perceptions of various integration initiatives were analyzed in annual surveys known as "Integration Barometers" conducted by the Eurasian Development Bank. According to the latest report published in 2017 (EDB 2017) the most interested countries in attracting labour migrants from the CIS countries were Kazakhstan (42 per cent), Belarus (41 per cent) and Kyrgyzstan (40 per cent). At the same time citizens of Russia (21 per cent) and Armenia (32 per cent) were much less inclined to accept labour migrants.

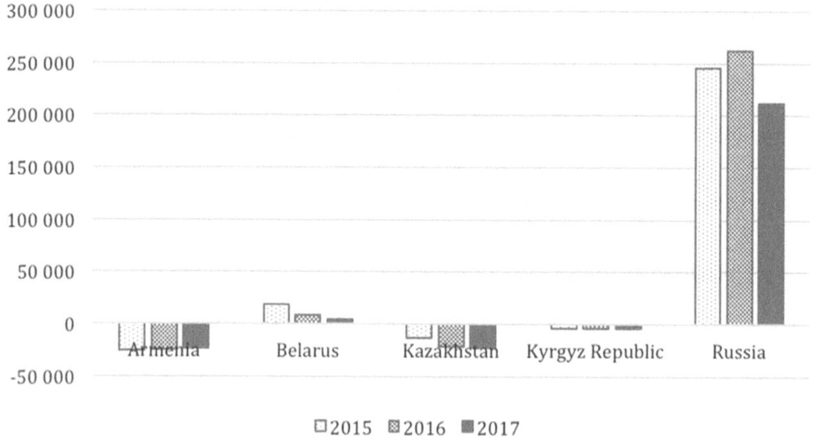

Fig. 9.2 Migration inflow (+) and outflow (-). (Source: Compiled by the author based on data from Eurasian Economic Commission. Retrieved from http://www.eurasiancommission.org/ru/act/integr_i_makroec/dep_stat/econstat/Pages/express_demography.aspx)

The demand for Russian specialists remains high. Around 40 per cent of respondents considered inflow of Russian workers to be positive for the economy.

The report also tried to estimate migration intentions of the population. The most popular destination for employment for the citizens of Kyrgyzstan (30 per cent) and Armenia (25 per cent) was said to be Russia. It looks like that in the long run Russia will be keeping a migration gain. In contrast, Kyrgyzstan and Armenia are expected to be experiencing a negative migratory balance while Kazakhstan and Belarus will keep a neutral migration gain (Balas et al. 2016).

Most migrants—especially from Kyrgyzstan—have been working in unskilled jobs for a pretty long time. The accession of the country to the EAEU positively impacted migrants' labour activities according to Abdygany Shakirov, Director of interregional public organization "Kyrgyz Birimdigi" in Moscow. He noted that "...if many of our migrants earlier worked as yardmen, cleaners and now we can see our citizens in good jobs particularly not only working at the cash registers of supermarkets and hypermarkets, but also managing departments. Many work in the banking sector" (Sagynbekova 2017).

Employment of migrants in low-skilled jobs can also be a result of the fact that labour migration is primarily driven not by better career opportunities or working conditions but by pure social and economic conditions.

Diasporas networks and friends serve as the main source for finding jobs. The dominant share of low skill-skilled workers in EAEU labour migration might cause serious challenges to the social and cultural adaption of those workers in host countries (Ryazantsev 2017). At the same time, excessive outflow of high-level professionals, or a "brain-drain", will complicate the economic development of the countries.

In order to make migration of workers more balanced, it would make sense to create a joint database at the EAEU level with information on available vacancies in all the member-states. The EAEU common labour market can only reach its full potential if the member-states constantly cooperate with each other on many issues including harmonization of legislation, protection of migrant workers' rights and social guarantees, and actively engage in social and cultural adaptation programs.

9.5 Conclusion

Prior to the establishment of the EAEU, the regulation of labour migration was primarily based on bilateral agreements between the former USSR republics. The Treaty of the EAEU considerably liberalized and unified the rules of labour migration between the five member-states. The Treaty prohibits governments from imposing any restrictions or using discriminative practices regarding workers coming from other member-states. EAEU labour migrants enjoy almost the same rights as national workers, including recognizing diplomas, the same rate of income taxes, free medical care, and a number of social benefits for their family members.

There are still some obstacles on the route to free movement of labour. First of all, unified regulation of pension provisions for migrant workers has been lacking. It is expected that the entry into force of the Agreement on Pension Provision in the EAEU will stipulate the terms and conditions of pension support. Another obstacle is related to different administrative procedures in internal borders between member-states.

Labour migration in the EAEU helps to address the issue of economic and social disparities between the countries. Differences in unemployment rates, salaries, the number of working population, and workers' qualifications lead to the situation when some countries as Russia and Kazakhstan become recipients of migrant workers while Kyrgyzstan and Armenia remain the main suppliers of labour force within the Union.

Remittances serve as an important instrument to improve living conditions of citizens in member-states with high unemployment rates, low salaries or to mitigate the effects of negative economic shocks. Money transfers sent by Kyrgyz workers employed in other EAEU countries accounted for 78 per cent of total inflow money transfers when the volume of remittances from Russia amounted to 25 per cent of GDP in 2017. Armenia is also quite dependent on remittances from Russia though to lesser extent than Kyrgyzstan.

It is expected that demand for foreign workers will remain in Russia as the main destination for labour migrants from the EAEU at the moment. In case of sustainable inflow of workers or increased labour migration, social and cultural tensions might increase in Russia as well as other migrant-accepting countries. Though the relatively recent opinion polls held in 2017 didn't show negative attitudes to labour migrants in EAEU countries, that sort of developments must be closely monitored.

The Eurasian Economic Commission, together with member-states, should intensify their efforts in the protection of workers' rights, fighting illegal migration, and employment without contracts, as well as finding common ground on approaches to further development of new opportunities that can be provided by the Common Labour Market.

References

Aliev, S. (2016). Trudovaya migratsia v Evraziyskov ekonomicheskom soyuze. *Pravovaya informatika, 2*, 34–45.

Balas, P., Emerson, M., Havlik, P., Kabat, P., Kofner, J., Pereboyev, V., Rovenskaya, E., Stepanova, A., & Vinokurov, E. (2016). *Labour Market and Migration across the Eurasian. Continent IIASA Project 'Challenges and Opportunities of Economic Integration within a Wider Eureopan and Eurasian Space' Workshop Report.* Retrieved from http://pure.iiasa.ac.at/id/eprint/13964/1/Laborpercent20marketpercent20andpercent20migrationpercent20acrosspercent20thepercent20Eurasianpercent20continent.pdf.

EDB. (2017). *Integration Barometer.* Report No. 46. Eurasian Development Bank. Retrieved from https://eabr.org/upload/iblock/3ef/EDB-Centre_2017_Report-46_EDB-Integration-Barometer_ENG_2.pdf.

Eurasian Economic Commission. (2017). *Barriers, Derogations and Restrictions in the Eurasian Economic Union.* Report. Retrieved from http://www.eurasian-commission.org/ru/Documents/BARRIERS,percent20DEROGATIONSpercent20ANDpercent20RESTRICTIONSpercent20INpercent20THEpercent20EURASIANpercent20ECONOMICpercent20UNIONpercent20ANNUALpercent20REPORTpercent202017.pdf.

Eurasian Economic Commission. (2018). Disposition No. 5 of the Intergovernmental Council of the Eurasian Economic Union on the issues related to the implementation of the Treaty on pension provisions to workers of the Member States of the Eurasian Economic Union. Retrieved from https://docs.eaeunion.org/en-us/Pages/DisplayDocument.aspx?s=percent7Be1f13d1d-5914-465c-835f-2aa3762edddapercent7D&w=9260b414-defe-45cc-88a3-eb5c73238076&l=percent7B8a412e96-924f-4b3c-8321-0d5e767e5f91percent7D&EntityID=16861.

Eurasian Economic Commission. (2019a). Statistics. Retrieved from http://www.eurasiancommission.org/ru/act/integr_i_makroec/dep_stat/econstat/Pages/express_inf.aspx.

Eurasian Economic Commission. (2019b). Statistics. Retrieved from http://www.eurasiancommission.org/ru/act/finpol/migration/tm/Documents/Сведенияpercent20opercent20численностиpercent20гражданpercent20государствpercent202013-percent201percent20полугодиеpercent202019.pdf.

Iontseva, S. V. (2016). Prospects for the formation of the common labor market of the EAEU: Legal features. *Migration and Social Development, 1*(2), 111–124.

Kasatkin, P. I., Kovalchuk, J. A., & Stepnov, I. M. (2019). The Modern Universities Role in the Formation of the Digital Wave of Kondratiev's Long Cycles. *Voprosy Ekonomiki*, 12, 123–140 (In Russian). https://doi.org/10.32609/0042-8736-2019-12-123-140.

KNOMAD. (2019). The Global Knowledge Partnership on Migration and Development (KNOMAD). *Data*. Retrieved from https://www.knomad.org/data/remittances.

Larry, N. (2007). *The Economics of Europe and the European Union* (p. 143). Cambridge University Press.

Luzina, T., Efimova, O., & Vysotskaya, V. (2019). Labour Market of the Eurasian Economic Union: The Leading Role of Migration. Advances in Social Science, Education and Humanities Research, Vol. 318. Retrieved from https://www.atlantis-press.com/proceedings.

Osadchaya, G. (2017). Formirovanie edinogo rynka truda Evraziyskogo ekonomicheskogo soyuza kak uslovie usprshnosti integratsionnykh protsessov EAES. Sotsiologicheskie issledovaniya [Sociological Studies]. No 11. pp. 53–64.

Putin, V. (2012, February 13). The President of the Russian Federation. Stroitel'stvo spravedlivosti. Sotsial'naya Politika dlya Rossii. Komsomolskaya Pravda.

Ryazantsev, S. (2017). Stsenarii razvitia migratsionnoi situatsii v EAES v usloviyakh usilenia ekonomicheskoi integratsii. In S. Ryazantsev, A. Ter-Akopov, E. Pis'mennaya, M. Khramova. Protsessy v migratsionnoy sfere i perspektivy evraziyskoy integratsii: opyt regionov. Analiticheskiy vestnik Soveta Federatsii Federalnogo Sobrania Rossiyskoy Federatsii. Vyp. 19 (676), 8–17. Retrieved from http://council.gov.ru/media/files/YGXXO4dC4P9FzpdRdYpa6pQIkaZFLzPA.pdf.

Sagynbekova, L. (2017). *International Labour Migration in the Context of the Eurasian Economic Union: Issues and Challenges of Kyrguz Migrants in Russia*. Working Paper No. 39. Institute of Public Diplomacy and Administration, University of Central Asia. Retrieved from https://www.ucentralasia.org/Content/Downloads/UCA-IPPA-WP-39percent20Internationalpercent20Labourpercent20Migrationpercent20in.pdf.

Talukdar, I. (2019). *Russia's State Migration Policy Concept 2019–2025*. The Russian International Affiars Council (RIAC). Retrieved from https://russiancouncil.ru/en/analytics-and-comments/columns/asian-kaleidoscope/russia-s-state-migration-policy-concept-2019-2025/.

Vinokurov, E. (2018). *Introduction to the Eurasian Economic Union*. Palgrave Macmillan.

World Bank. (2019). *Data*. Retrieved from https://data.worldbank.org/indicator/SL.EMP.SELF.ZS?end=2018&locations=AM-KG-BY-RU-KZ&start=1991&view=chart.

CHAPTER 10

Environmental Issues in the Eurasian Economic Union

Natalia A. Piskulova

10.1 Introduction

Most regional trade agreements (RTAs) incorporate environmental concerns, because countries use these agreements to cooperate on environmental matters and at the same time to prevent using environmental clauses as additional barriers in trade. The number of RTAs with various environmental provisions has been increasing since the 1990s. The most common types of provisions are associated with GATT Article XX and cover environmental cooperation. Several drivers may have contributed to implementing these provisions in RTAs: the necessity to comply with multilateral environmental agreements (MEAs), the deepening of cooperation between members, and the accumulation of positive experiences with the use of those provisions (George 2014a, b; Yoo and Kim 2016; Monteiro 2016).

A few studies evaluate the key implications of RTAs for the environment and conclude that RTAs can contribute to strengthening domestic

N. A. Piskulova (✉)
MGIMO University, Moscow, Russia

N. A. Piskulova (ed.), *The Economic Dimension of Eurasian Integration*, https://doi.org/10.1007/978-3-030-59886-0_10

environmental regulations and reducing environmental degradation (Martínez-Zarzoso 2018; Gallagher and Serret 2011). Some studies argue that RTAs promoted the enhancement of environmental cooperation among member countries, setting the example of East Asian countries (Yoo and Kim 2016).

There are numerous studies on the environmental aspects of integration in the "old" RTAs—EU, NAFTA, and others. However, there is relatively scarce research on the environmental topics in the EAEU. Most of them regard the legal aspects of environmental issues (Boklan 2015), mainly in the energy sector (Nazarkulova, Shugaipova 2016; Bordachev et al. 2019). Few experts explore the ways how the environmental problems of EAEU countries hinder sustainable development in this region and stress the need to solve them by joint efforts, as well as the strategies of each member country and the necessity of a transition to a green economy (Selishcheva 2018a, b).

Our intention is to provide a holistic study of the environmental aspects of EAEU integration, as well as its drivers and challenges, with a specific focus on the main areas of cooperation, including mutual trade in environmental goods, new projects and problems in this area.

10.2 Drivers of Cooperation

Currently, environment protection is not considered a major priority of cooperation between EAEU countries, as the main area of cooperation is economic development. However, environmental cooperation is one of the emerging areas of EAEU integration possibilities with a high potential: it can play a special role both for the economic development of the participating countries and greening the economy.

The main drivers of economic relations in the environmental field are persistent strong historical political, economic and cultural ties, rich environmental resources, the necessity to solve environmental problems alongside a view to prevent using environmental clauses as additional barriers in trade, orientation on economy modernization and export diversification, and a commitment to a green development path and increasing involvement in the global economy (Piskulova and Pak 2018a).

EAEU countries possess practically all types of natural and ecological resources. They account for a substantial global share of oil and gas mining, and the production of mineral fertilizers. Only Russia has the largest environmental resource base in the world, taking the leading place in territory and forest area, second place in water resources, and first place (or one of the first places) for many types of mineral resources—oil, natural gas, timber, iron, copper, lead, zinc, bauxite, nickel, tin, mercury, potassium salts, gold, platinum, palladium, silver, diamonds and so on (State Report 2016). The country possesses the largest untouched areas in the world; its ecosystem services play an important role for the world sustainability.

Other countries of the union also have resources that are important for economic development: Armenia has copper and molybdenum (5–9 per cent of global resources); Belarus has potassium salts; Kazakhstan has oil, coal, phosphorites, non-ferrous metals; Kyrgyzstan has mercury (1/5 of the global resources; Piskulova and Pak 2018a). EAEU countries have a leading global position for the annual river flow, possessing a high potential of underground water resources and lake water resources.

However, many of those resources are unevenly distributed; almost all countries experience a deficit of certain resources. Besides, vast resources stimulated material intensive type and inefficiency of the economy, and caused many environmental problems, including air pollution, water and soil contamination, depletion of natural resources (Piskulova and Pak 2018a).

The need for a joint effort to resolve ecological problems is due to their aggravation in practically all countries of the union. As an example, the volume of radioactive waste accumulated on the territory of Russia amounts to some 500 million tons (Federal Target Program 2018). In 21 per cent of the cities (with regular observations of air pollution), the air contamination is rated as high and very high (State Report 2018). In Kazakhstan, the most acute problems are the lack of water resources, radiation security and the quality of air in big cities. In Belarus, as the result of the Chernobyl accident, there is radiation contamination on some 22 per cent of its territory with a population of 2.2 million people (Nikitenko et al. 2017). In Armenia, the most acute problems are related to air pollution, habitat protection, and the over-usage of water resources. Up to 80 per cent of the soils are degraded to some extent and 44 per cent of the territory is subject to desertification. In the future, there is the possibility of swamping and even the full destruction of the unique eco-system of the Sevan Lake, where the water level has already dropped by 20 meters. In Kyrgyzstan, as the result of global warming, the Aral Sea is drying out. In the last 30 years, the volume of glaciers has shrunk by 25–30 per cent and their area by 40 per cent. The resource of interplastic artesian waters decreased by 40 per cent, which has aggravated the problem of drinking water. Some 1200 sources of radioactivity, created during the time of the Soviet Union, led to the issue of uranium tailings and toxic industrial waste. The total area of solid radioactive waste situated in seismically, torrent and flood-risk areas amounts to 650 hectares. In case of those tailings' dumps destruction, there is the danger of radioactive contamination, not just in Kyrgyzstan but also in the trans-border regions of Uzbekistan, Tajikistan, and Kazakhstan (Silishcheva 2018b).

Several environmental problems in separate countries of the Union have a trans-border character, affecting the interests of neighboring countries, so their resolution is possible by unified efforts only. EAEU countries share common water resources: for example, for Russia and Belarus a common river is the Dnepr alongside some smaller rivers (Boklan 2015); for Russia and Kazakhstan common rivers are the Ural, Irtysh and other rivers, as well as the Caspian Sea; for Kyrgyzstan and Kazakhstan common are rivers the Tchu and Talas. It is also worth mentioning that the realization of the "One Belt and One Road" concept, with the participation of EAEU countries, using outdated Chinese technologies, can have an additional negative effect on the environment of the countries of the Union.

One of the most used indexes, reflecting the environmental situation in specific countries, is the Environmental Performance Index (EPI) produced by Yale University and Columbia University in collaboration with the World Economic Forum. The index ranks 180 countries on 24 performance indicators, measuring environmental health (air quality, water and sanitation, heavy metals) and ecosystem vitality (biodiversity, forests, fisheries, climate and energy, air pollution, water resources, agriculture); this measurement provides a basis for adopting effective policy.

EAEU countries take different places in this ranking, from 44th for Belarus to 101th for Kazakhstan (Table 10.1).

According to measurements, air quality, biodiversity, and climate and energy remain the leading environmental threats to EAEU countries.

An important common issue is the resolution of issues related to greenhouse gas emissions. Currently by this measure[1] Russia is within the global top 5 (number four in the World), Kazakhstan is number 25, and Belarus 51, while Kyrgyzstan and Armenia take places 120 and 138, respectively (World Resources Institute 2019) (Table 10.2).

[1] The emissions data shown below do not include land-use change and forestry, nor emissions from the consumption of imported goods.

Table 10.1 Environmental Performance Index 2018

	Armenia	*Belarus*	*Kazakhstan*	*Kyrgyzstan*	*Russia*
Gross Domestic Product [PPP, constant 2011 int. $, in billions	23.5	159.17	417.22	20.02	3581.30
SDG Index (0–100, 100 is highest)	71.70	77.10	71.10	70.70	68.90
Environmental Performance Index	63	44	101	99	52
Environmental Health	109	67	79	114	44
Air Quality	142	82	90	132	54
Water and sanitation	60	46	56	104	52
Heavy Metals	44	36	50	80	24
Ecosystem Vitality	27	48	126	79	70
Biodiversity and Habitat	79	114	162	97	113
Forests	11	88	15	3	96
Fisheries	–	–	–	–	130
Climate and Energy	88	30	101	160	87
Air pollution	42	32	100	164	23
Water resources	55	18	67	88	24
Agriculture	68	101	120	25	30

Source: Wendling, Z. A., Emerson, J. W., Esty, D. C., Levy, M. A., de Sherbinin, A., et al. (2018). *2018 Environmental Performance Index*. New Haven, CT: Yale Center for Environmental Law & Policy. Retrieved from: https://epi.yale.edu/

At the same time, by per capita emissions, none of the EAEU countries is amongst the global top 10, although Kazakhstan's, Russia's and Belarus' numbers are quite high. In EAEU countries, the leading economic sectors with the highest emissions are the energy sector, transport, and construction. Resolving the issues of cutting emissions in those areas could form a joint base for the development of a joint or a coordinated policy.

Costs related to the solution of environmental issues on the path of developing a traditional economy are already very high; in the future they will increase further. In Russia, for example, costs associated with the decrease of natural environmental quality are estimated at 4–5 per cent of GDP per year, without taking health issues into consideration. Health-related costs due to air and water pollution amount in some years to 3–6 per cent of GDP (Government Expert Council 2018). This means that the total costs related to the deterioration of the environment can reach 7–11 per cent of GDP (Piskulova and Pak 2017), a number offering enormous potential for the economy subject to its restructuring on the green path.

Table 10.2 Greenhouse gas emissions in EAEU countries

	Country ranking in global GHG emissions (2017, per cent)	*Share in global GHG emissions (2017, per cent)*	*Country ranking in global GHG emissions per capita (2013)*	*Most polluting industries (GHG emissions, 2017)*
Armenia	138	0.02	116	Buildings, transport, power industry
Belarus	51	0.20	40	Power industry, transport, other industrial combustion
Kazakhstan	25	0.69	19	Other industrial combustion, power industry, buildings
Kyrgyzstan	120	0.03	125	Power industry, transport, buildings
Russia	4	4.86	23	Power industry, other industrial combustion, transport

Sources: World Resources Institute. Retrieved from: https://www.wri.org/resources/data-sets/cait-country-greenhouse-gas-emissions-data; Muntean, M., Guizzardi, D., Schaaf, E., Crippa, M., Solazzo, E., Olivier, J.G.J., Vignati, E. *Fossil CO2 emissions of all world countries—2018 Report*, EUR 29433 EN, Publications Office of the European Union, Luxembourg, 2018

In Kazakhstan, the inefficient use of resources is estimated to cost US $4–8 billion per year of lost profits; by 2030 this number could increase to US $14 billion. Costs associated with the low productivity of land amount to US $1.5–4 billion (Finreview 2019).

Costs associated with the implementation of environment protection measures can be substantially lower compared to environment deteriorations costs. For example, total annual land deterioration costs—due to its usage and deforestation on the Russian national and sub-national levels—amounted to $189 billion in 2001–2009, or $23.6 billion annually (in 2010 those expenses were equal to 2 per cent of GDP), while the costs of neutralizing land degradation are estimated to be five to six times lower during the next 30 years (Sorokin et al. 2016).

Global warming can require substantial costs. According to Russian experts' estimates, due to climate change in Russia annual economic losses can amount to 1–2 per cent of GDP, in certain areas up to 4–5 per cent (Timofeev 2014). Ecological change of the economy can lower such type of costs.

An important factor of EAEU countries' cooperation is the need to increase the speed of economic development and to modernize their economies, which is fully in line with one of the key targets of the Union: targeting entire modernization, cooperation and increased competitiveness of national economies in the global economy (Treaty 2018). The modernization requires substantial investments in new high technology industries and can contribute to economic development, economic diversification and an increase of competitiveness among EAEU countries. It also can help to find new profitable areas of mutual cooperation.

Currently, almost all countries of the Union have relatively low economic development rates, which is due both to internal and external circumstances. For example, in Russia, after moderate economic development in 2000s, internal and unfavorable external factors—including the financial and economic crisis of 2008–2009, the recent economic crisis, and Western sanctions (Piskulova and Pak 2018a)—hindered economic growth. In 2018, the GDP growth in the entire EAEU equaled 2.5 per cent against the lower rate of the development of the global economy, trade conflicts escalation and weaker dynamics of mutual trade *(Eurasian Commission* 2019e*)*.

A substantial proportion of the EAEU's economy is based on outdated technologies, which means that resource usage efficiency is relatively low. For example, in Russia, according to preliminary data, 47.4 per cent of fixed assets in 2018 were worn out (Federal State Statistics 2019), and in many sectors of the Kazakh economy at least 50 per cent of fixed assets are worn out *(*Kazakhstan Business Magazine 2019), which affects the green house gases emissions and general environmental situation.

In 1990–2016, the power intensity of all EAEU countries substantially decreased—Armenia by 4.6 times, Belarus by 3.4 times, Kyrgyzstan by 2.6 times, Kazakhstan by 1.8 times, and Russia by 1.4 times—which was due, first of all, to the change of GDP structure. However, in most countries this indicator is substantially above the global average, not to mention the average for more developed countries (Table 10.3).

While the average global indicator is 5.1 mJ/US$ (at the purchase power parity, 2011) in Russia the same is 8.6 mJ, in Kazakhstan 8.2 mJ, in Kyrgyzstan 8.0 mJ, and in Belarus 6.6 mJ. This indicator is similar to

Table 10.3 Energy intensity in the EAEU countries

Energy intensity MJ/$ 2011PPP					
	1990	*2000*	*2010*	*2015*	*2016*
Armenia	24.4	9.4	5.4	5.4	5.3
Belarus	22.4	13.7	7.5	6.5	6.6
Kazakhstan	14.4	10.1	8.8	7.9	8.2
Kyrgyzstan	20.5	9.6	7.6	8.6	8.0
Russian Federation	12.0	12.6	8.7	8.3	8.6
World	7.7	6.6	5.9	5.3	5.1

Source: IEA, IRENA, UNSD, WB, WHO (2019), Tracking SDG7: The Energy Progress Report 2019, Washington DC

world average in Armenia only (5.3 mJ) (IEA 2019), which is mainly due to the climate and the structure of national economies of those countries.

This is why the economy modernization can allow not just achieving economic development but also improving the ecological situation. EAEU countries face the challenge of increasing their ecological component in innovation activities, and the application of modern technologies in the power sector, which will allow the increase of production efficiency (Stepnov et al. 2019).

Another important factor and condition for the cooperation of EAEU countries in the environment protection area is the orientation on the development of the green economy, which was recently confirmed by practically all countries of the Union. Despite economic development currently being the main target, environment protection policy is part of all EAEU countries' strategy, which offers opportunities of cooperation between union member countries in this field.

Over the last years, despite serious economic problems, Russia declared its commitments to the green development path, which could contribute to solve issues of poverty, health, social security, environment, and rapid economic growth. Social and environmental targets of the green economy are included in fundamental conceptual documents—the Long-Term Concept for the Socio-Economic Development of the Country until 2020 (dated 2008) and the Strategy for Socio-Economic Development until 2020 (dated 2012), "Fundamentals of the State Policy in the Field of Environmental Development of the Russian Federation for the Period until 2030" (approved by the President of the Russian Federation in 2012),

Strategy of Ecological security of the Russian Federation for the period of up to 2025 (dated 2017)—among other documents—Energy Strategy of Russia until 2030 (dated 2010), the Russian Federation Presidential Decree "On Raising Energy and Environmental Efficiency" (dated 2008), the Law "On Energy Efficiency" (dated 2009) (Danilov-Danilyan et al. 2015). Over the last years, many new environmental laws and bylaws were adopted, concerning new economic stimuli in the environmental sphere, safe waste management, and the tightening of criminal liability for the illegal smuggling of rare animals (Piskulova and Pak 2018a). The national project "Ecology" has started, which provides for a solution for strategic goals in the ecological development of Russia until 2024, including drastic change to air and water quality, maintenance of biological diversity, improvement of waste treatment, and the introduction of best available technologies.

In the Republic of Belarus, increased attention is also paid to environment protection issues. The Strategy in the area of environmental protection of the Republic of Belarus until 2025 is in action, which is targeting issues such as the wide introduction of power and resource saving technologies, a decrease in the material and power intensity of products manufactured, and the National Plan of actions to develop green economy until 2020, providing for a change in consumer's behavior toward a more sustainable consumption model, the development of electrical vehicles infrastructure, realization of "smart cities" concept, and an increase in the potential of renewable energy sources usage.

Within the National Strategy of Kyrgyzstan until 2017, a Program and a Plan for the transition to sustainable development was adopted, and the National Council for the Sustainable Development with the President of the Republic of Kyrgyzstan was created.

In Kazakhstan, by the President's Decree of 2013, the Concept (among the first in the EAEU) for the transition of the Republic of Kazakhstan to "green economy" was adopted by the means of rational usage of natural resources (Piskulova and Pak 2018a), the international partnership program "The Green bridge" is being realized, which provides for the technology and experience exchange in the area of clean energy. In Armenia the development of green growth economic indicators is underway.

All Eurasian Economic Union (EAEU) countries have committed to climate action and to reduce greenhouse gases emissions within the framework of the Paris Agreement. Russia, Belarus, Kazakhstan and Kyrgyzstan have provided greenhouse gases emission reduction targets. Currently in most EAEU countries the share of renewable energy sources (RES) in the power balance is relatively low, except for Armenia, where in 2017 it accounted for some 32.5 per cent. In Belarus the share of RES is estimated at 4 per cent, and in Kazakhstan, Kyrgyzstan and Russia it is 1.3, 0.1, and 19 per cent, respectively (if the big hydroelectric power station are taken into the equation), while without counting this source this share is below 1 per cent (Eurasian Economic Commission 2019a). However, almost all EAEU countries carry out the policy of increasing the potential of renewable energy sources. For example, Armenia has declared its plan to double the share of RES in its power balance up to 70 per cent, Kazakhstan by 2050 up to 50 per cent. Those areas of activities can form an important base for the economic cooperation of EAEU in this sphere.

All EAEU countries realize their own state programs targeting energy saving and increasing energy efficiency, and some countries of the Union carry out research in this area and manufacture energy saving equipment.

One of the important reasons for greening economic collaboration in the environmental sphere is countries' growing integration in the global economy and the necessity to comply with international standards. Climate policy measures, when passed (standards, subsidies for the producers of renewable energy and other measures, affecting supply from other countries) will lead to the reduction of demand and prices on traditional energy goods. This can threaten the exports of EAEU countries, in most of which the export share of carbon intensive industries is very high, exceeding 60 per cent for the entire EAEU. According to preliminary data, in the exports structure of the EAEU to third countries, the share of mineral goods amounted to 67 percent in January–December 2018 (Eurasian Economic Commission 2019b). This is a special threat for Eurasian companies operating in the global market and working in the "dirty" industries (such as oil, metallurgy, transport, wood and paper, etc.). This factor, together with the decrease in hydrocarbons' production from traditional deposits poses a serious challenge to the EAEU.

However, the ecological path of economic development, including the introduction of carbon regulations, can reduce costs and increase competitive advantages, stimulating economic growth (by 2–3 per cent by 2050, according to OECD estimates in different G20 countries, on top of the reduction of the losses) and can more than overweigh the negative economic consequences (OECD 2017), although at the initial stage acceptance of such standards can lead to the decrease of competitive advantages.

Resolving the problems requires large investments, which are lacked in the EAEU in the current situation of economic recession. Those are, first of all, required to resolve the prevailing problems in EAEU countries related to the lack of clean water and power generation issues, which is in line with the UN Sustainable Development targets. As an example, just in Russia, to build water purification facilities, some 125 billion rubles of private investments are required (Federal Assembly of Russian Federation 2018). Necessary investments into the replacement of oil pipelines (95 per cent of oil spillage is due to their over-extended service life) should be in the range of 1.3 trillion rubles (Blokov 2018).

Some of the measures will not require substantial investments. As an example, the transfer to energy saving technologies, according to some estimates (including those by the World Bank), will not lead to substantial costs for Russian companies: at the same time, this will require changes in the management process (Piskulova and Pak 2018a). Previous studies have shown that realizing Russia's energy efficiency potential, amounting to 45 per cent of primary energy consumption in 2005, could save the economy up to $120–150 per year due to lower energy consumption and additional revenues from gas exports (World Bank 2008). Extra savings can be generated by gradually reducing fossil energy sources subsidies. FDI with modern environment-friendly technologies could help to solve the problems, but in the current conditions of Western sanctions, their inflows are at the very low level. In Kazakhstan, the potential of power usage savings amounts to $3–4 billion, and by 2030 this number could increase to $6–10 billion (Finreview 2019).

10.3 Common Policy and Actions

An important condition for the cooperation of the environment protection area of EAEU countries is the legal base at the EAEU level, as well as the current cooperation in this sphere taking shape. Despite fundamental EAEU documents, including the Eurasian Economic Union Agreement dated from 2014 (lacking specific environment-related provisions), some articles of the agreement do include references to the environment. In the Article 29, among the Exceptions to the Procedure of Functioning of the Internal Goods Market, the member-states may apply restrictions in mutual trade if required for the protection of human life and health, environmental protection, and the protection of animals and plants. In the Article 52, technical regulations of the Union shall be adopted only in order to protect life and/or health of people, property, environment, life and/or health of animals and plants, as well as for ensuring energy efficiency and resource conservation. The article is based on the WTO Agreement on Technical Barriers to Trade. The Article 56 provides for the adoption of sanitary, veterinary-sanitary and phytosanitary quarantine measures only to the extent required to protect life and health of humans, animals, and plants. Those ideas of the specific articles of the Agreement are generally in the compliance with the Article XX of WTO. The Article 62 stipulates that the main directions of the agreed macroeconomic policy of the member-states should include ensuring sustainable development of the economies of the member-states. The Article 68 on administrative cooperation sets up the actions of member-states on activities or investors that may harm the health or safety of people, animals, plants or the environment on the territory of that member-state or on the territories of other member-states. The Article 86 on the transport policy among its objectives stipulates ensuring transport safety and reduction of harmful effects generated by transport on the environment and human health (Treaty on the Eurasian Economic Union 2018).

A major target of joint electric power formation became the provision of economic sustainable development and power supply security, as well as the increase of economic efficiency. In the area of renewable power, currently there is almost no cooperation; to develop such cooperation it is planned to introduce amendments into the EAEU Agreement.

At the EAEU level there is a coordinated policy in the areas of sanitary, veterinary-sanitary, phytosanitary and quarantine measures. A unification of ecological standards is carried out, based on the GOST regulations and standards of the former Soviet Union, but with substantial changes over later years with increasing use of international and European standards (Emerson and Kofner 2018). Under the Eurasian Economic Commission's spotlight is the quality and safety of food products in the Eurasian market, as well as the identification of antibiotic residues and other hazardous substances, including transfats. As example, in 2018, some stringent standards for the permissible level of fatty acid transisomers established by the Union Technical Regulation for Fat and Oil Products came into force after the transitional period had elapsed (Eurasian Economic Commission 2019c). Some technical norms are already in place related to the safety of liquified hydrocarbon gases, oil, bottled drinking water, fish and fish products, children's playground equipment, and some others (GARANT 2019).

After June 2021, national standards will be replaced by 35 uniform mandatory safety requirements and technical regulations expected to enter into force, with the aim to ensure the safety and health of citizens, the security of assets, environmental protection, and the protection of plants and animals.

In order to harmonize with international legislation, the EAEU is cooperating with international organizations (with the European and Mediterranean organizations on the quarantine and protection of plant, with the UN FAO Regional Office for Europe and Central Asia), that is in the areas of sanitary, quarantine, phytosanitary and veterinary-sanitary measures (Azanov 2014).

10.4 Directions and Problems of Environmental Cooperation

EAEU countries have some experience of economic interaction in the area of environmental protection, although the level of such interaction is currently relatively low (Piskulova). The main areas of cooperation are trade and investment partnership.

An element of the economic interaction within EAEU in the environment protection area is the mutual trade in environmental goods, which includes almost all positions from the APEC list of environmental goods (using 6-digit Harmonized Commodity Description and Coding Systems (HS) Code[2]). Now, trade in those items accounts for rather small share of total mutual trade. It should be stressed, however, that the share of environmental goods in the years 2010–2016 increased from 0.04 per cent to about 1.8 per cent of EAEU's mutual exports (UN COMTRADE 2019). Even taking into consideration that the bulk of the EAEU's exports consists of raw materials and the prices for them fell in those years, the economic problems affected the environmental sector less than other sectors. In view of this, the mutual trade in environmental goods may have better perspectives than the total trade.

In the structure of the EAEU's environmental goods inter-trade in 2016, the following commodity groups prevailed: parts and accessories for liquid crystal devices "LCD", lasers and other appliances (901390); machinery and apparatus for filtering or purifying water (842121);

[2] The Harmonized System is an international nomenclature for the classification of products.

machines and mechanical appliances (847989); and parts of steam and other vapor turbines (840690). Those products are mostly traded between Russia and Belarus as well as between Russia and Kazakhstan.

Among relatively new prospective sectors of EAEU intra-trade, it might be worth mentioning the following environmentally clean goods not included into the APEC list, which are part of the traditional markets: agricultural goods, products of the fishing and wood industries, and tourism and other industries, which might be of interest to Eurasian exporters, as there is an increasing demand for environmental goods globally (Piskulova and Pak 2018b).

EAEU investment cooperation in the environment protection area is underdeveloped. Its main direction is efficient power usage, first of all higher energy efficiency. During the last two years the two-year project "Regulatory Framework to Promote Energy Efficiency in the Countries of Eurasian Economic Union" is being realized, which targets lower power consumption and, as a result, the reduction of greenhouse gas emission due to the increase of energy efficiency of lighting, household appliances and engineering equipment in the member countries through the introduction of energy efficient regulations and standards, and the development of trial capacities and the promotion of energy efficient technologies by the increasing awareness of the ultimate consumers. The total electric power saving volume, ten years after the project realization, will amount to 78 billion KWh, which corresponds to a reduction in emissions equivalent to some 43 million tones of CO_2 (UNDP 2019). New ecological projects are being realized with the EAEU's participation, including new environmental projects in the Arctic (The Arctic 2019).

At the EAEU level, technological cooperation includes measures to facilitate the development of environmental technologies. The Eurasian technological platform "Technologies for Environmental Development" (ETP) is enacted with the participation of state and business structures, based on which projects are developed to fight desertification and land degradation in arid zones (Piskulova and Pak 2018a). Currently, the first laboratory and experimental results have been obtained, which can help to improve the physical, chemical and biological characteristics of soils and plants; in the future those technologies can be also used on other markets. An action plan has been approved to stimulate the production and utilization of electric vehicles (Eurasian Economic Commission 2019d).

Active cooperation in the environment protection area is held back by a number of obstacles, including economic ones, that is, the limitations due to the existing production and technological base, limitations of the legal base, lack of political will and continuing orientation on the development of hydrocarbon power sources, uneven economic development of the Union countries, and the need to resolve the most urgent economic problems. In the area of the common legal base formation and cooperation in the environmental area, only the initial actions have been taken. It is clear that there is a lack of regulation in a whole range of environment protection segments on the EAEU level (e.g., in the area of water resources, in the common market of domestic waste); until now the resolution of ecological issues prevails on the national level. While the work is going on in this direction, it is lagging behind the urgent need to re-orient the economy toward the green development path and to stand up to new contemporary challenges.

Trade conflicts between the member countries also arise. For example, there were trade disputes over Kazakhstan blocking the access of Kyrgyz potatoes, and of Russia blocking Belarusian dairy products to its market on technical SPS grounds. At the same time, those trade disputes do not constitute any unresolvable obstacles in the economic relations of the Union countries in the environmental sphere.

10.5 Conclusion

Summarizing current EAEU cooperation in the environment protection is rather limited compared to the role of environment protection factor in the global economy. However, the development of cooperation in this area is in the general interests of EAEU countries. The main factors contributing to its promotion are the historic economic and cultural ties, the need to resolve environmental problems, vast natural resources, commitment to the ecologically oriented economic growth in line with the legal base being created, and the certain experience of economic interaction in the environment protection area. Subject to some conditions and responsible polices, ecological cooperation can contribute not just to the improvement of the environment and resolution of social issues, but also to the increase of efficiency and diversification of Union Economy.

The Union faces the challenge of achieving the balance between the economy and environmental protection, the full integration of environment protection targets into the common economic strategy, responsible use of international integration practices in the environmental area (Blokov 2018) including working out common standards and regulations as well as the formation of common environmental markets, the usage of the most advanced practices of EAEU countries, and attraction of foreign investments into economic projects with environmental content including projects targeting energy efficiency and the development of renewable power sources.

The main areas of EAEU economic cooperation in the environment protection area may become the trade in environmental goods, investment and technological cooperation. The five countries have good opportunities for expanding mutual ties in renewable energy and environmental protection.

Taking the above into consideration, EAEU countries should create conditions for the further harmonization of environmental standards, technical regulations and environmental labeling, with participation in those discussions of business community as well to stimulate exports of environmental goods, innovation and investment projects.

The adoption of a coordinated EAEU ecological policy can contribute to the realization of those targets, although such a policy could prevent the usage of protectionist measures, as well as the accumulation of finance, production and technological resources to be channeled to those sectors of EAEU economy which have the biggest potential for wider cooperation in the environmental sphere.

References

Azanov, B. K. (2014). Treaty on the Eurasian Economic Union: A Comprehensive Legal Analysis (Section I. General Provisions. Section II. Basic Principles, Objectives, Powers and Law of the Union). *Eurasian Law Journal, 4*(8(75)), 39–48. (in Russian).

Blokov, I. P. (2018). *Environment and Its Protection in Russia. Changes Over the 25 Years.* Moscow: OMHHO Greenpeace Council. (in Russian).

Boklan, D. S. (2015). Environmental Protection in the Context of Eurasian Economic Integration (International Legal Aspect). *Eurasian Law Journal, 1*(80), 25–28. (in Russian).

Bordachev T., Vishnevsky K., Glazatova M., et al. (2019, April 9–12). *Eurasian Economic Integration: Perspectives of Development and Strategic Aims for Russia.* XX Apr. International Scientific Conference on the Problems of Economy and Society Development. Moscow. Moscow: National Research University Higher School of Economics. (in Russian).

Danilov-Danilyan, V. I., Piskulova, N. A., et al. (2015). *Sustainable Development: New Challenges.* Moscow: Aspect-Press. (In Russian).

Emerson, M., & Kofner, J. (2018, March). *Technical Product Standards and Regulations in the EU and EAEU—Comparisons and Scope for Convergence*. International Institute for Applied Systems Analysis. Retrieved from http://greater-europe.org/wp-content/uploads/2018/06/2-Technical-Product-Standards-and-Regulations-in-the-EU.pdf.

Eurasian Economic Commission. (2019a, September 6). (in Russian). Retrieved from http://www.eurasiancommission.org/ru/nae/news/Pages/8-06-2018-5.aspx.

Eurasian Economic Commission. (2019b). Analytical Outlook. *The Results of Foreign Trade in Goods of the Eurasian Economic Union*, January–December, 2018.–February 26th. (in Russian).http://www.eurasiancommission.org/ru/act/integr_i_makroec/dep_stat/tradestat/analytics/Documents/2018/Analytics_E_201812.pdf.

Eurasian Economic Commission. (2019c). (in Russian). Retrieved from http://eec.eaeunion.org/en/nae/news/Pages/27-02-2019-1.aspx.

Eurasian Economic Commission (2019d). (in Russian). Retrieved from http://www.eurasiancommission.org/ru/nae/news/Pages/16-01-2017-2.aspx.

Eurasian Economic Commission. (2019e). (in Russian). Retrieved from http://www.eurasiancommission.org/ru/act/integr_i_makroec/dep_makroec_pol/economyPrognoz/Pages/Sred_prog.aspx.

Federal Assembly of Russian Federation. (2018). *Parlamentskaja gazeta*. (in Russian). Retrieved from https://www.pnp.ru/social/2017/04/25/60-zakonov-bylo-prinyato-za-poslednie-5-let-v-sfere-prirodopolzovaniya-minprirody.html.

Federal service of State Statistics.—GKS. (2019). (in Russian). Retrieved from http://www.gks.ru/wps/wcm/connect/rosstat_main/rosstat/ru/statistics/enterprise/fund/#.

Federal Target Program Ensuring Nuclear and Radiation Safety in 2016-2020 and up to 2030. (2018). (in Russian). Retrieved from http://фцп-ярб2030.рф/.

Finreview.info. (2019). (in Russian). Retrieved from https://dknews.kz/inner-news.php?id_cat=11 per cent20&& per cent20id=17796&fbclid=IwAR1RKT25Jv00M-i5M2q5XfESgOR3aNgtQh6ieLq7cSayGcJIeiax1ihfHBE.

Gallagher, P., & Y. Serret (2011). *Implementing Regional Trade Agreements with Environmental Provisions: A Framework for Evaluation*. OECD Trade and Environment Working Papers, No. 2011/06, OECD Publishing, Paris. https://doi.org/10.1787/5kg3n2crpxwk-en.

GARANT. (2019). Legal information portal. Retrieved from http://base.garant.ru/5425755/#friends.

George, C. (2014a). *Developments in Regional Trade Agreements and the Environment: 2013 Update*. OECD Trade and Environment Working Papers, No. 2014/01, OECD Publishing, Paris. https://doi.org/10.1787/5jz0v4qcg9zw-en.

George, C. (2014b). *Environment and Regional Trade Agreements: Emerging Trends and Policy Drivers*. OECD Trade and Environment Working Papers, No. 2014/02, OECD Publishing, Paris. https://doi.org/10.1787/5jz0v4q45g6h-en.

Government Expert Council. (2018). (in Russian). Retrieved from https://open.gov.ru/blogs/5513735/.

IEA, IRENA, UNSD, WB, WHO. (2019). *Tracking SDG7: The Energy Progress Report 2019*. Washington DC. Retrieved from https://www.irena.org/-/media/Files/IRENA/Agency/Publication/2019/May/2019-Tracking-SDG7-Report.pdf.

Kazakhstan Business Magazine. (2019). (in Russian). Retrieved from http://investkz.com/en/journals/51/393.html.

Martínez-Zarzoso, I. (2018. *Assessing the Effectiveness of Environmental Provisions in Regional Trade Agreements: An Empirical Analysis*. OECD Trade and Environment Working Papers, No. 2018/02, OECD Publishing, Paris. https://doi.org/10.1787/5ffc615c-en.

Monteiro J.-A. (2016, August). *Economic Research and Statistics Division*. World Trade Organization. Retrieved from https://www.wto.org/english/res_e/reser_e/ersd201613_e.pdf.

Muntean, M., Guizzardi, D., Schaaf, E., Crippa, M., Solazzo, E., Olivier, J. G. J., & Vignati, E. (2018). *Fossil CO2 Emissions of all World Countries—2018 Report*. EUR 29433 EN, Publications Office of the European Union, Luxembourg.

Nazarkulova, L. T., & Shugaipova, M. S. (2016). Environmental Issues in the Integration Processes in the Energy Sector in the Framework of the EAEU (Overview). *Vector of Science TGU, 4*(27), 63–65. (In Russian).

Nikitenko, P., Levkevich, V., Svetlosanov, V., Kudin, V., & Petrova, E. (2017). The Impact of Natural and Man-Made Risks on the Regional Development in Belarus and Russia. *Science & Innovations, 3*, 32–37. (In Russian).

OECD. (2017). *Investing in Climate, Investing in Growth* (p. 241). Paris. Retrieved from https://doi.org/10.1787/9789264273528-en.

Piskulova, N. A., & Pak, Y. V. (2017). Prospects of Russian Engagement in the Green Economy. *Intertrends., 12*, 40–58. (In Russian).

Piskulova, N. A., & Pak, Y. V. (2018a). Determinants of the EAEU-EU Mutual Trade in Environmental Goods. *Russian Foreign Economic Bulletin, 85*, 43–55. (In Russian).

Piskulova, N. A., & Pak, Y. V. (2018b). Key Trends in EAEU-EU Mutual Trade in Environmental Goods. *Russian Foreign Economic Bulletin, 9*, 98–105. (In Russian).

Selishcheva, T. A. (2018a). "Green" Economy as a Model of Sustainable Development in EEU Countries. *Problems of Modern Economy, 3*(67). (In Russian).

Selishcheva, T. A. (2018b). Problems of Sustainable Economic Development in EEC Countries. *Problems of Modern Economy, 2*(66). (In Russian).

Sorokin A., Bryzzhev A., Strokov A., Mirzabaev A., Johnson T., & Kiselev S. V. (2016). The Economics of Land Degradation in Russia. In E. Nkonya, A. Mirzabaev, & J. von Braun (Eds.), *Economics of Land Degradation and Improvement—A Global Assessment for Sustainable Development.* Cham: Springer. Retrieved from https://link.springer.com/chapter/10.1007/978-3-319-19168-3_18.

State Report. (2016). *On the State of the Environment and Its Protection in Russian Federation in 2015.* Moscow: Minprirody Rossii; NIA-Priroda. (in Russian).

State Report. (2018). *On the State of the Environment and Its Protection in Russian Federation in 2017.* M.: Minprirody Rossii; NPP "Kadastr". (In Russian).

Stepnov, I. M., Kovalchuk, J. A., & Gorchakova, E. A. (2019). On Assessing the Efficiency of Intracluster Interaction for Industrial Enterprises. *Studies on Russian Economic Development, 30*, 346–354. https://doi.org/10.1134/S107570071903016X.

The Arctic. (2019). Information Project. (In Russian). Retrieved from https://arctic.ru/international/20151116/225268.html.

Timofeev, A. D. (2014). Social and Economic effects of Climate Fluctuations in Russia. *Society. Environment. Development (Terra Humana), 2*, 174–178. (In Russian).

Treaty on the Eurasian Economic Union. (2018). 29.05.2014 (revised edition 15.03.2018). Legal Web Portal. (In Russian). Retrieved from https://docs.eaeunion.org/docs/ru-ru/0003610/itia_05062014.

UN COMTRADE Statistics. (2019). Retrieved from http://www.trademap.org/.

UNDP. (2019). *Standards and Regulatory Regime for Energy Efficiency Promotion in the EAEU Countries.* Retrieved from https://eaeueneff.org/o-proekte/.

Wendling, Z. A., Emerson, J. W., Esty, D. C., Levy, M. A., de Sherbinin, A., et al. (2018). *2018 Environmental Performance Index.* New Haven, CT: Yale Center for Environmental Law & Policy. Retrieved from https://epi.yale.edu/.

World Bank. (2008). *Energy Efficiency in Russia: Untapped Reserves, World Bank, International Finance Corporation* (pp. 6–7). Washington DC: World Bank.

World Resources Institute. (2019). *CAIT.* Country Greenhouse Gas Emissions Data. Retrieved from https://www.wri.org/resources/data-sets/cait-country-greenhouse-gas-emissions-data.

Yoo, I. T., & Kim, I. (2016). Free Trade Agreements for the Environment? Regional economic Integration and Environmental Cooperation in East Asia. *Int Environ Agreements, 16*, 721. https://doi.org/10.1007/s10784-015-9291-8.

CHAPTER 11

EAEU-Third Countries Cooperation: Opportunities and Limitations

Maria A. Maksakova and Stevan Gajić

11.1 Introduction

The early 1990s were marked by a significant extension of the regional integration groupings, as well as the development of the multilateral trading system, which was subject to the General Agreement on Tariffs and Trade (GATT), and later to a system of the World Trade Organization (WTO) agreements. This gave rise to the theoretical, economic, and political debate over the compatibility of the multilateral trading system with regional trade agreements (RTA). Some authors (Krugman 1991; Summers 1991; Lawrence 1996; Baldwin 1997; Ethier 1998) were optimistic about the prospects of regional trade integration and its favorable effect on the world trade and foresaw no threats to the multilateral trading

M. A. Maksakova (✉)
MGIMO University, Moscow, Russia

Institute of Economics of the Russian Academy of Sciences, Moscow, Russia
e-mail: m.maksakova@inno.mgimo.ru

S. Gajić
Institute of European Studies, Belgrade, Serbia

N. A. Piskulova (ed.), *The Economic Dimension of Eurasian Integration*, https://doi.org/10.1007/978-3-030-59886-0_11

system. Others, on the contrary, warned against RTAs' discriminatory nature and argued that trade preferences contradict the principles of the multilateral trading system (Bhagwati 1994; Bhagwati and Krueger 1995).

Nowadays, the "regionalism vs. multilateralism" issue is far from being exhausted. The basic principle that could be applied to solve this problem is a provision that goes back to early 2000s and reads: "WTO-consistent preferential trade agreements can complement but not substitute for coherent multilateral rules and progressive multilateral liberalization" (OECD 2003).

At the contemporary stage of global economic development, where the tendency toward regionalization is greatly intensifying and acquiring new outlines, many countries consider this process as one of the ways to uphold national interests in the global market. Profound forms of economic integration, such as a customs union, a common market, an economic union, and various forms of preferential relations without creating supranational institutions (free trade agreements, FTA, economic integration agreements, EIA), reflect two currently dominant concepts of integration—the so-called closed (old) and open (new) regionalism. Together, they form the situation of integration processes in the modern world.

The term "Old Regionalism" was used by Ethier in 1998 and was a synonymous with the term "First Regionalism", introduced by Bhagwati in 1991 to refer to the first wave of active development of regional integration (late 1950s–1960s) (Ethier 1998; Bhagwati 1991). The concept of traditional (closed, old) regionalism is based on the European experience and implies a consistent deepening of the integration level and the expansion of a number of areas in which interaction takes place in a preferential mode, with the formation of supranational regulatory bodies. In the context of traditional regionalism, the creation of a free trade zone is interpreted as an intermediate step toward deeper forms of integration.

The terms "Open Regionalism" and "New Regionalism" are synonymous and are used to refer to the second wave of integration initiatives (late 1980s, 1990s to the present time) (Bergsten 1997; Bhagwati 1993). Within the framework of the "Open Regionalism" concept, the intention is to agree on common approaches, but not to develop a single market policy. The emphasis is on expanding rather than deepening the integration process. This approach is aimed at maximizing the level of mutually beneficial trade and economic cooperation between countries, while fully preserving their sovereignty in all areas, and does not imply the development of deep integration forms. The phenomenon of "Open Regionalism" has been studied extensively, but discussions about its essence and prospects still ongoing.

However, recently the scientific community has also actively discussed an alternative view of the regionalization process, called "comparative regionalism". F. Laursen was one of the first to introduce this term into scientific circulation in the research "Comparative Regional Integration" (2005). The main aim of the study is to consider the integration processes from different theoretical positions, namely realism, institutionalism, and more. Researching the dynamics of the European Union, some authors proposed applying the method of comparative analysis of regional dynamics using social sciences (Warleigh-Lack and Van Langenhove 2010; Söderbaum and Sbragia 2010; De Lombaerde et al. 2009); for example, this would take into account and compare different countries and cultures in the analysis of regional construction. Other authors who study mainly integration processes in Asia (Acharya 2012) argue about the use of the EU experience as a model for the evolutionary regional construction. A. Acharya considers the theory of "comparative regionalism" in a broader sense. He believes that regional integration can go in different ways depending on historical, cultural, linguistic traditions. This is a kind of "non-European" type of regionalism that includes different types of regional construction.

Currently, all these concepts (old, new, and comparative regionalism) are implemented in parallel, sometimes within the framework of one integration project. In real practice, this situation can be observed within the Eurasian integration model, where a number of approaches inherent in closed regionalism are combined with a model of multi-level and multi-speed integration both within the union and on the external circuit of integration.

In modern publications, the problem of regional integration in the post-Soviet space is highly politicized, as researchers overestimate the role of political factors and underestimate the economic features of Eurasian integration, an objective analysis and scientific interpretation of which can contribute to the existing empirical and theoretical knowledge of regional economic integration and encourage search for ways of effectively solving practical tasks in this field.

The 1991 collapse of the Soviet Union left many economic ties between the republics destroyed. The 12 former Soviet Republics (with the exception of three Baltic States which joined the EU) formed the Commonwealth of Independent States (CIS), aimed at creating favorable conditions for regional integration development. However, liberalization of foreign trade and access to competitive foreign markets engaged these post-Soviet states in international exchange of goods and made them interested in global rather than intra-regional trade. Nevertheless, despite a decline in the CIS intra-regional trade share in the 1990s–early 2000s, the intensity of intra-regional trade remained relatively high and a large-scale Russian market continues to be a favorable factor for achieving the goals of trade diversification and structural reforms aimed at modernizing the economies of the EAEU countries (Gurova et al. 2018).

Nowadays, researchers have different deliberations regarding objectives and motives for establishing the EAEU, its peculiarities and prospects. One of the main objectives stated in the Treaty on the Eurasian Economic Union, is "to ensure comprehensive modernization, cooperation and more competitive national economies within the global economy" (EAEU 2014). The primary task for all EAEU countries is to modernize and diversify their economies and overcome specialization in commodities, fuels, and power, formed as a result of joining global trade. Indeed, when it comes to some aspects of modernization and diversification, EAEU states could also rely on regional opportunities. Intra-regional integration is viewed as a tool for achieving economic development goals through joint efforts. At the same time, in the context of solving this problem, it is impossible to discount the issues of forming the EAEU foreign economic agenda. Properly building a network of foreign economic relations and creating a system of preferential agreements with significant foreign partners can further increase the effectiveness of participation in cross-border value chains by removing barriers to cooperative products and harmonizing internal rules and procedures, thereby stimulating the modernization of the Union's economies. Modernization, in its turn, could be a positive factor in making the integration deeper.

The launch of the EAEU in 2015 coincided with worsening geopolitical and geoeconomic conditions, a slowdown in the member-states' economies against the background of weak growth of the global economy and rising geopolitical tensions, the imposition of trade restrictions and sanctions against Russia, and a substantial decline in world fuel and energy prices. In spite of these tough circumstances, some positive integration effects are expected. The Eurasian Economic Commission (EEC) forecasts that before 2030 integration will boost the member-states' GDP growth by an additional 13 per cent, the volume of trade in intermediate goods (fueled by production diversification) will increase by 80 per cent and the inflow of foreign direct investment (FDI) in the region from non-member countries is expected to increase by $90 billion (EAEU 2015).

11.2 Institutional Formats of EAEU International Cooperation

After the completion of the EAEU institutionalization process, the main question was how to embed the union in the global economy and multilateral trading system that is currently undergoing significant changes. These changes are connected with, among others, the challenges that arise in the world, and the inability of the WTO to fully contribute to the process of further liberalization. These factors predetermine countries and unions' desire to obtain the most favorable conditions on external markets by means of concluding various agreements accelerating the removal of barriers to goods and services trade, stimulating the development of investment, and scientific and technical cooperation.

An important stage in the development of economic cooperation is the creation of free trade zones with partners. Currently, this form of integration has become a long-term and promising trend in international trade, which certainly affects the EAEU. The subject of free trade became even more relevant after Russia's accession to the WTO. The creation of free trade zones allows the establishment of more liberal rules in trade with key partners based on the level of liberalization that already exists within the WTO. At the same time, it is important that such rules, when creating free trade zones with different partners, do not contradict each other and, above all, reflect the interests of the EAEU businesses.

In this context, the importance and need to establish effective cooperation between EAEU states, both within the framework of the union and with third countries, is becoming increasingly important each year. This aspect is regularly considered within the framework of the Supreme Eurasian Economic Council meetings and other high-level events. Currently, the EAEU is gradually increasing its international involvement: foreign countries show their growing interest in cooperation, negotiations about free trade zones with significant foreign partners are underway, and joint research groups are being formed to study the feasibility of concluding free trade agreements.

In May 2018, the Supreme Eurasian Economic Council approved a key document regulating the EAEU international cooperation sphere—the

Agreement "On the International Treaties of the Eurasian Economic Union with Third States, International Organizations or Integration Unions" (Electronic Fund of Legal and Technical Documentation 2018). The agreement defines the procedure for concluding, terminating, and suspending EAEU international agreements.

The procedure for international cooperation of the EAEU is established by a decision by the Supreme Eurasian Economic Council, which annually approves the document "Main directions of international activity of the Eurasian Economic Union" (EAEU 2019); this contains current forms of interaction with a wide range of countries and unions and determining target forms of cooperation (FTA, agreement on trade and economic cooperation, etc.).

Currently, the EAEU has several main institutional formats for building relationships with external partners:

1. Free Trade Agreements

Nowadays, modern free trade agreements (FTA) are complex and apply not only to trade in goods, but also to other areas: access to service markets, investment, movement of labor, competition policy, access to the government procurement market, protection of intellectual property rights and others. Following this global practice, the EAEU also seeks to conclude not only traditional FTAs covering mainly trade relations, but agreements with obligations in a number of other areas.

For now, the EAEU has a set of FTA in force with a number of countries in different regions: Vietnam (2015), the Islamic Republic of Iran (2018—Interim Agreement for a period of 3 years), the Republic of Singapore (2019), and the Republic of Serbia (2019). Generally, the terms and conditions of these agreements imply trade liberalization under the WTO-plus rules.

2. Agreements on Trade and Economic Cooperation / Non-preferential Trade Agreements.

As a rule, non-preferential trade agreements do not imply an automatic reduction or the abolition of customs duties. Still, though, there is the possibility of the targeted elimination of trade restrictions, and the removal of non-tariff barriers and the customs regulation. These agreements don't imply strict obligations to parties, but determine the cooperation mechanism on the basis of various kinds of advisory committees and working groups. Market access conditions and the level of transparency of the current trade policy can also be regulated due to the trade facilitation rules contained in the agreement.

In May 2018, the EAEU and the People's Republic of China (PRC) signed the Agreement on trade and economic cooperation. The agreement is non-preferential and does not imply any reduction in customs duties in trade. It includes a wide range of other issues: trade facilitation; increasing transparency and work on the mutual recognition of standards, technical regulations and conformity assessment procedures; protection of intellectual property rights; e-commerce regulation; cooperation in the sphere of public procurement.

3. Status of the Observer State.

According to the Treaty on the Eurasian Economic Union (EAEU 2014, Article 109), any state is entitled to apply to the chairman of the Supreme Eurasian Economic Council with a request to grant him the status of the observer state at the EAEU. This status allows the observer state to attend official meetings, and to receive documents without confidential status accepted by the EAEU, but does not give them the right to participate in decision-making in EAEU bodies.

In May 2018, the Republic of Moldova was granted the status of the observer state at the EAEU. Nowadays, the observer status is a convenient and compromised format for countries showing interest in EAEU activities, since, on the one hand, it allows building cooperation in certain mutually beneficial areas, and, on the other hand, does not impose any obligations on third countries for further agreement conclusion or membership in the union.

4. Memoranda of cooperation and mutual understanding with international organizations (UNECE, UNCTAD, FAO, ESCAP, IOM, ITC, etc.), regional unions (established working contacts with MERCOSUR, ASEAN, LAI, the Andean Community, Pacific Alliance) and third countries.

While memoranda with international organizations are important for strengthening the international legal personality of the EAEU, agreements with the other two types serve directly for the development of integration.

The purpose of the Memorandum is to create a platform for comprehensive economic cooperation development, and to identify and remove barriers to trade. Within the framework of the Memorandum, it is common practice to involve experts in bilateral consultations.

The EAEU's negotiations with integration unions suffer from global and regional risks, of both a political and economic nature. For example, in 2014, official relations began between MERCOSUR and the Eurasian Economic Commission (EEC). However, the development of relations actually stopped in 2016 due to the political crisis in South American countries and the suspension of Venezuela's membership in MERCOSUR. In November 2018, the dialogue received a new impetus; the parties agreed to expedite negotiations on the signing of a comprehensive trade agreement between the two unions (EEC 2018a)

The creation of a comprehensive FTA between the EAEU and ASEAN in the long-term also became more realistic after the signing of the Memorandum of Understanding by the EEC and ASEAN on November 14, 2018. It is assumed that cooperation will be developed in the following areas: customs regulation and trade facilitation, sanitary and phytosanitary measures, technical regulation, e-commerce, trade in services, investment, development of entrepreneurship, which will create the necessary conditions for the development of sustainable interaction at the level of micro, small, and medium enterprises (EEC 2018b). Deepening the dialogue with ASEAN for the EAEU opens up prospects for cooperation with China's macro-regional initiative—Regional Comprehensive Economic Partnership, which unites all ASEAN countries and six states that has already signed free trade agreements with ASEAN (Australia, India, China, New Zealand, Republic of Korea and Japan). Thus, it can be stated that the role of the EEC as an institutional mediator in establishing relations between integration unions remains quite popular and effective.

11.3 Priority Directions of EAEU International Cooperation

Given the ever wider spread of the FTA form of cooperation throughout the world, the complexity of the world trade structure, the decrease in the role of customs, tariff regulation tools with the increasing role of non-tariff barriers, and the growth of trade in services, the role of FTA for the EAEU in recent years has been steadily increasing. Now the most important target in the EAEU international agenda is to find a balance between the eastern and western directions with its own advantages and challenges.

At the current stage of the EAEU's foreign economic relations development, the main task for the union is to form a system of effective partnerships. It is important to interact with those countries that have good level of political dialogue with EAEU members, and deepening economic cooperation carries more benefits than potential threats and risks. Among the priority areas of cooperation, several key ones may be distinguished: Asian (Vietnam, China, Singapore, India, etc.), Middle East (Iran, Egypt, Israel), and European (Serbia, Moldova).

11.3.1 Asian Vector

Interaction with Asian countries is characterized by the desire to create a network of free trade zones and agreements on trade and economic cooperation, as well as linking the EAEU infrastructure and transport system with the Chinese initiative "One Belt, One Road" and the Indian project of the international transport corridor "North-South". A kind of "pilot project" and the starting point in establishing the FTA format in the Asian region was the experience of concluding the agreement with Vietnam.

The terms of the EAEU agreement with Vietnam imply trade liberalization under WTO-plus rules. On the one hand, the agreement covers a wide range of issues directly related to trade in goods: customs administration and trade facilitation, technical barriers to trade, sanitary and phytosanitary measures, etc. On the other hand, it goes further in regulation of the other spheres and provides for obligations regarding mutual liberalization of trade in services, investment regulation, movement of individuals, intellectual property rights, sustainable development, e-commerce, public procurement, and so on (EEC 2015). Moreover, this part of the agreement applies only to Russia and Vietnam; subsequently other EAEU countries will also be able to develop cooperation with Vietnam in these areas.

Some areas of economic cooperation remained outside the liberalization regime, included in the exemption lists or other trade protection measures. Thus, the most sensitive spheres were not affected. According to the experts of the Russian International Affairs Council: "The document did not become a breakthrough, although, probably, it should not have become one from the point of view of Russian-Vietnamese trade.

The value of this agreement lies in the reputational benefit for Vietnam, which has proved its importance as an Asian partner of Russia, as well as in developing negotiation practices and mechanisms for implementing such agreements for the EAEU" (RIAC 2015).

In May 2018, the Agreement on trade and economic cooperation between the EAEU and China was signed, providing mechanisms of interaction in various areas of state regulation that allow consideration of business interests, transparency, and the predictability of regulation at the national and supranational levels. The document is non-preferential in nature and does not automatically reduce trade barriers. However, it provides an opportunity to the targeted reduction of barriers to entry into the Chinese market for the EAEU businesses and increases the regulation transparency.

The agreement contains the legal framework for the further cooperation in such areas as trade protection measures, sanitary and phytosanitary measures, technical trade barriers, customs cooperation, e-commerce, intellectual property, industry cooperation, government procurement, and competition. The agreement also provides for a wide range of exemptions, including the following: to ensure national security, to protect public morality, to protect people, animals, plants, and so on. Contrary to expectations, the agreement does not imply significant measures of creating attractive conditions for mutual investments increase in the framework of the Silk Road Economic Belt project. Instead, the sections "Sectoral Cooperation", "Competition", and "Public Procurement" imply only an exchange of information and consultations within the framework of working groups.

The signing of the agreement between the EAEU and China is the next step in conjunction with the Eurasian Economic Union and the "One Belt—One Road" strategic initiative, and it is certainly a positive signal to companies to work more actively on joint projects. China also proposed creating a regional free trade zone within the Shanghai Cooperation Organization (SCO).

All the EAEU members eventually agreed that, in the face of a large deficit in the trade balance with China, the creation of a free trade zone between China and the EAEU would pose a serious challenge for many national industries and agriculture. However, in terms of cooperation in the field of investment and transport infrastructure, opinions diverged. Thus, Russia has traditionally been more cautious in expanding economic cooperation with China, fearing serious geo-economic consequences in the first place. That is why Russia is trying to fit the idea of partnership with China into the broader format of the EAEU—SCO—ASEAN as stated in the 2016 Foreign Policy Concept.

In October 2019, at the meeting of the Supreme Eurasian Economic Council, EAEU and Singapore signed an FTA. According to the document, Singapore provides duty-free access for all goods from the EAEU while Russian manufacturers will adapt gradually to the new trade regime. Immediately after the agreement enters into force, EAEU obligations envisage the provision of duty-free access for Singaporean goods constituting 40 per cent of the entire product range, and after the completion of all transitional periods (from 3 to 10 years) it will increase up to 87 per cent (EEC 2019).

The agreement also contains obligations to comply with international standards for the application of licensing procedures; prohibitions and quantitative restrictions; technical regulation, sanitary and phytosanitary measures; making transfers and payments for the supply of products; the application of antidumping, countervailing and special protective measures. The agreement also formed a significant groundwork for improving the quality and development of cooperation in such areas as E-commerce, the environment, countering anti-competitive practices, the transparency of public procurement, and protection of intellectual property rights that is especially relevant when discussing technology transfer issues.

The document was the first step toward the formation of a comprehensive FTA with Singapore in the format “goods + services + investment”, which will also regulate trade in services and investment conditions. With regard to trade in goods with Singapore, the effect of the free trade zone may be limited, but removing the barriers will increase mutual investment flows and will allow EAEU companies to enter the markets of other ASEAN countries through Singapore. In the future, the FTA will become an important factor in expanding the Russian presence in the Singaporean market and Asia-Pacific region as a whole. The FTA with individual ASEAN countries (Vietnam, Singapore) will become the basis for building cooperation at the level of the entire integration union.

11.3.2 Middle East Vector

In 2018, the Eurasian Economic Union and the Islamic Republic of Iran signed the Interim Agreement for a period of three years, with FTA establishing in the future. In October 2019, the agreement entered into force.

This agreement has become special for the EAEU, as it implies the creation of a free trade zone in two stages. At the first stage, the Interim Agreement will be valid for a certain list of goods to stimulate mutual trade (covers 50 per cent of mutual trade), within the so-called limited trade zone.

The list of goods for the EAEU includes certain types of agricultural products, as well as metallurgy products and some types of electronic and mechanical equipment. Iran has been granted tariff preferences for a wide range of food products, as well as building materials, and some non-ferrous metal products. For industrial goods, the average level of import duties in Iran will decrease from 22.4 to 15.4 per cent, in the EAEU from 8 to 4.7 per cent. For agricultural products, Iran will reduce duties on average from 32.2 to 13.2 per cent, the EAEU—from 9.6 to 4.6 per cent.

After a three-year transition period, it is planned to sign a full-format FTA between the EAEU and Iran. In future, trade may increase 1.5–2 times due to the growing supply of pharmaceutical, steel, automotive industry products, and various types of mechanical and electrical equipment. The implementation of infrastructure projects will also contribute to the growth of trade. The problem of transport and logistics infrastructure can be solved by organizing an effective railway transit through Georgia, Armenia, and Azerbaijan, as well as developing port infrastructure. The Meghri Special Economic Zone of Armenia will also be involved in cooperation with Iran by giving opportunities for businesses to organize joint production in its territory. Companies from Iran can export raw materials and components into the zone, and produce goods on its territory without customs and administrative procedures for further delivering to the EAEU market.

The first arrangements between EAEU countries and the Arab Republic of Egypt on the Free Trade Agreement were made in 2015. The first round of negotiations on the FTA was held in Cairo in early 2019, where the parties reiterated their desire to sign a progressive agreement.

According to preliminary estimates by the EEC, the EAEU export to Egypt may grow by 14.5 per cent, and imports from Egypt by 34 per cent due to the functioning of FTA. The EAEU countries have high potential for increasing exports to Egypt of food products, coal, ferrous metals, certain types of machinery and equipment. An analysis of the existing mechanisms and conditions for the access of agricultural products to the Egyptian market allows us to conclude that Egypt is a quite perspective direction for the EAEU agricultural products. Nowadays Egyptian agricultural industry is able to satisfy the country's food needs by no more than 60 per cent; therefore, Egypt is a major importer of food.

For the Eurasian Economic Union, the growth of imports from Egypt is projected due to the increasing supply of vegetables, nuts, fruits, and certain types of chemical products. Additional benefits may come from the use of the Russian industrial zone within the special economic zone of the Suez Canal. Certain opportunities for the EAEU export geography expansion may also arise from the using of a number of free trade agreements between Egypt and North Africa countries.

11.3.3 European Vector

The Asian and Middle East directions of the EAEU's foreign economic policy do not cancel the need to resume dialogue with Europe. Without European participation, the projects of infrastructural and economic integration of the Eurasian continent will largely lose their technological and investment attractiveness. However, in the short and medium term, the possibilities of implementing the concept of "integration of integration" or "conjugation" of the EU and the EAEU, when the Eurasian space is positioned as a bridge between Europe and the dynamically developing Asia-Pacific region, are currently extremely limited. Nevertheless, despite this, a certain success is observed in cooperation on the "external circuit" of the EU integration.

In this context, prospects for developing cooperation with partners in the European space are visible in the Balkans. In May 2016, the Supreme Eurasian Economic Council decided to launch negotiations with Serbia on unifying the trade regime in order to sign FTA in future (Lisovolik and Chimiris 2018). Finally, in October 2019, the EAEU and Serbia signed a Free Trade Agreement. The agreement fixes a set of obligations to comply with international standards for the application of licensing procedures; prohibitions and quantitative restrictions; technical regulation, sanitary and phytosanitary measures; fees related to customs clearance; application of anti-dumping, countervailing and special protective measures, protection of intellectual property rights.

For the EAEU, Serbia can be considered as a significant partner in terms of geoeconomics and geopolitics. For a number of years, only Russia has been among the largest partners of Serbia from all EAEU participants; however, the potential for developing mutual economic ties has not yet been exhausted. Economic cooperation with Serbia within the FTA can be beneficial in terms of diversifying investment ties with partners, deepening agricultural cooperation, expanding industrial interaction, intensifying technological and high-tech cooperation.

Through the establishment of a constructive dialogue and cooperation with countries of South-Eastern Europe, it would be possible in the future to bring negotiations on the conjugation of two integrations (European and Eurasian) to a new level. Still, it should be taken into account that concluding a non-preferential agreement between the EAEU and the EU would not deepen trade liberalization beyond the level established by the WTO, but would facilitate the development of cooperation in priority areas (infrastructure, energy, investment, scientific and technological fields), interesting to the member-states of both unions.

Among the important advantages of EAEU foreign economic relations can be matched the following:

- strengthening the role of the EAEU as a supporting logistics and infrastructure center of Greater Eurasia, linking Europe and Asia (transport, energy, digital infrastructure);
- effective integration of the economies of EAEU countries into international and regional production chains;
- attraction of foreign direct investment and technology;
- assistance in creating a belt of partnership around the EAEU, economic stability, and co-development.

11.4 Conclusion

In its foreign economic policy, the EAEU takes a flexible approach to the formation of external relations both bilaterally and multilaterally. At the same time, nowadays the EAEU gives priority to the bilateral agreements that take into account the specifics of a particular partner. This approach, based on the "new regionalism" principles, provides participation of the countries with different levels of development, leading role of economic motives, low level of institutionalization, intergovernmental decision-making format, and so on.

The most effective instrument of cooperation in this context is a Free Trade Agreement that goes beyond merchandise trade. The FTA network is designed to expand and simplify the access of EAEU manufacturers and exporters to other markets, to help Union countries integrate into regional and global production chains, and to attract investment. Finally, FTAs are aimed at solving two problems: an additional increase in exports, and investment increase, considered as drivers of economic growth.

EAEU countries have different visions on the format and speed which the union should use to build its international relations. EAEU member-states are trying to maintain national control over a number of areas such as trade in services and investment sphere that makes it more difficult to conclude progressive FTA at the supranational level. This creates not only organizational difficulties, but also a different degree of readiness among member-states to take on agreed obligations on trade in services and capital transfer.

The EAEU has a number of partners from different regions that can be divided into several priority groups, taking into consideration the level of cooperation and arising problems:

- the first group of countries (Vietnam, Egypt and Serbia) maintains good political relations with the EAEU (primarily Russia), has complementary trade flows, and large-scale opportunities to increase trade turnover in future;
- the second group of countries (India and Iran) also has good political relations with EAEU countries. They are of great interest to Russian exporters, especially in terms of non-fuel and high-tech exports. However, their markets are well protected by various tariff and non-tariff barriers. They also have a number of sensitive industries in trade relations with EAEU countries;
- the third group of countries (Singapore and Israel). Cooperation with these countries can be considered in terms of trade in services and investment interaction rather than trade in goods. The main difficulty in negotiating with these countries is to find the optimal balance between the partners' benefits;
- cooperation with two main partners (EU and China) should be built on a non-preferential basis. Rather than imply deepening trade liberalization beyond the level established by the WTO, this should nevertheless contribute to the development of cooperation in the priority areas, defined by the partners.

Moreover, cooperation between the EAEU and ASEAN has become more realistic in the long-term period after signing a set of agreements, including the one between the EAEU and Vietnam, a memorandum of understanding between the EEC and ASEAN, as well as a Free Trade

Agreement on goods and a framework agreement on comprehensive economic cooperation between the EAEU and Singapore. Deepening the dialogue with ASEAN opens prospects for cooperation within the macro-regional initiatives for the EAEU.

Based on the EAEU international agenda analysis, it seems quite perspective to develop one of such macro-regional initiatives—the Greater Eurasian Partnership where the EAEU with its network of FTAs may become one of the drivers of a wider integration circuit. The formation of the Greater Eurasian Partnership can be considered through the cooperation between the countries of the Eurasian Economic Union—Association of South East Asian Nations—Shanghai Cooperation Organization—Silk Road Economic Belt, with the possible involvement of the European Union in the future.

References

Acharya, A. (2012). Comparative Regionalism: A Field Whose Time Has Come? *The International Spectator: Italian Journal of International Affairs, 47*(1), 3–15.

Baldwin, R. E. (1997). The Causes of Regionalism. *World Economy, 20*(7), 865–888.

Bergsten, C. F. (1997). *Open Regionalism. The World Economy, 20*(5), 545–565.

Bhagwati, J. (1991). *The World Trading System at Risk.* USA: Princeton University Press.

Bhagwati, J. (1993). Regionalism and Multilateralism: An Overview. In J. De Melo & A. Panagariya (Eds.), *Chapter 2 in New Dimensions in Regional Integration.* UK: Cambridge University Press.

Bhagwati, J. (1994). Threats to the World Trading System: Income Distribution and the Selfish Hegemon. *Journal of International Affairs, 48*(Spring), 279–285.

Bhagwati, J., & Krueger, A. (1995). *The Dangerous Drift to Preferential Trade Agreements.* Washington, DC: American Enterprise Institute.

Comparative Regional Integration. (2005). Edited by F. Laursen. Ashgate.

De Lombaerde, P., Söderbaum, F. et al. (2009). *The Problem of Comparison in Comparative Regionalism.* University of Miami Under the Co-sponsorship of the Miami-European Union Center. Retrieved from http://aei.pitt.edu/14995/1/CompReg.pdf.

EAEU. (2014). *Treaty on the Eurasian Economic Union.* Retrieved from https://docs.eaeunion.org/docs/ru-ru/0003610/itia_05062014.

EAEU. (2015). *Main Directions of the EAEU Economic Development Before 2030.* Supreme Eurasian Economic Council's decree of October 16. Retrieved from http://eurasianeconomic.org/pdf/analiz02.pdf.

EAEU. (2019). *Main Directions of International Activity of the Eurasian Economic Union for 2020*. Retrieved from https://docs.eaeunion.org/docs/ru-ru/01123170/err_02102019_19_doc.pdf.

EEC. (2015). *Free Trade Agreement between the Eurasian Economic Union and Its Member States and the Socialist Republic of Viet Nam*. Retrieved from http://www.eurasiancommission.org/ru/act/trade/dotp/sogl_torg/Documents/EAEU-VN_FTA.pdf.

EEC. (2018a). *EAEU Develops Cooperation with MERCOSUR*. Retrieved from http://www.eurasiancommission.org/en/nae/news/Pages/02-11-2018-2.aspx.

EEC. (2018b). *EAEU and ASEAN Deepen Trade, Economic and Investment Cooperation*. Retrieved from http://www.eurasiancommission.org/en/nae/news/Pages/14-11-2018-1.aspx.

EEC. (2019). *EAEU and Singapore Signed Free Trade Agreement*. Retrieved from http://www.eurasiancommission.org/ru/nae/news/Pages/01.10.2019-2.aspx.

Electronic Fund of Legal and Technical Documentation. (2018). *Agreement on International Treaties of the Eurasian Economic Union with Third States, International Organizations or Integration Associations*. Retrieved from http://docs.cntd.ru/document/550970067.

Ethier, W. (1998). Regionalism in a Multilateral World. *Journal of Political Economy, 106*(6), 1214–1245.

Gurova, I., Platonova, I., & Maksakova, M. (2018). The Level of Trade Integration in the Eurasian Economic Union. *Studies on Russian Economic Development, 29*(4), 447–453.

Krugman, P. (1991). Is Bilateralism Bad? In E. Helpman & A. Razin (Eds.), *International Trade and Trade Policy*. Cambridge, MA: MIT Press.

Lawrence, R. (1996). *Regionalism, Multilateralism, and Deeper Integration*. Washington, DC: Brookings Institution.

Lisovolik, Y. D., & Chimiris, E. S. (2018). *Serbia–EAEU: Integration Prospects in a Free Trade Area*. Working Paper No. 37/2018. Edited by Ivanov, I.S. Russian International Affairs Council (RIAC). Moscow, RIAC NPP.

OECD. (2003). *Regionalism and the Multilateral Trading System*. Paris: OECD Publications.

RIAC. (2015). *Russian International Affairs Council*. Retrieved from http://russiancouncil.ru/analytics-and-comments/analytics/shest-voprosov-o-zst-eaes-vetnam/.

Söderbaum, F., & Sbragia, A. (2010). *Linking European Integration and Comparative Regionalism*. Paper for UACES Conference, Bruges. Retrieved from http://uaces.org/documents/papers/1001/soderbaum_f.pdf.

Summers, L. (1991). Regionalism and the World Trading System. In *Policy Implications of Trade and Currency Zones*. Wyoming: Federal Reserve Bank of Kansas City.

Warleigh-Lack, A., & Van Langenhove, L. (2010). Rethinking EU Studies: The Contribution of Comparative Regionalism. *Journal of European Integration, 32*(6), 541–562.

CHAPTER 12

Russia in the EAEU

Alexander S. Bulatov

12.1 Introduction

The foundation of the EAEU has generated numerous publications on its functioning, and much less on Russia's participation in the union. Some of them stress the economic domination of Russia to the EAEU (Dragneva and Volczuk 2017), as well as the geopolitical importance of the project for Russia (Sergi 2017). Others focus on the challenges for Russia at the EAEU (Busygina 2019) and possible ways to solve them (Li 2018).

Papers researching the economic prospects of the EAEU for Russia and other member countries can be divided into some groups. The first one covers papers that are skeptical about the economic foundations and prospects of the EAEU accentuating non-economic aspects of this integration grouping, and indicating that Russia basically pursues geopolitical aims at the EAEU (Inozemtsev 2014; Mostafa and Mahmood 2018). The second group of papers argues that the economic prospects of the EAEU are modestly optimistic (Hattory 2016; Rotaru 2018; Vinokurov 2017). The principal points of the chapter are the following: strong and weak aspects

A. S. Bulatov (✉)
MGIMO University, Moscow, Russia

N. A. Piskulova (ed.), *The Economic Dimension of Eurasian Integration*, https://doi.org/10.1007/978-3-030-59886-0_12

of Russia as a member of the EAEU; economic benefits and costs that Russia gets in the union; challenges for Russia in Eurasian economic integration.

12.2 Russia as a Center of the EAEU

By many indicators Russia leads in this part of Eurasia—by population (80 per cent of the EAEU), GDP (87 per cent), financial power (93 per cent of bank assets), R&D (97 per cent of R&D expenditures), and mutual trade (65 per cent of mutual trade) (Eurasian Economic Commission 2019).

The above statistics is reminiscent not of the European Union but of other integration unions with asymmetric memberships—USMCA (with US prevalence), MERCOSUR (Brazil), South African Customs Union (South Africa), or the Cooperation Council for the Arab States of the Gulf (Saudi Arabia). In turn, it bears asymmetry in integration union interdependence; economically the EAEU is less important for Russia than for other smaller member countries of the union (one can again draw a parallel with the USA, Brazil, South Africa, Saudi Arabia)—see Table 12.1.

Table 12.1 shows the low dependence the Russian has economy on goods and capital markets of other EAEU countries. Russia more strongly relies on the EAEU for economic dependence due to the labor market—CIS countries provide 8–12 million additional workers (by the author's estimation, about 1/4–1/3 of them are from the EAEU) for Russia with its decreasing labor force, constituting 10–15 per cent of labor (Bulatov 2019). This migration also brings substantial revenues for the mother countries of those workers via their remittances from Russia.

Table 12.1 Share of the EAEU in merchandise trade and FDI inflow of its member countries in 2018–2019 (per cent)

	Armenia	*Belarus*	*Kazakhstan*	*Kyrgyzstan*	*Russia*
Merchandise trade turnover[a]	30	50	21	37	8
FDI inflow[b]	21	37	10	–	1

Sources: Eurasian Economic Commission. On results of the EAEU mutual merchandise trade. July 25, 2019, p. 3 (in Russian); Eurasian Bank of Development. Center of integration research. Eurasian economic integration 2019. Report No.52. Moscow, 2019, pp. 82–85 (in Russian)

[a]January–May 2019

[b]January–September 2018

Besides the large size of the Russian economy, the comparatively limited interest of Russian business to Eurasian integration is accounted for through other serious reasons:

- Fuel and the material nature and technological weakness (except for some industries) of the Russian economy and its Eurasian partners limit the scope of Russian trade with them. For instance, Russian merchandise imports are aimed at machinery, equipment, and transport means—47.3 per cent of its volume in 2018 (Russia in figures 2019) and only a measly part of it ($4 billion out of $113 billion) is imported from other countries of the union. Vice versa, weak Russian manufacturing provides only a smaller part of machinery, equipment, and transport means imports of those countries;
- The Russian economy's financial immaturity and the orientation of its FDI outflow to capital flight toward offshores (Bulatov 2017) impedes Russian FDI flow to the Union (even if it is taken into consideration that some of FDI inflows from offshores are of Russian origin);
- In this decade, the macroeconomic instability of all EAEU members including Russia (low rates of growth, drop of production in 2015, currency devaluation) also provides the limited impetus for more close economic relations of Russian business with these countries.

Certainly, as with other integration unions, an economic interest co-exists with a geopolitical interest, which in the Russia-EAEU case is strong enough. For Russia, the EAEU is the territory of friendly states which are politically and culturally close and rely on Russia in the field of external security. Economic relations with those states support political influence of Russia in the region and vice versa.

It is reasonable to support these ideas with short analyses of economic benefits and costs of Russia in the EAEU.

12.3 Economic Benefits and Costs of Russia

From the author's point of view, this is the following combination of positives and negatives for the Russian economy. Some of these benefits and costs are connected:

- Being composed of fuel and raw materials, Russian merchandise exports contains only a small percentage of machinery, equipment, and transport means—5–9 per cent of the whole exports volume of Russia. At the same time, about 1/3 of these goods are exported to CIS countries (2/3 go to the EAEU), providing substantial support to Russian engineering. Annual quiz of Russian manufacturing enterprises indicates growing competition of respondents at CIS markets. If, at Russian markets, 91 per cent of respondents believe that their goods are competitive in 2019, then at West and East European markets this indicator is only 15 per cent but at CIS markets it is 51 per cent (38 per cent in 2009, 43 per cent in 2013) (Egorov 2019). On the other hand, Russian imports of machinery, equipment, and transport means from other CIS countries is meager and stagnating—about 5–9 per cent of these imported goods (Russia in figures 2019). One can suppose that this is the consequence of the low activity of global value chains of Russian engineering MNCs. This is decreasing the potential of economic relations between businesses of the EAEU countries:
- On the one hand, the trade balance of Russia with other member countries of the union is positive (merchandise exports–imports surplus was $12–19 billion in 2016–2018, that is, about 1/7–1/10 of the whole Russian foreign trade surplus) (Russia in figures 2019). On the other hand, most of those trade payments (and trade surplus) are in rubles, not in dollars or euros which are preferable for the current account surplus and official reserves of Russia;
- Potentially, the EAEU is a good field for Russian capital exports outflow, though nowadays Russian business prefers offshores and did not create enough global value chains in other union countries. However, these countries rely more on Russian financial aid than on Russian FDI. Belarus, the closest Russian economic partner in the EAEU, annually gets about $2 billion in financial aid from Russia in various ways (RBC 2019) when annual FDI inflow in Belarus (mainly from Russia) is less than $2 billion annually (UNCTAD 2018);
- Labor migration, especially short-term, from other post-Soviet countries is vitally important for the Russian economy, as was said above. Nevertheless, migration from Central Asia provides Russia with low-quality labor in general (with some exceptions, in medical and other services). It also hampers the wage (income) growth in Russia as well as the human capital development of the country.

This combination of benefits and costs could be detailed and continued. However, it will not give an answer to the question of whether the Russian economy *in general* has a positive or negative macroeconomic effect from participation in the EAEU. Nowadays, it does not look like a great positive surplus for Russia and it spurs Russian leadership to rationalize economic relationship with other members of the union—to diminish barriers in mutual trade, provide a more friendly investment climate in other union countries, and increase the educational level of potential emigrants in Asian member countries. However, the insufficient economic power of Russia disturbs these attempts and often compels Russian leadership to focus on other spheres of Eurasian integration where Russian power is more evident—mutual security and politics.

12.4 Challenges for Russian Economy

From the author's point of view, the most important external economic challenge for Russia in the EAEU is Chinese activity. This potentially loosens Russia's position in the economy of the states of the union, for example, in their foreign trade (see Table 12.2).

Although Chinese activity is more evident in merchandise imports than in exports of the union, the growing Chinese market re-orients trade flows of the EAEU members from third countries to the Chinese market and would partially re-orient these flows from Russia to China in the future.

Table 12.2 Share of Russia and China in foreign trade of some EAEU member countries (per cent)

	2010		*2014*		*2017*	
	exports	*imports*	*exports*	*imports*	*exports*	*imports*
Belarus						
Share of Russia	39.4	51.8	42.1	54.8	44.1	57.3
Share of China	1.9	4.9	4.8	5.9	1.2	8.0
Kazakhstan						
Share of Russia	9.5	39.4	8.0	33.4	9.6	39.6
Share of China	17.0	13.0	12.3	17.8	12.0	15.9

Sources: Foreign Trade of the Republic of Belarus. Statistical book. Minsk, 2018, 63–68; Foreign Trade of the Republic of Kazakhstan 2013–2017. Statistical abstract. Astana, 2018, 13–15 (in Kazakh and Russian); Foreign Trade of the Republic of Kazakhstan 2007–2011. Statistical abstract. Astana, 2012, 13–15 (in Kazakh and Russian)

Table 12.3 Annual GDP growth of the EAEU leading economies (per cent)

	2005	*2010*	*2014*	*2016*	*2018*	*2019 est.*
EAEU	6.7	4.8	1.1	0.3	2.5	
Armenia	3.9	2.2	3.6	0.2	5.2	6.0
Belarus	9.4	7.7	1.7	−2.5	3.0	1.5
Kazakhstan	9.7	7.3	4.2	1.1	4.1	3.8
Kyrgyzstan	−0.2	−0.5	4.0	4.3	3.5	3.8
Russia	6.4	4.5	0.7	0.3	2.3	1.1

Source: IMF. World Economic Outlook, October 2019

A more evident Chinese challenge is in capital movement, for example, accumulated Chinese FDI in Kazakhstan in 2016 reached $21 billion (Relationship EAEC and China 2017) whilst accumulated Russian FDI reached only $3 billion (Bulatov 2018). This disparity could appear in EAEU countries in the near future as a result of the Belt and Road Initiative.

The most evident intra-Eurasian challenge for Russia is the low growth of EAEU economies (including Russia), and their technological and financial weakness. Of them the most acute is low GDP dynamics in this decade (see Table 12.3).

Putting aside the small economies of Armenia and Kyrgyzstan, the trend for the largest economies of the EAEU is evident—their GDP growth is less nowadays than it was in the previous decade. In a world where this growth of developing economies was 3.9–4.6 per cent in this decade, the low economic dynamics of Russia, Belarus and Kazakhstan conserves the economic, technical, and financial backwardness of the EAEU.

These challenges seriously disturb any prospects of Russian economic relations with other member countries of the EAEU.

12.5 Economic Prospects of Russia in the EAEU

Being the dominant economy in the union, Russia determines the economic prospects of the whole EAEU to a great extent. In other words, the benefits and costs of Russia's participation in the EAEU depend on Russia itself.

Nowadays the economic prospects of Russia are unclear. On the one hand, initiated by the Russian president, federal national projects for 2019–2024 in various social and economic fields are based on the prerequisite of GDP growth in Russia speeding up—more than 3 per cent annually in the next decade (Ministry of Economic Development 2018). On the other hand, international organizations are more skeptical, and they forecast much less economic growth by Russia in the next decade—1.8 per cent in 2021 (World Bank 2019) and 1.6 per cent in 2024 (IMF 2019).

Such uncertain prospects for the Russian economy do not foster economic relations of other EAEU member countries with Russia—the low growth of Russian GDP may put a brake on their own dynamics. For instance, Belarus, highly connected with Russia economically, has bad forecasts from the World Bank (1.2 per cent growth of GDP in 2021) and IMF (1.6 per cent in 2024). This economic ambiguity is detrimental to Russia's relations with other EAEU countries. As a result, they are prudent in respect of Russian claims to accelerate mutual integration.

12.6 Conclusion

For Russia, the leading member country of the EAEU, the economic benefits and costs from the union are largely determined by Russia's economic power. Nowadays, the uncertainty of its prospects makes the contours of Russian economic participation in the EAEU uncertain too. In case of its own economic stagnation, Russia should focus on the political and humanitarian aspects of Eurasian integration. In case of its economic revival, Russia will intensify economic aspects of this integration.

References

Bulatov, A. (2017). Offshore orientation of Russian Federation FDI. *Transnational Corporations, 24*(2), 71–90.

Bulatov, A. (Ed.). (2018). *Russia in International Capital Movement in 2017-Beginning 2018.* Moscow: MGIMO-University.

Bulatov, A. (Ed.). (2019). *The Economy of Russia and Other Post-Soviet Countries.* Cambridge: Cambridge Scholars Publishing.

Busygina, I. (2019, February). *Russia in the Eurasian Economic Union: Lack of Trust in Russia Limits the Possible.* PONARS Eurasia, policy memo No.571. (in Russian). Retrieved from http://www.ponarseurasia.org/ru/node/10141209.

Dragneva, R., & Volczuk K. (2017). *The Eurasian Economic Union. Deals, Rules and the Exercise of Power*. Chatham House Research Paper. Retrieved from https://www.chathamhouse.org/sites/default/files/publications/research/2017-05-02-eurasian-economic-union-dragneva-wolczuk.pdf.

Egorov, A. (2019). Competition and Competitiveness of Enterprises in 2018–2019. *Russian Economic Barometer, 3*, 6–7. (in Russian).

Eurasian Economic Commission. (2019). *Short Statistical Digest* (pp. 11–16). Moscow. (in Russian).

Hattory, M. (2016, January). *The Role of the Eurasian Economic Union in Trade and Industrial Policy of Russia*. ResearchGate. Retrieved from https://www.researchgate.net/publication/325520794_The_Role_of_the_Eurasian_Economic_Union_in_Trade_and_Industrial_Policy_of_Russia.

IMF. (2019, April). *World Economic Outlook*, 160.

Inozemtsev, V. (2014). Eurasian Economic Union: Lost in the Middle of Nowhere. *Polis, 6*, 71–82.

Li, Y. (2018). The Greater Eurasian Partnership and the Belt and Road Initiative: Can Be the Two United? *Journal of Eurasian Studies, 9*, 94–99.

Mostafa, G., & Mahmood, M. (2018). Eurasian Economic Union: Evolution, Challenges and Possible Future Directions. *Journal of Eurasian Studies, 9*, 163–172.

RBC. (2019). *Russia presented to Belarus the plan of further integration* (in Russian). Retrieved from http://www.rbc.ru/economics/17/04/2019/5cb751019a7947caf9263ea3.

Relations of the EAEC and China. (2017). *Eurasian Studies*. Retrieved from http://eurasian-studies.org/archives/6142

Rotaru, V. (2018). The Eurasian Economic Union—A Sustainable Alternative for the Former Soviet Space. *Journal of Contemporary European Studies, 26*, 425–442.

Russia in figures. (2019). Moscow: Rosstat (in Rusian).

Sergi, B. (2017). Putin's and Russian-led Eurasian Economic Union: A hybrid half-economics and half-political "Janus Bifrons". *Journal of Eurasian Studies, 9*(1), 52–60.

The Ministry of Economic Development of the Russian Federation (2018). *The Forecast of Social and Economic Development of the Russian Federation for the Period up to 2024* (in Russian). Retrieved from http://economy.gov.ru/wps/wcm/connect/60223a2f-38c5-4685-96f4-6c6476ea3593/prognoz24svod.pdf?MOD=AJPERES&CACHEID=60223a2f-38c5-4685-96f4-6c6476ea3593.

UNCTAD. (2018). *World Investment Report*. Geneva.

Vinokurov, E. (2017). Eurasian Economic Union: Current State and Preliminary Results. *Russian Journal of Economics, 3*, 54–70.

World Bank. (2019, June 4–5). *Global Economic Prospects*.

Index[1]

C

Common energy market, 29, 108, 109
Common Labour Market, 28, 182–185, 187

D

Digital economy, v, 161–173

E

EAEU Digital Agenda, 14, 30, 151, 163, 167–172
Economic cooperation, 7, 18, 19, 27, 33, 57, 59, 76, 94, 114, 198, 204, 210, 213–218, 221, 224
Economic integration, v, 6, 13–15, 21, 22, 30, 58, 59, 62, 68, 93, 96, 98, 102, 103, 110, 111, 115, 116, 125, 126, 136, 139, 147, 162, 169, 210, 221, 228
Environment, 29, 138, 150, 155, 164, 169, 171, 189, 190, 192–194, 196, 197, 199–204, 219
Eurasian Economic Union (EAEU), v, 2–23, 27–64, 67–89, 93–105, 107–120, 125–139, 143–157, 161–173, 175–187, 189–204, 209–224, 227–233
Eurasian integration, v, 1–23, 36, 38, 53, 57, 60, 61, 104, 126, 128n1, 144, 145, 151, 154, 156, 211, 229, 231, 233
Eurasianism, 144, 145, 156

F

Foreign direct investments (FDI), v, 11, 15, 22, 33–35, 67–89, 97, 162, 172, 199, 213, 222, 228–230, 232
Free Trade Agreement (FTA), 9, 12, 18, 21–23, 57, 58, 210, 213, 214, 216, 217, 219–224

[1]Note: Page numbers followed by 'n' refer to notes.

N. A. Piskulova (ed.), *The Economic Dimension of Eurasian Integration*, https://doi.org/10.1007/978-3-030-59886-0

G

Green economy, 190, 196, 197

H

Higher education, 143, 145, 152, 153, 155, 156

I

Industrial cooperation, 3, 11, 14, 16, 42, 60, 61, 93–105, 149, 169

International Economic Relations (IER), v

Intra-regional/mutual trade, 4, 11, 13, 14, 16, 22, 27–64, 89, 95, 100–103, 112, 129, 131, 167, 190, 195, 199, 201, 212, 220, 228, 231

Investment regulation, 67–75, 78, 87, 217

L

Labour migration, 116, 169, 176, 181, 184–186, 230

Logistics, v, 23, 34, 36, 39, 82, 125–139, 168, 169, 172, 220, 222

P

Post-Soviet studies, v

R

Regionalism, 3–7, 17–22, 210, 211, 222

Russian economy, 32, 35, 71, 77–79, 229–233

S

Scientific cooperation, 150

T

Transport, v, 2, 4, 14–16, 22, 23, 28, 29, 34, 36, 39, 43, 61, 72, 82, 85, 98, 125–139, 147, 165, 169, 171, 193, 198, 200, 217, 218, 220, 222, 229, 230

The manufacturer's authorised representative in the EU is Springer Nature Customer Service Centre GmbH, Europaplatz 3, 69115 Heidelberg, Germany. If you have any concerns regarding our products, please contact ProductSafety@springernature.com

Printed and bound by CPI Group (UK) Ltd, Croydon, CR0 4YY
30/09/2026
02225702-0008